Remapping Persian Literary History, 1700–1900

Edinburgh Historical Studies of Iran and the Persian World

Published in association with Elahé Omidyar Mir-Djalali, Founder and Chair, Roshan Cultural Heritage Institute

Series General Editor: Stephanie Cronin, Elahé Omidyar Mir-Djalali Research Fellow, University of Oxford

Series Advisory Board: Professor Janet Afary (UC Santa Barbara), Professor Abbas Amanat (Yale University), Professor Touraj Atabaki (International Institute of Social History), Dr Joanna de Groot (University of York), Professor Vanessa Martin (Royal Holloway, University of London), Professor Rudi Matthee (University of Delaware), Professor Cyrus Schayegh (The Graduate Institute, Geneva)

Covering the history of Iran and the Persian world from the medieval period to the present, this series aims to become the pre-eminent place for publication in this field. As well as its core concern with Iran, it extends its concerns to encompass a much wider and more loosely defined cultural and linguistic world, to include Afghanistan, the Caucasus, Central Asia, Xinjiang and northern India. Books in the series present a range of conceptual and methodological approaches, looking not only at states, dynasties and elites, but at subalterns, minorities and everyday life.

Published and forthcoming titles

Religion, Orientalism and Modernity: The Case of the Babis and Baha'is in Iran
Geoffrey Nash

Remapping Persian Literary History, 1700–1900
Kevin L. Schwartz

Muslim–Christian Polemics in Safavid Iran
Alberto Tiburcio

edinburghuniversitypress.com/series/ehsipw

Remapping Persian Literary History, 1700–1900

Kevin L. Schwartz

EDINBURGH
University Press

For Sage and Ansel

Edinburgh University Press is one of the leading university presses in the UK. We publish academic books and journals in our selected subject areas across the humanities and social sciences, combining cutting-edge scholarship with high editorial and production values to produce academic works of lasting importance. For more information visit our website: edinburghuniversitypress.com

© Kevin L. Schwartz, 2020, 2022

Edinburgh University Press Ltd
The Tun – Holyrood Road
12 (2f) Jackson's Entry
Edinburgh EH8 8PJ

First published in hardback by Edinburgh University Press 2020

Typeset in 11/15 Adobe Garamond by
Servis Filmsetting Ltd, Stockport, Cheshire

A CIP record for this book is available from the British Library

ISBN 978 1 4744 5084 3 (hardback)
ISBN 978 1 4744 5085 0 (paperback)
ISBN 978 1 4744 5086 7 (webready PDF)
ISBN 978 1 4744 5087 4 (epub)

The right of Kevin L. Schwartz to be identified as author of this work has been asserted in accordance with the Copyright, Designs and Patents Act 1988 and the Copyright and Related Rights Regulations 2003 (SI No. 2498).

Contents

List of Figures	vi
Acknowledgements	vii
Note on Transliteration and Translation	xi
Introduction	1
1 Remembering Iran, Forgetting the Persianate: Persian Literary Historiography of the Eighteenth and Nineteenth Centuries	35
2 Reformation and Reconstruction of Poetic Networks: Isfahan *c.*1722–1801	81
3 A Market for the Masters: Afghanistan *c.*1839–1842	124
4 Debating Poetry on the Edge of the Persianate World: Arcot *c.*1850	163
Conclusion	202
Bibliography	208
Index	230

Figures

2.1 The Isfahani Circle of poets associated with Mushtaq's literary society — 101
2.2 Expansion of the Isfahani Circle of poets under the patronage of Mirza ʿAbd al-Wahhab — 101
2.3 Literary bonds among the Isfahani Circle of poets — 105
3.1 Cover of Hamid Allah Kashmiri's *Book of Akbar* (*Akbarnama*) published by the Historical Society of Afghanistan in 1951–2 — 126
3.2 Cover of *War Ballad* (*Jangnama*) by 'Ghulami' published by the Historical Society of Afghanistan in 1957 — 127
3.3 Frontispiece of Munshi ʿAbd al-Karim's *Battle of Kabul and Qandahar* (*Muharaba-yi Kabul va Qandahar*), lithographed at Lucknow 1850–1 — 149
3.4 Market-place of Anglo-Afghan war-ballads and other Persian imitations of the *Shahanama* in nineteenth-century Afghanistan and South Asia — 155
4.1 Portrait of the last Nawab of Arcot, Muhammad Ghaws Khan Bahadur 'Aʿzam' (d. 1855) — 168
4.2 General overview of the literary networks of Carnatic as reconstructed from the biographical anthology of Persian Poets, *Binish's Notices* (1848–9) — 173
4.3 Network map of instructional and family connections among poets in nineteenth-century Carnatic — 178
4.4 Network map of poetic instruction in nineteenth-century Carnatic and the isolation of the poet Vasif — 181

Acknowledgements

The transregional expanse and cultural reach of the Persianate world may not be what it once was, but networks of camaraderie, scholarship and exchange have remained available to a Persianist exploring its historical features, whether at Berkeley or inside the Beltway, across libraries and archives, during springtime in Washington, DC or winter in Prague. The route from Isfahan to Delhi – or any other of the myriad routes frequently traversed by Persian poets and littérateurs of a bygone era – it was not, but one of discovery, wandering, enrichment and distraction nonetheless.

At the University of California, Berkeley, I was fortunate to have a series of mentors and friends who inspired me to pursue this project from its earliest days and helped shape its completion: Wali Ahmadi, whose ways of problematising the categories of literary history and rethinking the boundaries of Persian literary belonging drew me to Berkeley in the first place; Hamid Algar, who taught me that one's scholarly sensibilities are defined as much by the accumulation of knowledge as by the ability and willingness to effectively share it; and Munis Faruqui, who reminded me that addressing complex historiographical questions is only worthwhile if one can do so in a practical and clear manner.

During the course of completing this project, I benefited from several sources of institutional support. My year as a Social Science Research Council Transregional Fellow, spent in residence at Roshan Institute for Persian Studies at the University of Maryland, provided me with the opportunity to connect and converse with like-minded colleagues studying the Persianate world. Many thanks to Ahmet Karamustafa, Fatemeh Keshavarz, Matt Miller and the participants of my workshop, 'Wide World of Persian: Connections and Contestations, 1500–Today', for the many wonderful conversations and enriching insights. To Ahmad Karimi-Hakkak, I am grateful for your mentorship during that year and all the guidance that has followed since.

The Library of Congress in Washington, DC, as will be clear from the opening pages of the Introduction, is about as dear to me as any place could be. I am grateful to the entire staff of the African and Middle East Division, led by the grace and guidance of Mary-Jane Deeb, who provided me with an unending amount of research assistance over the years. My thanks to Hirad Dinavari, who, in addition to supporting my research in every possible way, always welcomed me to the library like I was coming home. For a wonderful year at the Kluge Center as a Research Fellow, my thanks to Travis Hensley, Mary Lou Reker, Ted Widmer and my fellow cohort for providing such an enjoyable and active scholarly environment amid chaotic times.

New colleagues at the Oriental Institute of the Czech Academy Sciences welcomed me to Prague with open arms. Ondřej Beránek and Jan Zouplna helped make the transition across the Atlantic an easy one and remain great advocates of my research. Stefano Taglia, since the first days of my arrival, has offered indispensable advice and, just as importantly, ensured that I've grasped the finer points of Italian coffee-making. Táňa Dluhošová and Lenka Starkova went to great lengths to teach me about digital mapping and to help me visualise my research in new and exciting ways. For all your patience, especially when my data sets were a mess and I had no idea what I wanted to achieve, I am grateful.

A cast of colleagues and interlocutors have provided critical insights, commentary and encouragement at crucial moments over the years, without which this project would not have come to fruition. Aria Fani has been a valuable voice in pushing me to explore new directions in my work while keeping me moored to my truest beliefs. Samad Alavi, since the beginning, has been a constant presence to critique, advise and listen in the most understanding of ways. Mana Kia has served as a crucial interlocutor for many discussions about the Persianate world in ways of which I've lost count. Arthur Dudney has been my most adept guide through the wild world of South Asia literary culture, Persian or otherwise. Sunil Sharma always seems to be close at hand, ready to listen, enlighten and encourage. I have learned from a great many colleagues along the way, especially Faiz Ahmed, Sergio Alivernini, Hannah Archambault, Hunter Bandy, David Boyk, Dominic Brookshaw, Robert

Crews, Purnima Dhavan, Michael Hill, Sam Hodgkin, Domenico Ingenito, Nile Green, Walt Hakala, Daniel Majchrowicz, Alexander Jabbari, Houshang Jeirani, Prashant Keshavmurthy, Rajeev Kinra, Justine Landau, Ira Lapidus, Frank Lewis, Paul Losensky, Margaret Larkin, Afshin Marashi, Stefano Pellò, Jaleh Pirnazar, Nasrin Rahimieh, Simon Rettig, Giedrė Šabasevičiūtė, Elizabeth Saylor, Daniel Sheffield, Matthew Smith, Nathan Tabor, Kamran Talattof, Amin Tarzi, Mandy Terc, Ernie Tucker and Ahmed Zildzic.

Portions of this book have been presented in various conferences, colloquia and workshops. I would like to thank the many organisers, participants and audience members for inviting me to share my work and provide thoughtful feedback. Some portions of this book originally appeared elsewhere. An earlier version of Chapter 4 was originally published in *The Indian Economic and Social History Review* under the title 'The Curious Case of Carnatic: The Last Nawab of Arcot (d. 1855) and Persian Literary Culture'. Certain portions of Chapter 2 first appeared in the *Journal of Persianate Studies* under the title 'The Local Lives of a Transregional Poet: 'Abd al-Qader Bidel and the Writing of Persianate Literary History'. My sincere thanks to Sage Publishing and Brill, respectively, for the permission to reprint here. Many thanks to the entire editorial team at Edinburgh University Press, especially Nicola Ramsey, Kirsty Woods, Rebecca Mackenzie, Michael Ayton and Eddie Clark, and to Stephanie Cronin as editor of the series *Edinburgh Historical Studies of Iran and the Persianate World*.

Friends and family, from the Midwest to the Southwest and beyond, have held me close and kept me honest. I will always be the better for it. I am grateful for the lightheartedness and encouragement provided by Polly Dement, Karen Feldman, Simon Galed, Julie Goshorn, Ciara Knudsen, Ken and Terra Kuhne, Jason Ladnier, Janet Lewis, Larry Malm, John Mayer, Ahsiya and Omar Mencin, Gary Milante, Nadia Motraghi, Yaser Nosrati, Dari and Jon Pogach, Debby Rager, Gobind and Ravneet Sethi, Todd Shaw and Frank Sweet. To my DC collective, Dan Mahanty, Josh Volz and Patrick Worman – your friendship is as unvarnished as it is unwavering. There is simply no place like Salon 2110. To my family, Elizabeth, Joe and Abby Cason, Brian Harris, Everett Harris, Jessica Rocher, Andrew Schwartz, Erin Schwartz and Kersti Yllo, I am indebted to your unyielding affection. Special thanks to my father-in-law David Potter, who has been both a fierce advocate of the book and a fierce editor. You never shy away from a single piece of my writing, no matter how underdeveloped, and always find the best it, and me. To my parents, my most formative teachers in all matters personal and professional, I am forever grateful for your undying support and timely guidance.

Without the unflinching love and enduring companionship of my wife, Holly, the completion of this work simply would not have been possible. I owe you my deepest thanks for your support in this endeavour and all else. Finally, to Sage and Ansel, you continue to exceed my expectations. May you always strive to exceed your own. I dedicate this work to you.

Prague, Czech Republic
August 2019

Note on Transliteration and Translation

This book follows the *International Journal of Middle East Studies* (IJMES) system of transliteration, with the following modification: the letter 'he' (often referred to as the 'silent he') appearing at the end of many words in Persian is omitted. Personal names, place names and the titles of books and articles are transliterated without macrons and diacritics. Technical terms and translations are fully transliterated. All translations were made by the author, unless otherwise stated.

Introduction

During my time conducting research at the Library of Congress in Washington, DC, I came across a text I hadn't expected to find. The text in question was *A'zam's Rosegarden*, an anthology of Persian poets composed in South India in the nineteenth century. I had seen a copy once before, but only as a manuscript at Aligarh Muslim University in India, and, until this point, was unaware the text existed in print, and in the library, no less, where I spent most of my waking hours. I was relieved to be able to look over the text again and not be solely reliant on my notes made several months earlier. Maybe I missed something. I probably missed something.

Curiously, the book was not held in the African and Middle East Division (AMED), home to the library's Persian materials, where I sat staring at the catalogue screen, but in the library's Asian Division downstairs. By this point, I had been researching at the Library of Congress long enough to know which reading rooms held which materials, but not once had I discovered, nor been informed otherwise by the library's staff, that Persian books could be found anywhere other than in the AMED reading room. Persian materials, like those in Arabic, Hebrew and Turkish, were kept in the AMED reading room and that was that. I jotted down the call number and hurried out the door, around an exhibition on discovering the Americas, down a marble staircase and through a throng of visitors and students before finally arriving at the end of a long corridor where the Asian reading room was tucked away.

By now my small sojourn had elicited a larger, admittedly disproportional, sense of joy at making an unexpected discovery. I promptly filled out the request form and handed it over to the librarian at the circulation desk. Just as promptly, the little green slip was back in my hand, unprocessed. My clearly euphoric interest was met with a blank stare. 'This book isn't here.

Can't be. Persian materials are kept in the AMED reading room. Second floor', I was told. 'No, no, it's here, the catalogue says so', I replied. But now I was less sure of myself than when I had skipped past the crowd of tourists minutes earlier, and began wondering whether I had misread the record. It wouldn't have been the first time. I would now have to trudge back upstairs, past the tourists shuffling around with heads tilted upward to take in the elaborate friezes, murals and columns adorning the Library's Great Hall. I relinquished the request slip and beseeched the librarian to pull up the catalogue record. A blank stare. The librarian was now as incredulous as I had been that this Persian text – any Persian text – was actually to be found in the Asian reading room. He rang up the South Asian librarian to make sense of it. She looked over the record and rang up one of the library technicians. Twenty minutes later, the library technician emerged from the back with a microfiche of *A'zam's Rosegarden*. He explained that he had found the microfiche among some forgotten boxes he had never had occasion to open.

Grateful, I thanked everyone for helping. I sat down at the microfiche machine to spool the film. A blank stare. I slid over to the computer catalogue and searched for Persian materials, limiting the search to only those held in the Asian reading room. Hundreds of citations came up. It was like a secret cache of Persian materials hidden in the Asian reading room, waiting to be discovered. Almost all of the materials were either composed in the nineteenth century or printed in South Asia during the nineteenth century and after. This was not surprising: regardless of their content, the mere fact they had been composed or printed in South Asia during a time of rising national consciousness and the formation of borders explains them being sectioned off from Persian materials found elsewhere and designated, under some regionally based mandate, to the Asian reading room. When I later recounted what happened to some librarians in the African and Middle East Division, they were equally shocked at the discovery. How many Persian texts does the Asian Division actually have? Shouldn't the texts be *here* in the African and Middle East Division and not over *there*? Perhaps a repatriation process was in order.

I know no better now than I did then whether the Persian materials should be moved from the Asian Division to the African and Middle East Division. Such an approach merely swaps one regional designation for another – an admittedly ill-fitting treatment for a language that knew no such confines when operating as a lingua franca across Islamic Eurasia from pre-modern times to the late nineteenth century and connecting peoples, places and ideas on a transregional basis. What I know with more certainty is that understanding how these Persian texts may relate to other texts and phenomena occurring across the expanse of the Persianate world is of greater importance than figuring out in which section of a given library they belong. This is equally true for Persian materials of South Asia as for those from Afghanistan, Central Asia and elsewhere, which are too often defined by neat regional and national cantons, whether in libraries or universities, quarantined from one another and the potential larger multi-regional trends that connect them.

Remapping Persian Literary History is a modest contribution aimed at recovering multi-regional connections and complexities across the Persianate world by exploring trends in literary culture of the eighteenth and nineteenth centuries. It explains how Persian literary history of that period came to be conceptualised according to national and regional division, and how a more integrative literary history of the time can be written. It does so by analysing the development and impact of one particular idea that, more than most, has had an outsized influence on how we think about Persian literary history from the eighteenth century onward. This idea, known as 'literary return' (*bāzgasht-i adabī*), contends that poets in eighteenth- and nineteenth-century Iran revived Persian poetry by returning to the styles of the classical masters, while those outside Iran did not because they maintained an overwhelming allegiance to a poetic style seen as retrograde and overly complicated. Believing that Iranian poets rescued Persian poetry from stagnation and ill repute by enacting this 'return' to Persian literature's glorious past has at once territorialised Persian literary history for Iran and marginalised it elsewhere.

It has long been recognised that Persian literary culture in the pre-modern era shaped the socio-political and intellectual environments from the Balkans to Bengal, in particular in the territories and diverse societies of West, Central and South Asia. Dynasties from the Samanids to the Mughals patronised Persian poets and men of letters and made Persian the official language of their chancelleries.[1] Persian cultural and textual traditions helped dynasties manage empires, enabled inter-imperial communication and influenced a variety of customs, behaviours and textual products tied to a myriad other languages.[2] Patronage of the Persian arts, particularly poetry, elevated rulers' legitimacy and authority. Interest in Persian language and culture promoted cross-regional fertilisation among poets and littérateurs of this Persianate sphere.[3] This common language and cultural focus allowed such groups to travel across frontiers in search of professional opportunities or personal enrichment and buttressed transregional bonds in a wide range of ideational formations and social practices.[4] Over the centuries, despite political upheavals and dynastic conflicts, the position of Persian and Persianate sensibilities as the dominant cultural-linguistic idiom survived across large swaths of Eurasia.[5]

Nevertheless, stark changes in the eighteenth and nineteenth centuries – such as the increased use of vernacular languages, break-up of empires, rise of nationalism and European imperialism and colonialism – began to pull at the cohesiveness of the Persianate sphere. But even amid this period of political and linguistic fracture, one can locate different literary communities on a multi-regional basis that sought to relate their experiences and understand their position within a contracting Persianate world according to one of its most important and enduring literary frontiers: engagement with the classical masters of Persian poetry.[6] Despite these literary communities' spatial and temporal distance from one another, and the divergent social and political conditions shaping their experiences, their similar attentiveness to debating, engaging with and drawing inspiration from the classical masters of Persian poetry, at a time when the Persianate world was breaking apart, points to a wider, multi-regional lens through which to understand Persian literary history during this time.

Rather than accept the 'literary return' experience of Iran in the eighteenth and nineteenth centuries as an explanation of the period's *Persian* literary history – an invariably Irano-centric enterprise – this account looks to elsewhere in the Persianate world. It approaches the Iranian experience as less of a given than a variable and the territory of Iran as no more the epicentre of poetic experience than elsewhere.[7] This is of crucial importance if one seeks to better understand not just developments in Persianate literary history, but also other phenomena in a multi-regional Persianate world. As Nile Green explains in *The Persianate World: The Frontiers of a Eurasian Lingua Franca*, studies reliant on 'Persianate' as an investigative rubric are best served by pursuing methodologies that can both speak of developments in this vast geographic and cultural contact zone absent a singular 'centre' and 'analytically denaturalize Persian's civilizational ties to Islam and *denationalize its primordialist ties to Iran*'.[8]

By integrating tales of literary communities across Iran, Afghanistan and South Asia at a time when the Persianate world was contracting, *Remapping Literary History* offers a multi-regional account of the connected and contested space of Persian literary culture, as understood through engagement with the canonic masters of poetry. Accordingly, the task of this book is not only to analyse the way eighteenth- and nineteenth-century Persian literary history has been mythologised according to the Iranian nationalist frame of 'literary return', but to complicate this frame though the inclusion of other non-Iranian literary experiences excluded by way of its historiographical hegemony and cultural authoritativeness. For to only explore the pitfalls of the 'literary return' frame – without broadening our gaze to include literary phenomena outside of Iran – would do little to overturn Iran's own centrality in literary developments in the period under discussion. Pursuant to this goal, as will become clearer below and in the chapters that follow, the three case studies of literary community presented here converge to offer a more complete picture of Persian literary developments in the eighteenth and nineteenth centuries. They do so by collectively reworking the terms of engagement for finding meaning and understanding, however divergent in their particularities, in a community's relationship to the poetic practice, experiences and canonical voices of Persian's classical poets. In other words, on their own, each case may represent its own discrete snapshot of poetic community at a particular juncture in time, but spliced together they characterise a composite panoramic of how literary experiences, engagements and production connected to Persian's classical masters aligned and collided in the eighteenth and nineteenth centuries on a multi-regional basis, when, indeed, this multi-regional world was falling apart.

The remainder of the introduction is dedicated to explaining the idea of 'literary return' as a type of literary nationalism and how it fits alongside other nationalist discourses in Iran. This is followed by a discussion of how to pursue a more integrative literary history of the eighteenth- and nineteenth-century Persianate world.

'Literary Return' as Literary Nationalism

While scholarship continues to detail the emergence of nationalism in Iran through the prism of territorial anxieties, institution building, Orientalism and race theory, the analysis of literary nationalism has remained a curious gap. What is meant here by literary nationalism is not the formulation of a collective social and cultural identity around the promotion of Persian as the national *language* of Iran, though this is certainly a related venture, but rather the promotion of Persian *literature* as the exclusive and explicit domain of Iran as a national literature.

In discussing literary nationalism in Iran, Nasrin Rahimieh notes how Iranian literati from the nineteenth to the twenty-first century 'envisioned literary modernity as a means of liberating the nation' that resulted in efforts ranging from 'adopting a modern national literary sensibility to positing a national literature distinct from its modern European counterparts'.[9] Such efforts exemplify 'a nationalist tendency that actively rewrites history and occasionally offers anachronistic readings of pre-modern and early modern Persian literature'.[10] The crucial encounter initiating this process was, for Rahimieh, Iran's engagement with European concepts and literatures. This assessment is no doubt correct and, as will be seen below, also connects the emergence of literary nationalism with other burgeoning discourses of nationalism in late nineteenth- and early twentieth-century Iran. Often overlooked, however, by this steady focus on the encounter with Europe is the manner in which Persian literary nationalism emerged through a reconceptualisation of Iran's relationship to the Persianate world. Crucial to the formulation of literary nationalism in Iran was the necessary desire to truncate Persian literature in Iran from its non-Iranian past and establish the Persianate world outside of Iran's own borders as its 'other'. The idea of 'literary return' was foundational in this regard.

Studies of Iranian nationalism, even with an overwhelming focus on encounters with Europe, help frame the discussion for the emergence of Persian literary nationalism in Iran as they perceptively relate many of the political, intellectual and cultural practices and processes undergoing change in Iranian society in the nineteenth and twentieth centuries. Firoozeh Kashani-Sabet has detailed in *Frontier Fictions: Shaping the Iranian Nation*,

1804–1946 how territorial disputes and concessions to the Ottomans, British and Russia, in addition to the presence of separatist groups within Iran's borders, shaped a well-defined discourse around Iran's geography in the nineteenth and twentieth centuries.[11] These anxieties around Iran's territory precipitated a series of 'frontier fictions' by intellectuals and the state that led to discrete visualisations of Iran's geographic coherence as well as the implementation of attempts at creating a culturally coherent and homogeneous nation through language and culture, the diversity of its population notwithstanding.

Afshin Marashi, in *Nationalizing Iran: Culture, Power, and the State, 1870–1940*, explores the cultural and social transformations across the late nineteenth and early twentieth centuries to ascertain the social-structural apparatus within which nationalism, as a politics, came to circulate and helped make 'the category "the nation" a viable and tangible social abstraction'.[12] Marashi looks to the re-imagining of public urban space, the rising importance of Iran's pre-Islamic heritage, a burgeoning system of mass education and the 'grafting of Enlightenment and post-Enlightenment modes of thought onto a Persianate cultural idiom [that] recast Iran into modern national form'.[13]

How the ideas and language of the European enlightenment were applied to the Iranian context, often with an Orientalist sheen, is the major subject of Mostafa Vaziri's *Iran as Imagined Nation: The Construction of National Identity*. While Vaziri recognises how internal discord and imperialist threat assisted in the formation of national identity in Iran, the intellectual fermentation around European thought on rights, secularism and race served as the primary driving force. He understands the construction of Iranian national identity through the emergence of a discourse of secularism, print capitalism and Orientalist ideas about history and race. He does so by relying on the theory of nationalism as articulated in Benedict Anderson's *Imagined Communities*. The most prominent aspect of this process for Vaziri was how nationalist ideology in Iran 'boldly incorporated the constructed version of national history of Iran by the Orientalists' and how Orientalist scholarly discourses of race wedded Iranian identity to pre-Islamic times. Orientalist racial theory and its reliance on an ingrained juxtaposition between Aryan and Semitic peoples, thereby separating Iranians linguistically, culturally and racially from their Arab neighbours, provided Iranians with the necessary elixir of a national Iranian-ness.[14]

Vaziri's thesis of how Iranian national identity mainly resulted from the wholesale importation and imitation of Orientalist attitudes about the Aryan race and Iran's pre-Islamic past remains the subject of ongoing critique. Reza Zia-Ebrahimi, in *The Emergence of Iranian Nationalism: Race and the Politics of Dislocation*, seeks to reframe the impact of Orientalist thought in Iran by exploring how external ideas about race and nation were not imbibed fully, but tweaked, changed and redefined to fit the Iranian context. While seeing the elevation of Iran's pre-Islamic past and 'the racialization of Iranian history' as traceable to 'nineteenth-century European scholarship on the Orient and on race, and not to local traditions and narratives', Zia-Ebrahimi moves to highlight how these ideas were indigenised and hybridised by local interlocutors on the ground in Iran.[15]

Zia-Ebrahimi's look at how Iranian actors leveraged and reshaped European ideas for their own on-the-ground purposes continues an important trend in the study of Iranian nationalism that places interactions with Western ideas, practices, infringements and technological advancements front and centre. The loss of territory, political and economic concessions, educational and training techniques, translation to and from European languages, Enlightenment ideas and the sending of students abroad have all, to varying degrees, implicated the substantial role of how engagements with the West assisted in shaping attitudes and developments in Iranian nationalism and national identity. As Ali Ansari has aptly noted in a recent study, 'nationalism as understood in Iran has largely been driven by and defined against a normative frame of reference established by European intellectual and political culture'.[16]

Abetting a European frame of reference in defining the contours of Iranian nationalism are a variety of exchanges whose roots lie outside of the West. The impact of Kemal Atatürk's language reform efforts on that of Reza Shah Pahlavi (r. 1925–41) have long been known, while the transregional connections impacting the intellectual ferment of Iran's Constitutional Revolution (1905–11) have come under increased attention in the past decades.[17] Recent scholarship has begun to fruitfully expand on Indo-Iranian exchanges to demonstrate the extra-territorial roots and routes of Iranian nationalism and nation-building. Historians such as Nile Green, Afshin Marashi and Farzin Vejdani have explored the connections, conversations, and textual and religious economies bridging Iran and South Asia to help better situate the growth of Iranian national attitudes, memory and identity in the realm of transregional interaction and exchange in the nineteenth and twentieth centuries.[18] In other words, some of the roots of nationalism in the territorially restrictive space of Iran benefited from sources and routes circulating from outside of it. Understanding these circulatory trends and cross-regional currents helps redefine Iranian nationalism 'as a transnational cultural and intellectual enterprise'.[19]

Perhaps the most prominent example in this regard is the role played by South Asian scholars and writers, that would feature heavily in emergent attitudes of linguistic, ethnic and cultural nationalism in Iran. Historical, lexicographic and philological texts by scholars based in South Asia helped establish the Indo-European roots of the Persian language. This linguistic discovery, underwritten by theories of race as promoted by the likes of the famed Orientalist William Jones (d. 1794), assisted in rationalising and developing an Aryan myth that allowed Iran to demonstrate 'a common and noble origin' with Europeans.[20] With such a linguistic theory of race in hand, Iranian nationalists, on a presumed evidentiary basis, could more easily 'dislocate' Iran from the East and associate it more fully with Europe.[21] Complementing this linguistic turn were texts produced and published in South Asia that emplotted the narratives of Iran's glorious pre-Islamic past on the (re)writing of Iranian history and refashioned a national cultural attitude on firm non-Islamic grounds. Collectively, these efforts, as Mohamad Tavakoli-Targhi notes, contributed to a burgeoning discourse in Iran seeking to 'project Iran's "decadence" onto Arabs and Islam and introject attributes of Europeans on the pre-Islamic Self'.[22] By formulating Iranian identity around the trident of the Persian language, Aryanism and a pre-Islamic past, the nation could distance itself from its relationship to Arabic and Islam and instead recast its destiny more fittingly alongside Europe as it sought to stride into modernity.[23] Thanks to scholarly output in South Asia that linked Iran to Europe through racialised theories of language and reasserted its pre-Islamic heritage, conceptual categories of the European enlightenment, like progress and secularism, could be more easily ascribed to a nascent Iranian nation, while the decadence and degradation of Arabic and Islam could be readily discarded.

The interactions and textual flows between Iran and India, new re-imaginings of language and history, engagement with Enlightenment concepts and technological advancements in Europe all blended together to initiate a robust discourse of linguistic and ethnic-cultural nationalism in Iran during the Qajar (1789–1925) and early Pahlavi (1925–79) eras. It was in such an environment that many of the parameters were formulated for a distinct literary nationalism to emerge as yet another attempt to define the boundaries of the Iranian nation. This was perhaps no better seen than in efforts to reform the Persian language in late nineteenth- and twentieth-century Iran. The obvious general intertwining between reforming a language and nurturing national literature aside, the case of Persian language reform is particularly instructive in terms of how many of the conceptual categories used to justify its efforts would similarly feature in framing a new narrative of literary nationalism centred on the idea 'literary return'.

Seen as the great preserve of Iranian cultural identity and independence during centuries of foreign invasion and occupation by Iranian intellectuals, the Persian language was considered a worthy target for reform.[24] Efforts to transform the language no doubt mirrored other attempts seeking to use Iran's linguistic and pre-Islamic heritage to create a closer conceptual proximity to Europe. As the literary scholar Ahmad Karimi-Hakkak explains, the country was 'entering the twentieth century with a consciousness that reform of its official language, Persian, was an integral part of the total social drive toward democracy within the framework of a modern nation-state'.[25] Reforming Persian, initially at least, meant purifying the language of its Arabic and Turkish 'accretions'.[26] Doing so would shed aspects of Iran's association not only with Arabic, but with the religion (Islam) and social class (clerics) accompanying it. In other words, distancing Persian from Arabic was meant to decouple Iranian national consciousness and identity from the foreignness of Arabs and Islam and reconnect it to a pre-Islamic past when the Persian language was supposedly pure and unadulterated. One of the earliest works demonstrating the convergence of glorifying Iran's pre-Islamic past and a non-Arabic inflected 'pure' Persian was the *Book of Kings* (*Nama-yi khusruvan*) by the Qajar prince Jalal al-Din Mirza (d. 1871). In explaining his decision to compose the work in 'pure' Persian, the Qajar prince wrote in a letter to the famed reformer and playwright Mirza Fath Ali Akhundzada (d. 1878) that 'I have used the language of our ancestors which like everything else has been violated and plundered by the Arabs'.[27]

Jalal al-Din Mirza found a sympathetic ear in Akhundzada. The Azerbaijani playwright, who wrote mainly in Azeri Turkish and spent most of his life in Tbilisi, saw in Arabic and Islamic culture the source of Iran's backwardness and an obstacle in the path towards progress, secularism and reform. The ideals of 'civilization' and 'progress', as well as other similar abstract notions which Akhundzada drew from his engagement with European thought, had to be found in Iran's pre-Islamic past, not its Islamic present.[28] As Marashi notes, 'Iranian authenticity, for Akhunzadeh, could thus be represented as congruent with modernity, whereas the Arab-Islamic elements in Iranian culture came to represent the inauthentic and anti-modern'.[29] The desire to locate ideals like 'civilization' and 'progress' in Iran's pre-Islamic past extended to a desire to do away with the Arabic script in both Persian and Turkish. The role of Arabic in Iranian society was particularly troublesome for Akhundzada. According to him, the primacy of Arabic allowed the clerical class to maintain a monopoly over Islamic law in Iran and contributed to high rates of illiteracy in Muslim societies that used the Arabic script.[30]

While Akhundzada was ultimately unsuccessful in convincing either Ottoman or Iranian authorities to do away with the Arabic script, less extreme examples of language reform in early twentieth-century Iran gained traction. Already in the Qajar period members of the courtly elite, like Jalal al-Din Mirza and Qa'im Maqam (d. 1835), had endeavoured to write in more simplified Persian. Soon, however, secular intellectuals connected these efforts to a larger agenda by demonstrating a 'profound interest in the cause of language simplification ... as an indispensable part of their quest for liberty and democracy'.[31] If the Persian language could be simplified, then ideas of secularism and democracy could be expressed all the more easily. For many, language reform became, in the words of Karimi-Hakkak, 'the pursuit of simplicity, direct expression, and naturalness which ... characterized both the speech of the man in the street as well as that of the great poets and prose-stylists of a glorious past'.[32] The social agenda underpinning these efforts was not necessarily distinct from that of Akhundzada, even if the means differed:

simplifying the Persian language, of which moving away from Arabic word-usage was a part, could help dismantle the clerical elite's hold over society and redirect it towards a more secular future. A corrupted language and style of writing needed to be uncorrupted.

Here, in the convergence of Persian language reform, the desire for simplified expression and more general efforts to recalibrate Iranian national identity around a glorious past, the idea of 'literary return' as an expression of literary nationalism can be located. The idea of 'literary return' is, at its most basic level, the belief that Persian poetry needed to return to the simplified styles of the ancients by distancing itself from the complex, convoluted and unwelcome style that had taken over in its stead. Supposedly nurtured at once by a lack of poetic talent, the debilitating impact of foreign invasion (the Mongols) and the rise of a religiously-minded dynasty more interested in propagating Islam (the Safavids), a stylistic return to the 'roots' of sound classical poetry as articulated by the ancients was deemed in order. In this way, the idea of 'literary return' was conceptualised according to the same motifs found in articulations of Iranian racial and linguistic national identity, namely, (re)connections with an ancient past through the eradication of unsavoury and intervening 'foreign' corruptions, such as Islam and the Arabic language. Persian poetry too had been overtaken by its own corrupting forces to the point of unintelligibility. A renewal was needed to rectify this sorry state of poetic affairs. Poets in eighteenth- and nineteenth-century Iran, we are told, having dutifully assessed the debilitating state of a Persian poetry mired in complexity and declining in stature, advocated a 'return' to the simple styles of the ancients. Their efforts, as contemporary commentators and those later in the twentieth century made clear, rescued Persian poetry and re-established it on the path towards progress. Thanks to the 'literary return' movement, Persian poetry in Iran was able to narrowly avoid its death knell and recalibrate Iran's literary environment.

The contrasting terminology of 'decline'/'renewal' and 'simplicity'/'complexity', used to promote the idea of an awakened sense of Iranian nationalist identity around racial, cultural and linguistic lines certainly inflected conceptualisations of 'literary return'. References to how Persian poetry was overcome by 'weakness' (*sustī*), mired in 'decline' (*inḥitāt*), overtaken by complexity (*pīchīdigī*) and in need of a 'revival' (*iḥyā'*) litter contemporary accounts of 'literary return' in the nineteenth century, as they do for commentators in the twentieth century seeking to explain the movement's germination.³³

The attitudes of Muhammad Taqi Bahar (d. 1951) and Riza-Zadah Shafaq (d. 1971), writing in the 1930s and 1940s, demonstrate how the binaries of 'decline'/'renewal' and 'simplicity'/'complexity' mapped onto the depiction of a uniquely national literary movement in Iran. In such accounts, the decline of Persian poetry can be traced to the Mongol invasions of Iran, which led to the raiding of libraries, the scattering of books on the Persian language and sound composition, the disappearance of a scholarly class and the fleeing of poets from Iran. A few esteemed classical masters, like Rumi (d. 1273), Sa'di (d. 1291–2) and Hafiz (d. 1390), may have been able to thrive during this time, but the overall appearance of great poetry was significantly diminished. Due to the lack of adequate materials and teachers to cultivate good poetry, and the strengthened position of Arabic during this time, the Persian language (and its poetry) became corrupted and weak. Gradually, according to Bahar, the Persian language and the methods used for its pleasant cultivation were forgotten.³⁴

If the scourge of the Mongol invasions led to the depreciation of poetry through a physical depletion of literary materials and scholars from Iran, we are told, then the religious proclivities of the Safavid dynasty (r. 1501–1722) sent Persian poetry into a tailspin. As Shafaq put it in his *History of Persian Literature*:

> With all of this [the promotion of Shi'ism and religiosity] one can consider from a general perspective the Safavid period to be one of Persian literary decline (*inḥitāt*) … not only is this period devoid of esteemed poets, but the important issue of the ancients' poetry, in the lyric and mystical poetry, was discarded because the Safavids opposed them both. Persian prose and poetry were significantly downgraded.³⁵

The Safavids' adherence to Shi'ism and supposed shunning of poetry on account of their piety remains one of the most recurrent myths concerning the state of Persian poetry in the early modern period. The Safavids' disdain for poetry altogether, or an exclusive focus on poetry in praise of religious figures, pepper the well-established literary histories composed throughout the 1960s, 1970s, 1980s and later, in works such as Zarrinkub's *Literary Criticism*, Farshidvard's *On Literature and Literary Criticism*, Aryanpur's *From Saba to Nima* and Shamisa's *Stylistics of Poetry*.[36] Implied in many of these impressions is that the arrival of Arab clerics in Safavid Iran played a disastrous role for poetic production, echoing Akhundzada's criticism of the clerical elite's negative impact on Iranian society in the nineteenth century.[37] While assessments of the Safavids' disdain for poetry and the precise impact on poetic production vary, the general result as presented in literary histories of Iran was that Persian poetry starting in the sixteenth century entered a period of decline and stagnation.[38] As Hamid Dabashi summarily puts it in *The World of Persian Literary Humanism*, 'from the rise to power of Shah Ismail [r. 1501–24] to the ascendancy of Fath Ali Shah [r. 1797–1834], a period of some 300 years, no great poet or literary prose stylist of any enduring significance emerged in Iran'.[39]

It is in such an environment, defined by uncultivated literary sensibilities, a religiously-minded dynastic court and the supposed corrupting force of Arabic and Islam, that the style known to history as the 'Indian Style' filled the void. Known for 'advancing weakness and complexity in the lyric day after day', to borrow the words of Bahar, the 'Indian Style' would come to dominate Iran, South Asia and much of the Persianate world for the next two centuries.[40] In the opinion of Bahar and his contemporaries, the period may have produced its share of decent poets, like 'Urfi Shirazi (d. 1591) and Kalim Kashani (d. 1651), who rose to the position of poet laureate under the Mughals (r. 1526–1857), but as in the preceding post-Mongol period these examples were few.[41] There were even those who tried in earnest to compose poetry in the style of the ancients, but neither could this development disrupt the Indian style's overall 'corrupting' influence on Persian poetry writ large.[42]

The proliferation of the transregionally prevalent 'Indian Style', supposedly beset by strange meanings, ambiguity, weakness of language, wordplay and incongruent metaphors, has been put forward as the rationale for poets in eighteenth- and nineteenth-century Iran seeking a 'literary return' to the styles of ancients. 'It is obvious that if the literary return movement didn't appear and the vulgarity of the Indian style had gradually gained strength', a recent appraisal of the movement notes, 'then today the fate (*sar-nivisht*) of Persian poetry and prose would have precipitously fallen.'[43] Absent the occurrence of 'literary return', Persian poetry would not have progressed and developed. Consequently, it has been argued, a re-introduction to the foundations and constructions of classical Persian prose and poetry was crucial.[44]

It bears mention that not every element abetting the standardised narrative of 'literary return' presented here has been immune from critical scholarship and re-evaluations. The Safavids' supposed disdain for anything but religious poetry has been revealed as a myth.[45] So has the general notion that the period of their reign in Iran militated against literary production.[46] New scholarship has begun to critically re-evaluate the poetics of the 'Indian Style' (more appropriately termed *tāza-gū'ī* or 'fresh-speak') and its position within Persian literary history.[47] Likewise, the narrative of 'literary return' and desire to nationalise Persian literature should not be regarded as having unfolded in any linear fashion. Individuals like Bahar and Shafaq, perhaps two of the most crucial figures in the articulation of the parameters of 'literary return', display a level of uncertainty and ambiguity in detailing its rise in some of their early writings. Neither, it bears mention, was this process solely undertaken by Iranian scholars, but it benefited from the contributions of other Western and non-Western scholars. For example, the South Asian scholar Shibli Nuʿmani (d. 1914) noted in his five-volume *Poetry of Persians* (originally published in Urdu) that 'poetry and the art of versifying in Iran began with Rudaki and ended with Mirza Saʾib [d. 1677–8]. There were poets before Rudaki and after Saʾib, but these two periods count for nothing.'[48] In other words, no poetry of consequence was produced after the mid-seventeenth century when the 'Indian Style' supposedly reigned supreme. The impact of exchanges with Western scholars in particular would feature in the national project to redefine Persian literary history as Iran's own, most notably in the work of Edward Granville Browne (d. 1926).[49] All told, Persian literature and literary history as a discipline and object of inquiry was institutionalised through transregional exchanges among Iranians, Afghans, South Asians and westerners.[50] Even with these necessary caveats, indeed in spite of them, the backbone of the 'literary return' narrative as a crucial interpolation in the development of Persian literature and proxy for literary nationalism in Iran endures.

The case of 'literary return' contains many of the hallmarks defining different permutations of Iranian nationalism active in the nineteenth and twentieth centuries: the impact of foreign invasion, the deleterious effects of Islam and Arabic and the overall corruption of an element of Iranian national identity, in this case poetry, removed from its rightful and purified origins. But there is also something noticeably distinctive about retellings of 'literary return' as an instantiation of literary nationalism. Unlike its territorial, linguistic, ethnic and racial counterparts, the narrative of 'literary return' takes as its ultimate counterpoint not Arabs, the Arabic language or the Islamic religion, but the cosmopolitan Persianate world existent beyond Iran's borders. To truly nationalise and territorialise Persian literature as Iran's own is to recognise the phenomenon of a glorious 'return' to an ancient poetic past as an exclusively Iranian experience. As Karimi-Hakkak explains, the poets of the 'return' movement 'tended to reject the immediate past as alien, employing instead the styles associated with earlier poetic schools', and 'endeavored to restore the millennium-long tradition of Persian poetry to what they perceived as its "original" simplicity'.[51]

The 'literary return' movement, as even some of the most sceptical critics would agree, pertains to Iran alone.[52] The rest of the Persianate world, whether in South Asia, Central Asia or elsewhere, did not participate in this important stage of Persian literary development. Any development occurring outside of Iran during or after the 'literary return' period, that is, during or after the eighteenth century, is deemed outside of Persian literary history. This attitude reflects a type of conceptual rendering of literary history that, as the literary scholar David Perkins reminds us, is capable of highlighting 'only those texts that fit its concepts, sees in texts only what its concepts reflect, and inevitably falls short of the multiplicity, diversity, and ambiguity of the past'.[53] Moreover, in promoting the phenomenon of 'literary return' as an exclusively Iranian endeavour, the literary history of Persian becomes synonymous with Iran's own and is truncated from the rest of the Persianate world. Unlike iterations of Iranian nationalism constructed around race and language, which benefited through real or imagined connections with South Asia, this type of literary nationalism seeks to wholly divide Iran's literary destiny from places outside its borders.

This does not mean that some incontrovertible binary pitting Iranian 'selves' in opposition to Persianate 'others' defined all interactions and exchanges between Iranians and non-Iranians in the eighteenth and nineteenth centuries. On the contrary, as Mana Kia has shown, a dialogue of intimacy, commonality, similarity and friendship defined relationships among Iranians and other members of the Persianate sphere across a range of epistemological discourses.[54] But the process of redefining the literary history of the Persianate sphere as Iran's own was not of this mould: it was not a process of construction or one fashioned around commonality, but one of destruction and difference, increasingly laid bare in territorialised and nationalist terms. Matthew Smith concisely sums up the process by noting how 'rather than attempt to expand their awareness of an Iranian nation in order to correspond with the geographical reach of Persian literature, *bazgasht* [return] authors instead reversed the process and allowed the shrinking physical borders of the nation to provide the limits of what was understood to be a proper body of literature'.[55] It is a statement that can equally be applied to the many literary histories recounting the rise and importance of the 'literary return' movement; their uncritical appraisal necessarily obstructs our ability to recognise literary phenomena occurring outside of Iran in the eighteenth and nineteenth centuries. Our vision of literary history during this period is constricted.

Cosmopolitanism, Canon, Community

In discussing the global process of transition from cosmopolitan to national literatures, Alexander Beecroft in *An Ecology of World Literature: From Antiquity to the Present Day* notes how emerging nation-states began to demonstrate a more restrictive view of literature and literary production. 'Wherever nation-states emerged', he writes, 'their scholars tended to valorize texts in the national vernacular over those in a cosmopolitan language … both in the nation that claimed the cosmopolitan language as its own and in the other nations that now privileged their vernacular histories.'[56] In other words, whether in a place like Iran, where Persian remains the language of national literature, or erstwhile places of the Persianate world such as today's Turkey or India where it does not, supplanting the cosmopolitan past represents for Beecroft the critical index for establishing the domain and ideology of national literature.[57] To this end, national literatures worked to marginalise the large quantity of information that did not correspond to readings and interpretations of texts 'through the lens of the nation-state, whether as that state's embodiment, as the dissent tolerated within its public sphere, as its legitimating precursors, or as its future aspirations'.[58] For Beecroft, like others, a crucial element for the creation and formulation of national literature in this regard is the writing of literary history.[59] For those seeking to constrict national literature to only those texts pertaining to the nation it is deemed to embody, other texts and literary experiences understood as incapable of fulfilling this aim must be reduced, elided and ultimately edited out.[60] As Ríos-Font points out, literary history constructs a narrative plot around the protagonist of the imagined nation, which 'appears from the outset in a competitive struggle with others' and utilises 'literary history as an instrument at the service of this contest'.[61]

Beecroft's frame for explaining the emergence of a national literature out of a cosmopolitan environment is a crucial intervention in understanding how Persian literary history writing truncated Iran from its cosmopolitan past and assisted in nationalising Persian literature for Iran. Suddenly it seems, as if in one fell swoop, the shared experiences, encounters and engagements connecting people and places across the Persianate sphere dissipated. The interpolation of the idea of 'literary return' in Persian literary history writing was the key ingredient creating a 'rupture with the cosmopolitan past, by the assertion of the national literary language as superior to its cosmopolitan antecedents'.[62] Iran inaugurated a movement to 'return' to the classical styles of the ancients, as if such poets reside in an unmediated and timeless entity sealed from the periods before and after them; the rest of the Persianate world outside of Iran's borders decidedly did not.

The critical distinction being made between poetic production in different locales across the Persianate sphere as accounted for in Persian literary history, as noted above, is undoubtedly one based on style (*sabk*). The so-called 'Indian Style' remained prevalent outside of Iran, while inside of Iran it was shunned for a 'return' to the style of the ancients, so the story goes. Following from this distinction are, of course, a series of aesthetic judgements and qualifications that pit the simplicity and purity of the 'return' style against the complication and weakness of the 'Indian Style'. Perhaps for the first time, according to William Hanaway, 'clear stylistic boundaries were drawn by the poets within Iran, and the models for good poetry were specified'.[63]

But it is not enough to understand the distinction being made between poetic production in Iran and the rest of the cosmopolitan world of Persian as simply a matter of stylistic difference. The rupturing of Persian literary history in Iran from its cosmopolitan legacy is more than the recognition of the stylistic asymmetry between two geographic areas. Underwriting the aesthetic distinction between the 'literary return' and 'Indian Style', and the geographic entities to which they remain connected, is the internal logic of Persian literary history itself, a logic that equates development and progress with stylistic change. The very title of Bahar's influential work, which sets the tone for much of Persian literary history in the twentieth century, is often referenced with the truncated title of *Stylistics* (*Sabk-shinasi*), but the fuller title of *Stylistics or the History of the Evolution of Persian Writing* (*Sabk-shinasi ya tarikh-i tatavvur-i nasr-i Farsi*) is a stark reminder of how he and others recognised the unfolding of Persian literary history over time.[64] Stylistic change, as much for Bahar as others relying on his model, is what determines a new stage in Persian literary evolution. Persian literary history is not simply a story of stylistics, but of stylistic change.

What may appear like a subtle and even obvious point is nonetheless a crucial one for understanding how the literary history of the eighteenth- and nineteenth-century Persianate world has come to be written. What abetted the ability to conceptualise Persian literature in Iran as breaking away from literature elsewhere in the Persianate sphere was as much the idea of aesthetic difference as stylistic change. The newness of the 'literary return' style is what secured its place as a *new* period of Persian literary evolution. The 'Indian Style', by contrast, warrants no further consideration on account of supposedly being frozen in stylistic time. In other words, the perseverance of the 'Indian Style' during the same time as 'literary return' comes onto the scene in Iran is incapable of being incorporated into a model of Persian literary history that sees stylistic change as the engine of evolution. As curious as it sounds, the style replicating poetic models of the ancients (*mutaqaddimīn*) in the eighteenth and nineteenth centuries is what qualifies as 'newness', whereas the style perpetuated through the often-disparaged moderns (*muta'akhkhirīn*) making topics 'new' or 'fresh' is determined as unchanging. But such is the result of equating a new literary style with literary evolution. Persian literary history only lurches forward when stark stylistic changes are observed, which in the case of the eighteenth and nineteenth centuries often means participating in the stylistic innovation of a 'new' and emergent 'literary return'.

The idea of stylistic change as the driving force for understanding Persian literary production in the eighteenth and nineteenth centuries is necessarily limiting in scope. It presents two major problems, one related to analyses of poetry outside of Iran's borders and the other to analyses of poetry in Iran itself. First, literary production during this time that does not adhere to the newly emergent poetic trend (i.e. 'literary return') is deemed uneventful. In other words, poetry outside of Iran is penalised for presuming to maintain some variation of the status quo (i.e. the 'Indian Style') and not engaging in the style of 'literary return'. As recent scholarship makes clear, poetic production within the frame of the 'fresh-speak' style continued to develop, refashion and reinvent itself in the eighteenth and nineteenth centuries, often by remaining connected to modes of authorities and models that can be traced back to the ancients.[65] Such impressions, however, have been continually elided and obfuscated in the grand narrative of Persian literary history. Poetic practice outside of Iran as understood by Bahar and his successors has been consigned to an unchanging and uneventful 'Indian Style'.

Second, the insistence on understanding the emergence of 'literary return' as one of stylistic change necessarily focuses analyses of eighteenth- and nineteenth-century poetry in Iran on the stylistics of individual authors. As the defining characteristic, and crucial undertaking, of the 'literary return' movement is presumed to be a stylistic shift towards the simplified verse of the ancients, proving the ancients were indeed replicated is paramount. In other words, poets are only deemed to participate in the 'literary return' provided they display a stylistic affinity for the ancients in their poetry. Here is Saba (d. 1822) imitating Firdawsi (d. 1019 or 1025), Qa'ani (d. 1854) replicating the verse of 'Unsuri (d. 1039), Surush (d. 1868) recalling Mu'izzi (d. *c.*1125–7) and Nashat (d. 1828–9) harking back to the verse of Hafiz (d. 1390).[66] This type of approach, which permeates analyses of 'literary return', not only necessarily restricts the definition of what is meant by the period and style itself, but narrowly defines the parameters on which a poet can engage with the poetic canon of the ancients in the eighteenth and nineteenth centuries. Only the appearance of stylistic proof of the ancients in the verse of an individual poet of several centuries later is what meets the criteria for being a poet of record in eighteenth- and nineteenth-century Persian literary history.

It bears mention that, until recently, there has been very little pushback to this understanding of Persian literary history, either by scholars and poets in Iran, as made clear above, or by those in Afghanistan and South Asia, whether in the nineteenth or twentieth centuries. On the contrary, the narrative of 'literary return' has been able to survive as it has through a significant level of direct or indirect buy-in by Afghan and South Asian literary historiography. This will be further explained in later chapters, but two brief examples warrant mention. First, Afghan literary historians in the twentieth century deferred to the 'literary return' narrative either by depicting it as a uniquely Iranian phenomenon or by seeking to rediscover its Afghan equivalent. In the latter case, this was pursued by searching for an 'Afghan literary return' as narrowly defined by the 'individual poet imitating an individual master' paradigm, thereby hoping to secure a place for Afghanistan in the established grand narrative of Persian literary history. Either way, Afghan literary historiography of the eighteenth and nineteenth centuries was being constructed on terms set forth by a conceptualisation of 'literary return' as pertaining to developments in Iran. Second, South Asian poets of the nineteenth century, in many ways precipitating the Iranian-centrism coursing through literary historiography later on, began deferring to native speakers of Persian to define the parameters of what constituted acceptable Persian verse.[67] This does not imply any awareness on their part of 'literary return' developments in nineteenth-century Iran. Nonetheless, this example helps explain how a narrative of Persian literary history that would increasingly privilege the voices of Iranian poets and scholarship at the expense of South Asian poets could so easily take hold later on, as seen in the work of Shibli Nuʿmani, and the demonisation of the so-called 'Indian Style'. In other words, Persian literary historiography in both Afghanistan and South Asia either constructed itself to directly complement the Iranian-centricity of Persian literary history or had developed characteristics primed to indirectly accept it. No major criticisms of 'literary return' would emerge from Afghanistan and South Asia until much later in the twentieth century.

The need to identify an esteemed ancient in the verse of an eighteenth- and nineteenth-century poet is mutually reinforcing for defining the Persian poetic canon. While a full assessment of Persian canon formation lies outside of this study, it is sufficient to note that identifying a one-to-one correspondence between a nineteenth-century poet in Iran and an ancient one of several centuries past is one of the many accumulated instances giving the canon its shape, a process that reaches its fullest maturation in the early twentieth century.[68] The conceptualisation of 'literary return' as a distinct period in Persian literary history certainly played its part: as much as the verse of an ancient poet brings the 'literary return' poet to life, a 'literary return' poet provides the vehicle through which the status of an ancient poet is further reified in the canon through such recognition. The result is a self-reinforcing paradigm defined by a closed circuit of stylistic engagement between individual Iranian authors of the eighteenth and nineteenth centuries and the increasingly canonised ancients. In this way, Persian literary history of this period has been distilled to an account of poetic production in Iran and a narrow focus on the stylistics of individual Iranian poets engaging with the poetry of an individual ancient poet at that. This is not an argument for the complete eradication of the important scholarly practice dedicated to ascertaining stylistic change in Persian poetry, but rather a desire to see its investigation in the greater context of shifting social-political settings and debates, literary or otherwise, contemporaneous with an author's writing.[69]

One of the aims of this study is to depart from such a restrictive rendering of Persian literary history. It seeks to do so by at once exploring literary production beyond Iran's borders and, at the same time, moving away from a primary focus on the stylistics of individual authors. In the first instance, the inclusion of Persian literary phenomena outside of Iran in the eighteenth and nineteenth centuries not only justifiably re-integrates the non-Iranian world into the realm of Persian literary history, but also demonstrates how engagement with the ancients during this time was not the sole domain of Iranian poets. In the second instance, assessing Persian poetic culture outside the narrow close-circuitry of stylistics between individual poets and ancient masters broadens an understanding of how engagement with the ancients operated on a wider multi-regional scale across variegated social and political contexts.

Rather than adhere to a model of eighteenth- and nineteenth-century Persian literary history that privileges stylistic change and the writing of poetry by individual authors, this study shifts its gaze to communities engaging with the ancients on a wider basis. It moves away from a narrative privileging the writing of poetry towards the reception and reading of it, from stylistics imitating the ancients to the broader engagement with their work and legacy, from connecting individual poets to the Persian canon to literary communities debating and engaging an open-ended canon according to their own social and political contexts. By looking at cases of literary communities in Iran, Afghanistan and South Asia across the eighteenth and nineteenth centuries, it aims to wrestle away Persian literary history from its fixation on the restrictive category of 'literary return' and the prevalent logic which states that literary culture during this time is defined by the experience of Iranian poets imitating an 'ancient' style. To be clear: this study is not a critical examination of the variegated aesthetics and stylistics of 'literary return' poetry per se and, as such, does not focus on poetic practice at the Qajar court in the mid-to-late nineteenth century when the style achieved primacy. Rather, the concern here is to unpack the category of 'literary return' and unravel the myth-making it emplotted on Persian literary history. As New Historicism reminds us, when a text or literary category ceases to be seen as 'sacred, self-enclosed, and self-justifying ... it begins to lose at least some of the special power ascribed to it, its boundaries begin to seem less secure and it loses exclusive rights to the experience of wonder'.[70]

One way to move away from a rendering of Persian literary history focused on the style of individual poets towards one exploring the activity of literary communities is by relying on the genre of biographical anthologies (*tadhkira*). Unlike an individual collection of poetry (*dīvān*), these texts provide a firmer basis for exploring the social bonds among communities of poets, the poetic debates occupying their energies and how they collectively related themselves to larger literary and cultural environments. Coming from the Arabic root dh-k-r, meaning 'to recall' or 'to remember', *tadhkira*s are one of the most prevalent genres of texts in Islamic societies. These texts appear in different languages and in slightly different formats, but may best be described as texts seeking to 'remember' certain individuals, by virtue of which those individuals are established as a 'class', whether they be Sufis, scholars or poets, either throughout history or contemporary with an author's writing. According to Chase Robinson, this feature of *tadhkira*s helps define them as prosopographic texts in Islamic historiography. 'Whereas', Robinson notes, 'biography is about exemplary or otherwise distinctive individuals whose lives – however exceptional or heroic – take meaning from their times, prosopography compiles and organizes those items of biographical data that mark an individual's belonging to a group.'[71]

*Tadhkira*s are produced for wide-ranging purposes, maintain differing emphases, vary in scope and diverge in their methods for composition and cataloguing. The biographical anthologies utilised for this study are those that focus on the lives of Persian poets. Long undervalued as texts serving as little more than repositories for the basic details of a poet's life and verse, *tadhkira*s of Persian poets have proved of late to be a valuable resource for charting a vast array of literary, social, cultural and political phenomena across the early modern and modern Persianate world.[72] Recent scholarship has relied on these texts to explore a wealth of topics, ranging from studies in cultural memory and literary reception to the exploration of the 'urban life' of poets and conceptualisation of geographic space.[73] Here, *tadhkira*s of Persian poets will be used to reconstruct social and literary communities across the eighteenth- and nineteenth-century Persianate world, whose networks will be visualised in a series of network maps. Demonstrating how biographical anthologies can serve to reconstruct social and literary connections among groups of poets, as well as recover forgotten genealogies of literary attitudes and sensibilities, will highlight the many ways in which this genre of texts can contribute to a remapping of literary history in the eighteenth and nineteenth centuries. Doing so will help better position the field of Persian literary studies so as to institute a necessary shift away from focusing on individual 'canonic' voices and instead emphasise aspects of literary community, both locally and across borders, more reflective of the vast, integrated and ever-morphing Persianate world in the early modern and modern periods.

Organisation of the Study

Before presenting the cases of three distinct literary communities engaging with the poetry of the ancients across the Persianate world, the first chapter provides the historiographical backdrop for how the idea of 'literary return' impacted the writing of Persian literary history in Iran, Afghanistan and South Asia. Chapter 1, 'Remembering Iran, Forgetting the Persianate: Persian Literary Historiography of the Eighteenth and Nineteenth Centuries', explains how the insertion of 'literary return' as a category helped truncate the multi-regional integrity of the Persianate sphere and chart different nationalist and regionalist readings of Persian literary history in those places. Each section presents the historiography of Persian literary culture in Iran, Afghanistan and South Asia in turn and provides the framework for locating the experiences of each individual literary community addressed in subsequent chapters. The chapter begins by expanding on the narrative account of 'literary return' presented above by analysing some of the earliest accounts of the movement in eighteenth- and nineteenth-century Iranian sources.

While the idea of 'literary return' reached its full fruition in twentieth-century Iran, its germination process begins a century and half earlier, when ideas about Iranian poets seeking to return to styles of the ancients start to appear in biographical anthologies. Excavating the genealogy of 'literary return' in the writings of various poets and anthologists in the eighteenth and nineteenth centuries elucidates how some impressions of the movement in its gestational phase were cast aside by later authors. Recovering these forgotten elements allows for a re-investigation of what motivated poets in eighteenth- and nineteenth-century Iran to 'return' to the styles of the ancients in the first place. The chapter next turns to the legacy of 'literary return' in Afghanistan and how Afghan literary historians have promoted the idea of a specifically 'Afghan literary return'. Even though the idea of an Afghan 'literary return' remains a questionable historical occurrence, and is derided by some as simple mimicry, its promotion by Afghan historians displays an effort by non-Iranians to grapple with an Iranian-centric literary category and rewrite Afghanistan into the main narrative of Persian literary history. The chapter concludes with a discussion of Persian literary historiography in South Asia and how the idea of 'literary return' helped consolidate a long-held view of Persian's decline in the Subcontinent. While recognising the increased stress felt by Persian literary culture due to the rise of British colonialism and the Urdu language, it challenges the idea that either of these factors led to Persian's complete eradication in nineteenth-century South Asia.

Chapter 1, having established the historiographical stakes for different readings of literary history in the eighteenth- and nineteenth-century Persianate world, Chapter 2 re-investigates poetic culture in post-Safavid Isfahan. 'Reformation and Reconstruction of Poetic Networks: Isfahan *c.*1722–1801' provides a retelling of the literary and social circumstances that led a group of poets in post-Safavid Isfahan to return poetry to the style of the ancients. The typical account of this literary occurrence relies on the erroneous belief that a group of 'Iranian' poets sought to rescue Persian poetry in response to the deleterious stylistics of 'Indian' poets and trends in poetic culture outside of Iran's borders. This retroactive insertion of proto-nationalist rivalry into the narration of an eighteenth-century movement incorrectly depicts what inspired a close network of poets to undertake a 'return' to classical styles of the ancients in the first place. Through a close reading of historical texts, biographical dictionaries and the authors' poetry, the chapter argues for viewing this movement of poets as one significantly more concerned with the politics, prestige, and opportunities for patronage in these poets' own local environment. Rather than displaying an interest in literary activity outside of Iran's borders, this community sought to re-establish the role of the poet in Isfahan. In pursuing this claim, the chapter challenges a long-held assumption about Iranian history in the eighteenth century: that the period between the downfall of the Safavids and the rise of the Qajars represents a stark break in history and disallows any social and literary continuity between the two dynasties. Overturning such a long-standing belief assists in better depicting the larger social, literary and political circumstances that allowed a localised Iranian 'return' movement to flourish. Indeed, the eighteenth century is generally depicted as a 'black hole' in Iranian history and discarded as a period defined by political turmoil and chaos. But as Michael Axworthy notes in his recent volume reassessing the period, 'periods of crisis, turmoil, and trauma are often formative and decisive – they create opportunities as well as misery'.[74]

Moving away from an explanation that stylistic imitation is what led a group of poets in Isfahan to return to the styles of the ancients allows for a broader investigation of how communities of poets elsewhere similarly engaged with the ancients around the same time. Chapter 3, 'A Market for the Masters: Afghanistan *c.*1839–1842', turns its gaze to mid-nineteenth-century Afghanistan and explores the literary production of a series of war-ballads (*jangnāmas*) written in response to the first Anglo-Afghan War (1839–42). While the invasion, occupation and retreat of the British from Afghanistan has been depicted in various historical and fictionalised accounts, the consideration and analysis of these local Afghan literary responses has remained a noticeable gap in scholarship. Of greater importance for this study is that these war-ballads were composed in imitation of Firdawsi's *Book of Kings* (*Shahnama*), arguably the most famous model for war-ballads in classical Persian literature. The composition of these texts in clear imitation of the style of a classical master represents a consequential occurrence of how engagement with the poetry of the ancients was not restricted to Iran during this time. But beyond any similarity in style, an exploration of the production, circulation and reception of these war-ballads demonstrates the remarkable degree to which the ancient masters of Persian poetry were valued by Afghan poets, audiences and patrons. These texts, which circulated in oral, manuscript and printed form and drew upon a diverse group of patrons, point to a transregional 'market of the masters' stretching across Afghanistan and South Asia. The existence of such a market for these texts nullifies the claim that no engagement with the style and form of the ancients existed outside of Iran. Crucially, the composition of these texts and their afterlives point to how Afghan poets in a moment of political crisis, not unlike their counterparts in Isfahan, sought to engage the poetry of the ancients to make sense of their own experiences. Moreover, this case offers for Persianate studies an individual example of how texts, authors and patrons cohered to form a multi-regional network of literary production.

Chapter 4, 'Debating Poetry on the Edge of the Persianate World: Arcot *c.*1850', offers one last case of a literary community engaging with the canon of Persian poetry in a moment of literary and cultural crisis. While it is commonly held that Persian literary culture had become more or less irrelevant in South Asia by the mid-nineteenth century, especially in the south of the Subcontinent, the situation at the court of the last ruler of the kingdom of Arcot dispels such a myth. The Arcot state, as well as the seat of British power in nearby Madras, provided a hospitable climate for Persian literary production. The last Nawab of Arcot (d. 1855) promoted Persian literary life by constituting a poetic assembly whose members engaged one another in vibrant debate over the Persian poetic canon. The literary climate of mid-nineteenth-century Arcot makes clear that following the break-up of the Mughal Empire, Persian literary culture did not merely decline but found new avenues for re-articulation, renewal and re-organisation. More importantly, the situation at Arcot not only contradicts the prevalent notion that poetic culture in nineteenth-century South Asia stagnated, but reveals how literary voices in this 'far-off' locale sought to decipher their place in the Persianate literary sphere. Not unlike their counterparts in Isfahan and Afghanistan, the community of poets at Arcot responded to the changing cultural, social and political parameters of their literary world by exploring their own relationship to the ancients of Persian literary history. The case study of Arcot, however, should not be taken as demonstrative of the state of Persian literary culture across South Asia in the nineteenth century. Both the cultural status and elite usage of Persian were in retreat in the Subcontinent during this time. But herein lies the value of the Arcot case: it offers an example of Persian literary production in a place and at a time when the language's status and usage were at a breaking point. It allows one to observe how the literary experience of one community – in a place where Persian would *not* serve as a future national language – compares to other communities engaging with a similar set of subjects connected to a cosmopolitan and multi-regional literary past. As the historian Assef Ashraf notes, 'being attuned to differences within the Persianate world, and to change over time, is essential if scholars are to avoid monolithic and unchanging depictions of Persianate culture'.[75]

Nonetheless, the case studies presented here do raise the *possibility* that communities of poets across the eighteenth- and nineteenth-century Persianate sphere all activated engagements with the ancients in response to moments of crisis in some relatable fashion, which has remained obscure by the inclusion and justification of the category of 'literary return' in Persian literary history. This remains a possibility. However, it would be inaccurate to conclude that poetic communities in these three disparate locales participated in some Persianate-wide 'return' to the styles of the ancients. Nor is it my purpose to make this particular case for shared *collective* experience one way or the other. What is offered instead is the plausibility of this occurrence made thinkable through the recognition of coterminous multi-regional phenomena of Persianate literary culture. It is a venture made possible by moving away from the strictly narrativised chronological account of Persian literary history that unfolds in stages of development and establishes discrete periods with beginnings and ends.[76] Rather, *Remapping Persian Literary History* looks to the experiences of literary community across the multi-regional Persianate sphere as a series of relatable episodes. In this way, the case studies of literary community in Iran, Afghanistan and South Asia found here should not be understood as directly and indiscriminately linked, but, to borrow the words from Robert Levine, read in

> relatively suppositional and conditional terms … as 'episodes' in which the linkages between discrete moments are not overly insisted upon, in which outcomes remain vague and unpredictable, and in which the authors themselves have no clear sense of connections between their contemporary present moments and possible pasts and futures.[77]

The episodes offered here are but one example of how the experiences of literary communities across the multi-regional Persianate sphere are relatable in the eighteenth and nineteenth centuries. There are others.

Notes

1. For a brief introduction to the spread of Persian throughout the Islamic world and the emergence of the Persianate sphere see Spooner and Hanaway, 'Introduction: Persian as *Koine*'.
2. On the importance of multilingualism for understanding the origins, growth and perpetuation of the Persianate world, see Green, 'Introduction: The Frontiers of the Persianate World (ca. 800–1900)', pp. 9–24. Eaton, 'The Persian Cosmopolis (900–1900) and the Sanskrit Cosmopolis (400–1400)'.
3. My understanding of the term 'Persianate' follows the usage articulated by Marshall Hodgson as referring to 'cultural traditions in Persian or reflecting Persian inspiration', in such fields as literature, administration, history writing or the arts. Hodgson, *The Venture of Islam*, p. 293. For two recent discussions as to the value, relevance and applicability of 'Persianate' as an analytical category as well as its limits as a rubric for investigation see Green, 'Introduction: The Frontiers of the Persianate World (ca. 800–1900)'. Ashraf, 'Introduction: Pathways to the Persianate'.
4. E.g. Alam and Subrahmanyan, *Indo-Persian Travels*. Dale, *The Muslim Empires of the Ottomans, Safavids, and Mughals*. Moin, *The Millennial Sovereign*. Khazeni, *Sky Blue Stone*.
5. For two brief opinions on how political events did not affect the cultural and literary connections between Iran and Central Asia in the post-Timurid period,

see Becka, 'Tajik Literature from the 16th Century to the Present'. Mazzaoui, 'Islamic Culture and Literature in Iran and Central Asia'.
6. On the usefulness of the concept of 'frontiers' as a rubric for understanding developments in the Persianate sphere and its constitution as a whole see Green, 'Introduction: The Frontiers of the Persianate World (ca. 800–1900)', pp. 1–9.
7. Ibid., p. 8.
8. Ibid., pp. xv and 7. Italics mine.
9. Rahimieh, 'Four Iterations of Persian Literary Nationalism', pp. 40–1.
10. Ibid., p. 40.
11. Kashani-Sabet, *Frontier Fictions*.
12. Marashi, *Nationalizing Iran*, pp. 10–11.
13. Ibid., p. 66.
14. Vaziri, *Iran as Imagined Nation*, p. 66.
15. Zia-Ebrahimi, *The Emergence of Iranian Nationalism*, p. 3.
16. Ansari, *The Politics of Iranian Nationalism*, p. 3.
17. See Perry, 'Language Reform in Turkey and Iran'. Gheissari, 'Iran's Dialectic of the Enlightenment: Constitutional Experience'.
18. Marashi, 'Parsi Textual Philanthropy'. Vejdani, 'Indo-Iranian Linguistic, Literary, and Religious Entanglements'. Vejdani, *Making History in Iran*. Ringer, 'Reform Transplanted'. Green, *Bombay Islam*. Green, *The Love of Strangers*.
19. Marashi, 'Patron and Patriot', p. 187.
20. Ansari, *Iranian Nationalism*, p. 13.
21. I borrow this idea of 'dislocation' from Zia-Ebrahimi, *The Emergence of Iranian Nationalism*.
22. Tavakoli-Targhi, 'Contested Memories', p. 175.
23. Ibid.
24. For an overview of the overwhelming importance accorded to the Persian language in the development of Iranian national identity and consciousness, see the arguments in Meskoob, *Iranian National Identity and the Persian Language*. Reassessing the value and role of the Persian language in the nineteenth and twentieth centuries was not, of course, restricted to deliberations in Iran alone, but extended to other societies across the Persianate sphere as well. See Spooner, 'Persian, Farsi, Dari, Tajiki: Language Names and Language Policies'.
25. Karimi-Hakkak, 'Language Reform Movement and its Language', p. 88.
26. This debate was multi-faceted and the outcomes of language reform remained uncertain, as participants offered starkly different approaches to solving the matter. On the nature of the debates, see Mehrdad Kia, 'Persian Nationalism'.

For the historical trajectory of the movement up until the later twentieth century, see Karimi-Hakkak, 'Language Reform Movement and its Language'.
27. Cited in Mehrdad Kia, 'Persian Nationalism', p. 12. The *Nama-yi khusruvan* was also unique for the way it periodised Iranian history into one continuous flow of time, thereby shaping it 'into a national unit with an uninterrupted history that would later serve as a template for the nationalist narrative', and 'its reconstruction of the Iranian past for political purposes'. See Zia-Ebrahami, *The Emergence of Iranian Nationalism*, pp. 36–40.
28. See Marashi, *Nationalizing Iran*, pp. 70–1.
29. Ibid., p. 72.
30. Algar, 'Akundzada'.
31. Karimi-Hakkak, 'Language Reform Movement and its Language', pp. 91–2. For information on Qa'im Maqam in simplifying Persian prose see Khatami, *Pizhuhishi dar nasr va nazm*, pp. 26–33.
32. Karimi-Hakkak, 'Language Reform Movement and its Language', p. 87.
33. This does not mean that nineteenth-century observers of 'literary return', such as the corps of biographical anthologists who first began to articulate its occurrence, self-consciously did so as a nationalist literary movement simply because they employed a lexicon to be used by more nationalist-minded commentators later on. Rather, the implication is that the job of later twentieth-century critics, who would go on to conceptualise the national value of 'literary return', would be all the easier, as they could leverage a type of language already in the 'sources' to serve their own myth-making purpose of a national literary history.
34. Bahar, *Bahar va adab-i Farsi*, vol. 1, p. 53.
35. Shafaq, *Tarikh-i adabiyat-i Iran*, p. 364.
36. Zarrinkub, *Naqd-i adabi*. Farshidvard, *Darbara-yi adabiyat va naqd-i adabi*. Aryanpur, *Az Saba ta Nima*. Shamisa, *Sabk-shinasi-i shi'r*. For a good collection of remarks by Iranian and non-Iranian literary scholars on the 'decline' of poetry in Safavid times see Shafieioun, 'Some Critical Remarks on the Migration of Iranian Poets', pp. 156–61.
37. For the important role played by Arab clerics in Safavid Iran see Abisaab, *Converting Persia*.
38. For an overview of the range of depictions of the Safavids in twentieth-century Iran and their relation to popular cultural memory, see Amin, '*Mujassama-i bud mujassama-i nabud*'.
39. Dabashi, *The World of Persian Literary Humanism*, p. 243.
40. Bahar, *Bahar va adab-i Farsi*, vol. 1, p. 53.

41. It is typically these poets, along with Fayzi, who receive commendation for producing choice poetry during the period, but they are regarded as the exception not the norm. See e.g. Shafaq, *Tarikh-i adabiyat-i Iran*, p. 365. On the poetry and personas of Kalim and ʿUrfi, see Sharma, *Mughal Arcadia*.
42. For an account of poetry in Safavid Iran outside of the court, which included the 'bazaarisation' of classical masters like Saʿdi and Hafiz, see Shams-Langarudi, *Maktab-i bazgasht*, pp. 16–33.
43. Baygdili, 'Nigarish bar bazgasht-i adabi', p. 35.
44. As articulated, for example, in Baygdili, 'Nigarish bar bazgasht-i adabi' and Dihgan-Nizhad et al., 'Bar-rassi-i tarikhi', p. 40.
45. On the piety myth in the Safavid promotion of literature see Losensky, 'Poetic and Eros in Early Modern Persia'.
46. See e.g. the account of the 'realist school' (*maktab-i vuqūʿ*) in Gulchin-i Maʿani, *Maktab-i vuquʿ*. For some general comments about poetic production in Safavid Isfahan see Schwartz, 'Bazgasht-i Adabi', pp. 33–43. The precise relationship between the Safavid court and poetic patronage continues to be an unsettled matter. For example, compare the arguments offered by Tamimdari, 'Adabiyat-i ʿasr-i Safavi', and Tughyan, 'Isfahan va tahavvul-i shiʿr', appearing in the same two-volume collection. For more information on rethinking the Safavid monarchy's relationship to literature and intellectual output in general see Savory, *Iran under the Safavids*, pp. 203–25.
47. E.g. Keshavmurthy, *Persian Authorship and Canonicity*. Dudney, 'Sabk-e Hendi'. Kinra, 'Make it Fresh'. Faruqi, 'A Stranger in the City'.
48. Nuʿmani, *Shiʿr-i ʿAjam*, vol. 3, p. 158. Quoted in Hanaway, 'Bazgasht-e Adabi'. For more on the Iran-centric nature of Nuʿmani's work and the impact it had on Urdu literary scholarship disparaging the 'Indian Style' see Keshavmurthy, *Persian Authorship and Canonicity*, p. 6.
49. See Vejdani, *Making History in Iran*, Chs 1 and 6. Jabbari, 'The Making of Modernity in Persianate Literary History'. Ferdowsi, 'Emblem of the Manifestation of the Iranian Spirit'.
50. The institutionalisation of Persian literature in the late nineteenth and early twentieth centuries as understood through exchanges among Iranian and Afghan scholars is explored in Fani, 'Becoming Literature'.
51. Karimi-Hakkak, *Recasting Persian Poetry*, p. 28.
52. See e.g. Khatami, *Pizhuhishi dar nasr va nazm*, p. 201. Asghari, 'Jaigah-i dawra-yi bazgasht'. While both authors are critical of some of the conceptual parameters that have come to define 'literary return' as either a period or style in Persian

literary history, neither questions its existence or whether it can apply to literary movements outside of Iran.
53. Perkins, *Is Literary History Possible?*, p. 51.
54. Mana Kia, 'Indian Friends, Iranian Selves'.
55. Smith, 'Literary Courage', p. 58.
56. Beecroft, *An Ecology of World Literature*, p. 123.
57. Ibid., p. 202.
58. Ibid., pp. 197–8.
59. See e.g. Hohendahl, *Building a National Literature*.
60. Beecroft, *An Ecology of World Literature*, p. 198.
61. Ríos-Font, 'Literary History and Canon Formation', p. 16.
62. Beecroft, *An Ecology of World Literature*, p. 200.
63. Hanaway, 'Is There a Canon of Persian Poetry?', p. 9.
64. For a discussion of Bahar's *Sabk-shinasi* as a text detailing both Persian literature's evolution and development and its disciplinary emergence as a national institution see Ahmadi, 'The Institution of Persian Literature'.
65. See e.g Dudney, 'Sabk-e Hindi'. Dudney, 'Metaphorical Language'. Faruqi, 'A Stranger in the City'.
66. Among the many examples of this method see Khatami, *Pizhuhishi dar nasr va nazm*, pp. 203–8. Asghari, 'Jaigah-i dawra-yi bazgasht', pp. 6–7.
67. See Faruqi, 'Unprivileged Power'.
68. On the notion of canon formation as a cumulative historical process as formulated by a 'continuum of judgements and rewritings over extended periods of time', see Ch. 3 in Kolbas, *Critical Theory and the Literary Canon*.
69. For two recent studies in this regard, see Karimi-Hakkak, 'Continuity and Creativity'. Keshavmurthy, *Persian Authorship and Canonicity*.
70. Gallagher and Greenblatt, *Practicing New Historicism*, p. 12.
71. Robinson, *Islamic Historiography*, p. xxv. Italics in original.
72. In dismissing the value of Persian biographical anthologies, Ann K. S. Lambton noted that 'their interest, if any to the historian is the witness they bear to the special literary bent of the Persian people and the place of the poet of society'. Lambton, 'Persian Biographical Literature', p. 143.
73. See e.g. Schwartz, 'The Local Lives of a Transregional Poet'. Pellò, 'Persian Poets on the Streets'. Kia, 'Imagining Iran before Nationalism'. Hermansen and Lawrence, 'Indo-Persian Tazkiras as Memorative Communications'. Losensky, 'Welcoming Fighani'. Beers, 'The Biography of Vahshi Bāfqi'. Sharma, 'From ʿĀesha to Nur Jahān'.

74. Michael Axworthy (ed.), 'Crisis, Collapse, Militarism and Civil War', p. 2.
75. Ashraf, 'Introduction: Pathways to the Persianate', p. 10.
76. See e.g. Dighan-Nizhad et al., 'Bar-rassi-i tarikhi'. In an otherwise excellent rethinking of the transition points between different periods or stages of Persian literary history, the article nonetheless adheres to the standard narrativised account of literary history unfolding in stages of development made to fit the national trajectory of poetic production in Iran.
77. Levine, *Dislocating Race and Nation*, p. 12.

1

Remembering Iran, Forgetting the Persianate: Persian Literary Historiography of the Eighteenth and Nineteenth Centuries

The purpose of this chapter is to provide a historiographical overview of some of the major shifts and developments in Persian literary culture in eighteenth- and nineteenth-century Iran, Afghanistan and South Asia. It highlights the formation and consolidation of the 'literary return' narrative in Iran, trends and debates in Afghan literary historiography and the narrative of 'decline' of Persian in post-Mughal South Asia. Exploring side by side the general matrices of Persian literary culture in these three locales elucidates the far-reaching impact of the idea of 'literary return' upon national, regional and global renderings of Persian literary culture in the eighteenth and nineteenth centuries. While the narrative of 'literary return' remains the overarching frame for truncating the historiography of the Persianate world in the eighteenth and nineteenth centuries, it is not the only one. Abetting it are the separate historiographies of Persian literary culture in Afghanistan and South Asia that have followed their own more circumscribed paths. Charting the major ongoing debates in Persian literary history writing points to the various shortcomings of these frameworks and highlights the gaps into which the topics of the three subsequent chapters will be placed. In essence, the three literary historiographies presented here serve as the roadmaps for navigating the corresponding individual chapters that follow.

'Literary Return' and the 'Indian Style'

The idea of 'literary return' was given its name, and most prominently formulated, by the poet and literary historian Muhammad Taqi Bahar (d. 1951) in the early part of the twentieth century. Starting in the 1930s, Bahar began articulating some of the characteristics of 'literary return' and, alongside it, developed his criteria for evaluating 'good' poetry.¹ But it was most notably in his groundbreaking work *Stylistics or the History of Evolution of Persian Writing* (*Sabk-shinasi ya tarikh-i tatavvur-i nasr-i Farsi*) that Bahar devised a schematic for understanding Persian literary history by dividing its evolution into four distinct categories, which included 'literary return'. About a decade prior to the appearance of *Stylistics* in the 1940s, Riza-Zadah Shafaq began articulating an idea of 'literary return' as well, but had not yet narrativised and periodised the movement in any orderly fashion as his contemporary Bahar would.² While Bahar built upon the earlier work of biographical anthologists in this endeavour, as will be seen below, he is nonetheless the first individual to give a concrete historiographical voice to the idea of 'literary return' as a distinct period and movement in Persian literary history. Like any good literary historian, Bahar leveraged the messier details of poets' lives, relationships and verse from earlier texts to create a macroscopic vision of the evolution of Persian literature. It was as much an effort to shape a narrative of Persian literature's development as it was indicative of a break from the older model of biographical anthologies, which had dominated Persian literary history writing for several centuries. Bahar's work was emblematic of the more *en vogue* form of temporalising literary history (*tarikh-i adabīyāt*) into distinct periods, rather than simply recording the work and lives of individual poets.³

Bahar understood the evolution of Persian literature as unfolding according to four distinct categories. Each category constituted a different school or style of poetry, maintained its own special characteristics and roughly corresponded to a different period in history. The Khurasani style, dominant from the ninth to the thirteenth century, was primarily defined by the ode (*qaṣīda*) performed for patrons in a courtly setting. The theme of naturalism, battlefield triumphs, grand feasts, hunting, royal merry-making and wine-drinking predominated. The 'Iraqi style, which prevailed from the thirteenth to the fifteenth century, marked a shift from a gaze dedicated to recording worldly splendour to one more inward-looking and mystically inclined. This shift in the zeitgeist of Persian poetic practice is seen as resulting from the chaos and destruction wrought by the Mongol invasions and the desire to explain an existence impacted by cataclysmic tumult. The dominant form of this period was no longer the ode but the lyric (*ghazal*), which served as a more suitable means of expressing the period's themes. The lyric continued its dominance during the heyday of the so-called 'Indian Style' (*sabk-i Hindī*) from the fifteenth to the eighteenth century. Challenging metaphors, literary acrobatics, wordplays, puzzles and all types of mannerisms defined its highly intellectualised style. The final category is 'literary return', which was active in Iran in the eighteenth and nineteenth centuries. The essence of the style and movement, according to Bahar, was that it sought a 'return' to the simpler models of the Khurasani ode and 'Iraqi lyric of centuries past.

This classification inaugurated by Bahar is problematic from a number of perspectives, not least the way it appears to create isolated categories of poetic form and style to refer to a select period alone, and not others. Any student of Persian literature recognises that courtly odes and mystical lyrics can be found throughout the history of Persian literature, not just in the Khurasani and 'Iraqi periods respectively. Bahar recognised this fact as well. His categories of Khurasani and 'Iraqi were meant to be no more hermetically sealed to the poetic trends ascribed to those particular periods than restricted to the locales from which the categories derived their names.[4] Odes delivered under the patronage of a ruler could easily be found outside of ninth- to thirteenth-century Khurasan, as could mystical lyrics outside of thirteenth- to fifteenth-century 'Iraqi-i 'Ajam. But such is the result of an attempt to define the entirety of Persian literary evolution according to four temporal periods and find the poetic and social zeitgeist capturing each one. No different from earlier anthologists dividing poets into ancients (*mutaqaddimīn*), moderns (*muta'akhkhirīn*) and contemporaries (*mu'asirīn*), albeit in a less determinative fashion, Bahar sought to provide an access-point for understanding the development of Persian literature over a 1,000-year period. He did so by focusing on what he determined as being the four most prominent trends in poetic practice defining select eras.

Significantly more problematic is the manner in which Bahar's category of 'literary return' transforms his developmental account of Persian literary history into a narrative of *Iranian* literary history. While the Khurasani, 'Iraqi and Indian styles reference developments pertaining to Persian literary practice in geographies across the Persianate world, the category of 'literary return' narrows its focus to Iran alone. 'Literary return' pertains only to poetic developments in one particular place (Iran) and time (eighteenth and nineteenth centuries). In this sense, the category of 'literary return' is set apart: unlike the other three categories preceding it, 'literary return' is presented as stylistically, geographically and temporally restricted to Iran.

The idea of 'literary return' as a conceptual category bifurcates the literary history of the Persianate world between Iran and everywhere else from the eighteenth century onward. As Iranian poets returned to the style of the poetry found in the Khurasani and 'Iraqi periods, the rest of the Persianate world did not. As Iranian poets returned to composing poetry in imitation of the classical masters, like Firdawsi (d. 1019 or 1025), Anvari (d. *c.*1180) and Hafiz (d. 1390), Persian poets elsewhere did not. With a not so subtle shift, Bahar transitions his description of Persian literary history into one tailor-made for describing the literary history of Iran and its formation.

The recognition that Iran alone experienced a 'literary return' signifies more than a new and revitalised direction for the country's literature. It also implies that other regions, having not experienced a literary renewal, remained dedicated to practising another type of poetry. In defining 'literary return', articulating what Iranian poets 'returned to' was as important as explaining what the poets 'returned from'. Bahar had a ready-made solution to this problem by conceptualising 'literary return' as a response to the so-called 'Indian Style'. If 'literary return' is defined by renewal, rejuvenation and the re-centring of Persian poetry in Iran by going back to the styles of the masters, then the 'Indian Style' is its opposite. It is Persian poetry gone astray and in decline. It is a style overtaken by complication, unhinged from classical models, mired in stagnation and incapable of progression. The 'return' movement, according to Bahar and later literary historians, stemmed nearly entirely from poets' weariness and displeasure with the 'Indian Style'. In this way the 'Indian Style' has served as an easy contrast with the Iranian-born return movement. Its dissatisfying complexity and questionable language-play juxtapose nicely with poets returning to the more simplified, classical styles appearing in formats tried and true.[5]

Broadly speaking, the so-called 'Indian Style' flourished mostly from the sixteenth to the eighteenth century in South Asia, practised both by poets born there and by Iranian-born poets who travelled to South Asia to spend most of their creative life there.[6] Practitioners of this style appeared elsewhere, such as in Iran or Central Asia, but the epicentre of this style of poetry existed in South Asia, which at this time was the epicentre of Persian literary culture more broadly. Even though it was in South Asia that the style primarily flourished, and probably for this reason that it earned such an appellation, many scholars assume that it was an exclusively South Asian or Indian phenomenon, or, at the very least, more pervasive in the non-Iranian eastern Persianate world.[7]

The 'Indian Style' has long been chastised for being overly complicated, mired in wordplay and highly abstract. Western and non-Western critics posit that this not only made the poetry itself unenjoyable and difficult to understand, but also led to the decline of Persian poetry. The style of poetry has been bemoaned as exhibiting the 'hopelessness of bizarre poetical expressions'[8] or as too 'grotesque' to exhibit any 'good taste or unity'.[9] As will be seen below, this legacy of a complicated style of poetry, which later historians have deemed synonymous with the 'Indian Style', can be traced to earlier authors in Iran in the eighteenth and nineteenth centuries.

Recent scholarship has questioned critics who demonise the 'Indian Style' by noting that those wishing to chastise the style for its complicated metaphors and linguistic deficiency do so by haphazardly offering a line of poetry here or there out of context.[10] Others have noted how the characteristics attributed to the 'Indian Style' can be found in other styles of Persian poetry, whether classical or modern.[11] The literary critic Shamsur Rahman Faruqi believes the 'Indian Style' in many ways offers the most ingenious and inventive examples of Persian poetry.[12] Rather than corrupting the classical tropes of Persian poetry, the style in fact expanded upon it and enriched it through a habit of 'theme-creating' (*mazmūn āfarīnī*). By highlighting the way in which the 'Indian Style' built upon some of the traits of classical Persian poetry, Faruqi offers an apt reminder that it cannot simply be relegated to the 'foreign' or 'strange'. Instead of the fascination of poets with the use of mixed metaphors or abstract language being viewed as a detriment, these techniques may be seen as examples of the ingenuity of a style consistently seeking to make poetry, including that of the classical canon, 'fresh' (*tāza*). As the literary scholar Prashant Keshavmurthy reminds us, the 'fresh' style in fact 'derived its name from its predominant trait of playing on the reader's awareness of the … classical canon' in order to 'evoke new topoi, new logics of intertextual relation and new metaphors and syntax'.[13]

In such a counter-narrative, the 'Indian Style' is regarded as the vehicle via which innovative poets and critics could push the aesthetic and cerebral elements of Persian poetry to its utmost limits. It also serves as a testament to the centrality of South Asia in shaping the contours of one of the early modern period's most pervasive world literatures, as the location where the 'fresh' style most resplendently flourished. Since the terms '*sabk-i Hindī*' and 'Indian Style' are ill-fitting and problematic, their usage will be restricted to designating a category in Persian literary historiography. In referring to the 'Indian Style' of poetry practised throughout the early modern period, or that which eighteenth- and nineteenth-century writers were responding to during the time of their writing, the more appropriate 'fresh' style or 'fresh-speak' (*tāza-gū'ī*) will be used.

Despite new scholarship peeling away old attitudes regarding the 'Indian Style', even doing away with its name, these revisions are occurring long after Bahar secured a place for it in Persian literary history as a retrograde type of verse overwhelmingly associated with decline. This identification of the 'Indian Style' made easy the juxtaposition with 'literary return' as a movement invested in Persian poetry's renewal. Indeed, the predominance of the supposedly deleterious 'Indian Style' in the Persianate world is offered as the raison d'être for Iranian poets instigating a 'return'. The 'Indian Style' mired the non-Iranian world in literary decline only to be saved by an Iranian-born 'return' movement to reawaken poetry.

Strangely embedded within Bahar's account is a recognition that prior to the emergence of the 'return' movement, South Asia was the centre of poetic production in the Persianate world. It may be tempting to see here the non-Iranian world receiving its due for contributing to Persian literary evolution and innovations in poetics. But it is less a praiseworthy accolade than a back-handed compliment: South Asia was the centre of the Persianate world only insofar as it 'originated' and cultivated what would eventually become known as a corrupting style of poetry. Recognising the 'corrupting' centrality of South Asia to poetic (and prose) composition in this way helped Iranian literary historians acknowledge that the number of Persian manuscripts produced in South Asia dwarfed that of those produced in Iran during the early modern era.[14]

Iranian Story

By the late nineteenth century all the trademarks of what would come to define 'literary return' as conceptualised by commentators like Bahar in the twentieth century were falling into place. While the narrative of 'literary return' was not yet fully formed, authors in Zand (r. 1751–94) and Qajar Iran began to articulate the idea that the revival of Persian poetry and a return to the style of the masters were occurring before their eyes, to wipe away the last vestiges of the bad stylistics dominating the Persianate sphere. Historians, littérateurs and anthologists like Lutf Ali 'Azar' Baygdili (d. 1781), 'Abd al-Razzaq 'Maftun' Dunbuli (d. 1827–8), Muhammad Fazil Khan Garrusi (d. 1843) and Riza Quli Khan Hidayat (d. 1871) offered varying impressions about the stylistic shift under way and the poetic communities responsible for carrying it out. These authors' keen observations of literary developments demonstrate how the politically tenuous times of eighteenth- and nineteenth-century Iran did not hinder their ability to offer critical opinions about the major trends in poetry happening around them. In actuality, the lack of political stability in eighteenth-century Iran was a crucial factor in instigating a movement of poets there to 'return' to the classical styles of the masters, as will be seen in the following chapter.

The Isfahan-born, peripatetic poet Azar was perhaps the first author in Iran to intimate a need to return to the masters in response to the *en vogue* poetic practice later associated with the 'Indian Style'. Writing in his *Firetemple* (*Atishkada*), the only major biographical anthology to emerge in Iran in the eighteenth century, he notes that poets in his home town of Isfahan 'had a great zeal for the construction of poetry', but because 'the method of the ancient writers was abolished during this time, there was no outpouring of excellent poetry from them'.[15] Azar's praise of the talents of poets while at once bemoaning their detachment from the style of 'the ancient writers' represents yet another of the back-handed compliments in the historiography of the so-called 'Indian Style'.

The historian and littérateur Dunbuli, one of Azar's companions, offers no pretence of praise.[16] Instead, he avers an adamant disavowal of the poets practising what would be known to history as the 'Indian Style' and relates a specific critique of its debilitating features. The clear juxtaposition Dunbuli creates between these two styles of poetry – one debilitating and one reviving – would serve as a major feature for conceptualising 'literary return' later on. Dunbuli's critique is perhaps one of the most often-repeated statements by twentieth-century authors cataloguing the rise of 'literary return' in response to the 'Indian Style'. It reads:

> When the carpet of poetry was trampled upon from the audacity of absurd ideas [put forth by] Shawkat, Saʿib, Vahid and others like them, and together with frigid metaphors and stale similes fell from freshness and lustre, Mushtaq came to the site of poetry's rose-bed. He enveloped the writings of that group like a rosebud and spread a carpet of poetry that he himself had been good at and that is the method of Zamiri and Naziri. At the head of the garden of speech he built melodies and constructed tunes such that the mellifluous nightingales of the age followed him. His colourful poems adorned the melodies of Barbad-like minstrels of the time and his sweet songs graced the society of clever ones.[17]

Building upon Dunbuli's stance, the Qajar secretary and poet Muhammad Fazil Khan Garrusi presents an equally scathing and confident take on the state of Persian poetry and its revival. Garrusi, like Dunbuli, champions the role of Mushtaq, who by 'mental exertion' caused 'the arm of eloquence to be strengthened and the torn garments of poetry to be remade' in order to achieve the 'revival of tradition and renewal of custom'. Writing at the Qajar court of Fath Ali Shah (r. 1797–1834), when the 'literary return' was in full swing, Garrusi noted:

> Following the displeasing usages and unsuitable inventions of mediocre ones, eloquence in language succumbed to disgrace, the transmission of pleasant oration was cut off, the splendour of great writers' thoughts was extinguished and the works from the ages of esteemed writers became unnecessary. He [Mushtaq] made, by his mental exertion, the arm of eloquence to be strengthened and the torn garments of poetry to be remade. Although his excellency, with respect to poetry, would not bestow this praise upon himself, in the revival of tradition and renewal of custom [his role] is unquestionable. Prior to this, first-rate noble contemporaries like Azar, ʿAshiq, Hatif and those like them were joined together as attendees of [his] assembly and confessors of [his] mastery.[18]

The definitive role accorded to Sayyid Ali Mushtaq Isfahani (d. *c.*1757–8) and his small band of followers in reviving Persian poetry remains one of the major historiographical legacies from the nineteenth century. Twentieth-century literary historians credit Mushtaq with teaching a small circle of Isfahani-based poets 'the rules of poetry and prose', founded upon the method and style of the old masters. Mushtaq supposedly even specified which masters to follow: Saʿdi (d. 1291–2) in the lyric, Anvari (d. *c.*1180) in the ode, Firdawsi (d. 1019 or 1025) in depicting battles, Nizami (d. 1209) in describing feasts and ʿUmar Khayyam (d. 1131) in the quatrain.[19] To not draw inspiration from past masters would lead one to 'traverse the path of error'.[20] In language reminiscent of the effulgent praise found in literary anthologies of nearly two hundred years ago, contemporary authors talk of Mushtaq's 'eloquent efforts and great striving' to establish a literary society via which a return to the classical styles of the masters could be achieved.[21] Without his leadership and 'the management and encouragement of talented youth' to follow him, it seems, a 'literary return' in Iran would never have happened.[22] This role accorded to Mushtaq has been heavily overstated.

The other major legacy from Zand- and Qajar-era texts shaping ideas about 'literary return' is the juxtaposition between a style of 'frigid metaphors and stale similes' (read: 'Indian Style') and the 'revival of tradition and renewal of custom' (read: 'literary return'). Azar hinted at it, Dunbuli refined it and Garrusi emboldened it. But it was the Qajar diplomat and historian Riza Quli Khan Hidayat, writing at the court of Nasir al-Din Shah (r. 1848–96), who brought it together. In the best tradition of the biographical anthology genre, Hidayat built upon the ideas and language of Dunbuli and Garrusi to offer a culminating overview of a poetic revival in Iran in the midst of literary stagnation.

In the introduction to his six-volume *Assembly of the Eloquent* (*Majmaʿ al-fusaha*), the most comprehensive Qajar-era biographical anthology, Riza Quli Khan Hidayat makes the idea of 'literary return' in Iran thinkable for later generations of historians. At the Qajar court in Tehran, the diplomat and historian Hidayat was at the nexus of several Qajar efforts seeking to bolster the dynasty's place in Persian and Iranian historiography.[23] His role in articulating the idea of 'literary return' was a similar endeavour. In capturing the rise of 'literary return', Hidayat first relates how Iran entered a period of decline, exemplified by poetic unintelligibility and lyrics (*ghazal*s) epitomised by 'confused speech, idle prattle and vain oratory' during Safavid and Afsharid (r. 1736–96) times. Next, there came a period of renewal when poets in Iran broke free from the 'reproachable style of the moderns' and 'became inclined toward the pleasant style of the old masters'. This phenomenon occurred slightly before the rise of the Qajars, but naturally achieved its fullest fruition under the sponsorship of Hidayat's dynastic employers. Hidayat, whose perch at the court afforded him access to a wide array of texts being produced across Iran, proved more than capable of establishing the parameters of 'literary return' for future commentators by relying on the opinions of earlier anthologists.[24] It is not difficult to hear the echoes of earlier anthologists, like Garrusi and Dunbuli, in Hidayat's remarks several decades later. Hidayat's statement below, like Dunbuli's above, is one of the most often-cited statements in explaining the rise of 'literary return'. It reads:

> During the Safavid period reproachable methods became manifest. The well-considered manner of writing a splendid ode and the eloquent method of composing writings on admonition, advice, governance, pious devotions and epics, which were the custom of our preceding writers, were entirely supplanted. Versifiers became inclined toward ... the outlining of riddles and the conjuring up of misnomers. Because the *ghazal* lacked a fixed arrangement, they established [a style of] confused speech, idle prattle, and vain oratory after a manner of sickly dispositions ... in lieu of the acquisition of truths, frigid meanings came about, and in lieu of rhetorical flourishes and pleasant rarities, detestable topics and opaque intentions were used. In particular, during the end of the Safavid and Afsharid periods ... the ascendant star of these poets' fortune was the cause of the setting star of excellence, wisdom, eloquence, rhetoric, philosophy and knowledge. Every learned person chose a cell and every adept master hid in a corner [while] every prattler became renowned ... [until] several people settled on the restoration of the ancients' method (*iḥyā-yi shīva-yi mutaqaddimīn*). They became aware of the tastelessness of the moderns' style (*bī-mazagī-hā-yi ṭarz-i muta'akhkhirīn*) and their contemptible fashion. They struggled to the utmost limit and donned the robe of earnest striving and forbade other people from the reproachable style of the moderns. They became inclined

toward the pleasant style of the old masters. Nevertheless, despite their laborious efforts in doing this, they did not reach high ranks.[25]

Hidayat's impression of 'literary return' is of equal consequence for the manner in which it articulates a poetic trend of returning to the masters as it is for defining a more discernible and established poetic movement. This was partially the result of circumstance. With the institutionalisation of the 'literary return' style at the court of Fath Ali Shah in the rearview mirror, and its continued prominence at the court of Nasir al-Din Shah, Hidayat had the luxury of writing with more temporal distance and literary data at his disposal than his predecessors. He begins to see the shift in poetic styles less as the result of any individual poet, but rather as the result of a movement. Unlike Dunbuli and Garrusi, who linked the return movement to the personality of Mushtaq and a small collection of poets in Isfahan, Hidayat felt confident in describing the movement in more abstract terms. 'Literary return' is not solely the domain of a particular poet like Mushtaq, or his literary circle, but an established paradigm guiding poetic activity. It is no wonder that his entry on Mushtaq, by contrast, is sparser than his predecessors and contains little of their fanfare.[26]

Hidayat's description of the literary return movement in Iran, which would go on to provide the blueprint for later commentators, displays the manner in which he whittled down the narrative from a collection of observations and commentaries to a concretised account. There is no mention in Hidayat's introduction of the role of Mushtaq's associates like Azar, 'Ashiq and Hatif. There is no mention of Mushtaq's poetic affinity for the style of Zamiri (d. 1579) or Naziri (d. c.1612–14), which undercuts certain aspects of the movement's creation narrative, as will be seen in the next chapter. By removing these references, Hidayat expunges any semblance of continuity between Mushtaq and the poets of the preceding period, not to mention two poets (Zamiri and Naziri) who were known to engage with the poetry of the classical masters.[27]

The absence of this type of information has reduced the narrative of 'literary return' to a story lacking its proper social, cultural and political context. Some content has been adapted, some has been edited out, and important social and cultural data has been elided until a more cohesive and digestible narrative is left standing. In essence, the rise of the 'literary return' movement has been whittled down from its treatment in Zand- and Qajar-era biographical anthologies to a few interconnected, unquestioned and established truths curated by Hidayat and later consolidated by Bahar and others. As the literary critic and translation theorist André Lefevere notes, 'once a culture has arrived at a canonized image of its past, it tends to edit out those figures and features of the past that do not fit the image'.[28] It is this practice of rewriting and refining the story of 'literary return', which Hidayat and later historians achieved so effectively, that has ensured the concept's survival in literary history, more so than the 'intrinsic value' of any particular work of literature from the period.[29]

The impact of Zand- and Qajar-era anthologists on twentieth-century renderings of 'literary return' can be seen in subtler, no less illuminating ways as well. The long statement by Hidayat is once again instructive in this manner. Moving beyond his general framework of the 'why' (poetic decline) and the 'how' (renewal of past poetic models) of the 'return' movement, he offers the curious final remark: 'Despite their laborious efforts [following the ancients], they did not reach high ranks.' It is a somewhat odd addendum concluding a passionate recounting of the brief history of 'literary return' to note that in the end its poets did not really amount to much. The implication here is most certainly not that the 'literary return' poets failed to reshape the poetic landscape of nineteenth-century Iran. The institutionalisation of the style of poetry at the court of Fath Ali Shah, and the continued patronage it received at the Qajar court into the twentieth century, is suitable evidence to suggest the movement's lasting impact. The influence of the 'literary return' style during the Qajar period spread to perhaps as many as a hundred poets, who sought to compose odes and lyrics in the styles of the classical masters.[30] Rather, Hidayat's final comment is an aesthetic judgement on the merit of the poetry, not the movement's historical impact. Poets may have revived past models and relieved Iran from a period of poetic decline, but the quality of their poetry left something to be desired. It is an odd paradox for a movement credited with reviving the glory of Persian poetry and rescuing it from debilitation.

Echoes of Hidayat's criticism that the 'literary return' poetry was merely imitative in nature resonate throughout modern scholarship. Critics note that 'literary return' poets were so enamoured of imitation, through the use of the language, rhyme scheme and metres of previous poets, that they disregarded the social conditions and concerns of their own time. Instead they steeped themselves in the world-views of the poets they imitated. This has led several scholars to claim that the 'literary return' movement achieved nothing more than glorified imitation detached from the social concerns of the existent world. While the poets they imitated were interested in relating poetic content to a world-view contemporaneous with their own times, the 'literary return' poets were not. Instead, the 'literary return' poets favoured a frame of reference more closely related to the Ghaznavid (r. 977–1186) or Seljuk (r. c.1040–1157) periods.[31] With a total disregard for the world existing outside of the court, notes one modern commentator, these poets were more in tune with depicting the feast, battle, wine and the hunt.[32] The 'literary return' poets praised the Qajars as if they were the Ghaznavids, notes another.[33] Indeed, poets and writers during the time of Fath Ali Shah sought to specifically connect the image of his court to that of the Ghaznavids, as well as the personage of Fath Ali Shah himself to the ruler Mahmud (r. 998–1030), in order to at once glorify the prowess of Qajar patronage and establish its superiority over a dynastic predecessor.[34]

Other critics note how the poets of the 'return' movement cannot be deemed initiators of anything new, since their style and method relied upon an imitation of language and structures from an earlier period. This impression is perhaps best summed up by the observation of the modern poet Mehdi Akhavan-Sales (d. 1990) that the 'literary return' period in Iran was nothing more than the appearance of 'false-Saʿdis' and 'false-Manuchihris'.[35] In other words, 'false masters'. Nevertheless, the 'literary return' poets are credited with protecting and preserving the language of classical Persian and freeing it from frailty and weakness.[36] Poets of eighteenth- and nineteenth-century Iran initiated a 'literary resurrection' (*rastā-khīz-i ababī*) of Persian poetry, even if they did little for the perpetuation of its 'life' (*ḥayāt*) and 'fecundity' (*barūmandī*).[37] Put simply, they composed works wholly imitative in nature without the same effect as that of the poets they imitated.

Critics also take issue with the way 'literary return' poets did not use language and constructions to the same effect as the older poets being imitated.

While the old poets properly placed words and heeded rules of grammar, the poetry of the 'return' poets is full of grammatical errors.[38] This too was pointed out by earlier Zand and Qajar commentators: Dunbuli, for example, made note of 'return' poets' misuse of language and grammatical challenges.[39] Clearly, the biographical anthologies from the eighteenth and nineteenth centuries provide crucial information concerning 'literary return', often as foundational sources for explaining the rise of the movement. But the opinions of authors like Azar, Dunbuli and Hidayat have more or less dominated the discourse around 'literary return' for more than a century without any critical appraisal.

The commonalities between the criticisms of anthologists, historians and poets across nearly two centuries point to the degree to which scholarly understanding of 'literary return' has persisted over time. The 'return' poets' place in history is secured by the fact that they rescued Persian poetry from decline by returning to the classical styles of the masters. It is a legacy constricted to an ability to re-establish the historical trajectory of Persian poetic development, but not advance it aesthetically or stylistically in any significant way. They succeeded through the imitation of a previous style, rather than initiating a new one. In other words, poets in eighteenth- and nineteenth-century Iran merely reasserted the masters to their purported proper place at the centre of Persian poetic development, but in no way upset their enshrinement in the Persian canon. In this way, the 'return' poets are deemed no more than stewards reasserting the unassailable march of literary evolution in Iran, having averted a nearly disastrous detour. Their added value was an ability to reassert the centrality of the classical masters and maintain Persian literary development in a holding pattern. It would be left to the next generation of poets during the Constitutional period and afterwards to experiment with thematic content and forms and truly thrust Persian poetry into the modern era.[40]

The idea of 'literary return' may well be a crucial linchpin in the story of Iranian literary salvation without which there would be a cavernous gap in the narrative of Persian poetic development. But it is also a movement that at its inception was nurtured by the social and historical circumstances of post-Safavid Isfahan in the mid-to-late eighteenth century. To exclude such a fact in any retelling demonstrates a wilful neglect to historicise the 'return' movement at the expense of its status as an abstract category glueing the narrative of Persian literary history together.

Returning to the social and political circumstances of the movement's gestational phase in post-Safavid Isfahan recovers a narrative passed over by later anthologists and literary historians, such as Hidayat and Bahar. Information on the formation of the 'return' movement as found in early biographical anthologies, like those of Dunbuli and Garrusi, brings the exigent historical circumstances shaping the experiences of the first 'return' poets to the fore and highlights the contingent nature of the movement as one born out of a local context. They maintain traces of important features of the movement's formation, such as their literary networks and patronage prospects, beyond a (supposed) mere disdain for a certain type of poetics. The verse of the early 'return' poets themselves, equally incongruent with the abstract role consigned to 'literary return' in history writing, is another site rife with alternative impressions of how and why the movement took shape as it did. Their verse demonstrates how their deep personal bonds and shared social experiences helped a group of like-minded poets coalesce into a community during an unsettling time.

Usually depicted as a group of poets consciously seeking a 'return' to past poetic models when faced with a burdensome literary style, these early Isfahani poets invested themselves significantly more in reconstituting poetic community and the role of the professional poet in the unsettling political environment of post-Safavid Iran. In seeking to achieve this end, they relied on the past model of the classical masters to guide their way through uncertain times. Recognising the early 'return' movement as an outgrowth of localised circumstances and concerns not only assists in re-historicising literary developments in eighteenth- and nineteenth-century Iran, but points to larger literary-sociological processes at work. Neither an abstract idea nor a placeholder in Persian literary history waiting to welcome the next stage of poetic evolution, the emergence of the 'literary return' movement in Iran is indicative of a larger global practice of seeking out the masters to establish one's place in the uncertain times of the eighteenth- and nineteenth-century Persianate world.

Afghan Legacy

The insertion of 'literary return' as a conceptual category in literary history writing has not only served to reassert the centrality of Iran for the development of Persian poetry. It has also been particularly effective in obscuring the complex dynamics of eighteenth- and nineteenth- century Persian literary culture outside of Iran too. For as much as 'literary return' creates an Iranian national imaginary by returning to the styles of the classical masters, it also wilfully forgets trends in literary culture occurring elsewhere. This is largely achieved by associating the nineteenth-century, non-Iranian Persianate world with stagnation resulting from the supposed dominance of the 'Indian Style'. In relegating the non-Iranian Persianate world to one mired in stagnation, an Iranian-centric Persian literary history is absolved from exploring manifestations in Persian literary culture occurring outside of Iran itself.

The state of Persian literary culture in nineteenth-century Afghanistan fulfils the clichéd expectation of a country located at the intersection of West, Central and South Asia, a heritage as much coloured by the richness of indigenous dynasties and courtly traditions as it is by interactions with outsiders. The historical development of Persian literary culture in Afghanistan has been Persianate in the fullest sense, accumulated over time as a result of Afghanistan's proximity to some of the most notable events and places in the region: Mahmud of Ghazna's foray into South Asia, the resplendent court of Husayn Bayqara (r. 1470–1506) at Herat, incursions undertaken by the Safavids and Mughals, proximity to Samarqand and Bukhara and the oral traditions of Khurasan.

In the eighteenth century, following what is considered the founding of the modern state of Afghanistan by Ahmad Shah Durrani (r. 1747–72), Persian literary activity displayed coherence in its output due to both the state's patronage and preference for a particular style. This is as much true for the state's rise under Ahmad Shah and his progeny as it is for poetic practice under the rule of 'Abd al-Rahman Khan (r. 1880–1901) and later with the state-sponsored poetic activities of Mahmud Tarzi (d. 1933).[41] While not the only factor affecting trends in Persian literary culture in eighteenth- and nineteenth-century Afghanistan, the impact of the state on Persian poetic practice was nonetheless a crucial factor. Nowhere is this better suggested than in the state's efforts to raise the poetry of the South Asian poet 'Abd al-Qadir

Bidil (d. 1721) to the highest realms. The promotion of the poetry of Bidil by the Afghan state, as well as the overall high regard in which the poet's oeuvre continues to be held, has preoccupied literary historians. This preoccupation has prevented the assessment of other literary trends in Afghanistan that run counter to the impression of a country solely dedicated to the promotion and use of the 'Indian Style', of which Bidil is seen as the apogee.

The Rise of the Durrani State and Bidilism

The post-1747 Durrani rulers of Afghanistan were active literary patrons. In an effort to bolster their regal and cultural bona fides, rulers sought to attract men of letters and artisans, not unlike other dynasties throughout the Islamicate world. Literary activity, specifically related to Persian, was further bolstered by the fact that the early Sadduzai rulers of Afghanistan composed Persian poetry themselves. Ahmad Shah Durrani composed two collections of poetry, one each in Persian and Pashto, establishing a tradition that would be followed by his Sadduzai heirs, such as his son Timur Shah (r. 1772–93) and grandson Shah Shuja' (r. 1803–9 and 1839–42).[42]

During the rule of Timur Shah, with the initial turbulent phase of state formation in slight retreat, greater centralisation of political and economic authority followed. The social and cultural activity of the bazaars, craft-making and schools of learning blossomed.[43] Accompanying such changes was the emergence of state-sponsored poetry and literature. Profiting from a more stable courtly atmosphere than his predecessors, Timur Shah was able to attract a variety of poets, Sufis, history-writers and others to his court.[44] Most notable was the pleasure displayed by Timur Shah for the poetry of Bidil, solidifying Afghanistan's long-lasting relationship with the great poet that continues until today.[45] Of all the literary activity at his court, Timur Shah reserved the utmost attention to organising gatherings devoted to reciting and analysing Bidil's verse.

The spread, influence and popularity of the poetry of Bidil may be considered one of the primary features of literary culture in eighteenth- and nineteenth-century Afghanistan and traced to scholars and poets returning to Afghanistan from centres of learning abroad, including Delhi, Samarqand and Bukhara.[46] Poets, such as Gul Muhammad Afghan (d. c.1834–5), who spent time in centres of learning in Central Asia, helped circulate Bidil's poetry in Afghanistan.⁴⁷ Originally from Qandahar, Gul Muhammad travelled to Bukhara where he met poets like ʿIsa Makhdum Balkhi and ʿAbd al-Qadir Suda Bukhari, two prominent poets dedicated to understanding and imitating Bidil's verse.⁴⁸ Makhdum, in particular, has come to be regarded as one of the most adept poets at understanding and deciphering the verse of Bidil during his lifetime.⁴⁹ Back in Afghanistan, Gul Muhammad Afghan remained committed to the style, word-choice and overall demeanour of the poetry he had honed abroad.

Timur Shah was not the first Afghan ruler to display an interest in the poetry of Bidil, but rather he built upon the precedent set by his father Ahmad Shah. It has been posited that the founder of the modern Afghan state brought some collections of Bidil's poetry from South Asia to the Royal Library in Qandahar. When Timur Shah moved the seat of his power from Qandahar to Kabul, the Royal Library accompanied him and presumably Bidil's collected works came along with it.⁵⁰ In Kabul, Timur Shah set about capitalising on the appearance of Bidil's poetry and style in Afghanistan. The new Afghan ruler's promotion of Bidil's verse was typified by his sponsoring of gatherings solely devoted to the reading of Bidil's poetry, known as 'Bidil-recitation assemblies' (*majlis-i Bīdil-khānī*). These gatherings were no doubt aided by returning individuals who had witnessed similar assemblies previously in other parts of Central Asia.⁵¹ In such ways, the poetry of Bidil spread and gained in popularity.

Timur Shah was assisted in his endeavours to promote and imitate the poetry of Bidil by his close companion Mir Hutak (d. 1826–7). An aficionado of Bidil's poetry, Mir Hutak hosted the Bidil gatherings at his house, where poets met to read Bidil's work, analyse it and attempt to understand it in a communal setting.⁵² The poets who came to be affiliated with this circle and benefited from the patronage of Timur Shah came from across what is today modern-day Afghanistan. ʿAyda Ghaznavi, who was appointed as one of the Shah's teachers, arrived at the court from Ghazna, as did ʿIshrat Khan ʿIshrat, who would go on to record events relating to Timur Shah's coronation and death.⁵³ The female poet ʿAisha Durrani (fl. late 18th century), who was married to Timur Shah, was also a member of these literary gatherings. In one instance at least, albeit that of ruling monarch's wife, the gatherings were not solely restricted to male participants.⁵⁴

Upon Timur Shah's death, and the battle for the throne that followed, poetry and literary activity at the court came to a standstill. The circle of poets around Timur Shah dispersed.[55] However, the poetry of Bidil, to whom the court had dedicated its most directed care, did not disappear but continued in Afghanistan well beyond the poetic gatherings sponsored by the Afghan ruler. The imitation of Bidil's style and the spread of Bidil-recitation circles persisted throughout society. Later, Bidil's verse would become the first collection of poetry printed in Afghanistan.[56] For such reasons, it has become commonplace among literary historians to anecdotally posit that the popularity of Bidil in Afghanistan is on a par with that of the Shiraz-born Hafiz.

An 'Afghan Literary Return'?

Afghan literary culture in the nineteenth century was more than just the imitation and spread of the poetry of Bidil, whether at the state level or throughout society. While many literary historians argue that the non-Iranian world was fixated on the so-called 'Indian Style', as evidenced by Bidil's stature in Afghanistan, other trends in Persian poetic practice were also emerging. The aforementioned 'Aisha Durrani, who participated in the gatherings of Timur Shah and witnessed the rise of Bidil's poetry at the state level, remained dedicated to following the poetic style of Hafiz in the lyric and Manuchihri in the ode, two undisputed 'masters' of the Persian canon.[57]

Further pointing to the multiplicity of trends in Persian poetic practice in Afghanistan is the work of a little-known poet by the name of Vasfi. His corpus undoubtedly complicates the notion that following the 'ancients', on the one hand, and the 'fresh-speak' style, on the other, was somehow contradictory. Little is known about Vasfi's life outside of the poetry he left behind, but he was likely born some time during the early reign of Timur Shah and probably died around 1844. The Afghan literary scholar Husayn Na'il notes that Vasfi sought to imitate and respond to about ninety different poets, some known throughout Persian literary history and some lesser-known.[58] Among those well-known poets are Anvari (d. c.1180), Khaqani (d. c.1190), Rumi (d. 1273), Sa'di (d. 1291–2), Amir Khusraw (d. 1325), Hafiz (d. 1390), Baba Fighani (d. 1519), 'Urfi (d. 1591), Kalim (d. 1651) and Sa'ib (d. 1677–8), a healthy mix of poets occupying different temporal and geographic spaces, not to mention ones often viewed as practising different, seemingly opposed, styles of poetry.⁵⁹ Indeed, Vasfi sought to imitate and respond to contemporary poets too, including many of the 'literary return' poets of Iran who will be introduced in the following chapter, such as Azar, Mushtaq and Rafiq.⁶⁰ How Vasfi became acquainted with the work of such poets is not known, but his engagement points either to the wider Persianate canvas on which a 'return' to the 'masters' may have operated or to how engagement with the classical canon simply persisted as it always had. Either way, the collection of Vasfi begins to complicate the idea that only poets in eighteenth- and nineteenth-century Iran sought to engage the great masters.

The idea of a 'literary return' in nineteenth-century Afghanistan is not unknown. Though it has been granted significantly less attention than its Iranian counterpart, scholars have noted how various poets in Afghanistan attempted to move away from the poetry of Bidil and the style he represented. Instead they wished to instigate a 'return' to the past styles of the ancients. There is no consensus among literary historians as to the nature of this 'Afghan literary return' or even whether it occurred at all. What is abundantly clear, nonetheless, is the manner in which Afghan and other scholars have sought to use the category of 'literary return' to assess developments in Afghanistan in the nineteenth century. Places outside of Iran grappling with and debating the four schools of Persian literary evolution first conceived by Bahar typically receive scant, if any, attention.

As in the case of 'literary return' in Iran, the recognition of a possible 'Afghan return' is as much the result of actual literary preference as it is an *ex post facto* historiographic construction. The occurrence of an 'Afghan literary return' is presumed to have occurred later in the nineteenth century following the deaths of ʿAisha Durrani and Vasfi, two poets noted above who engaged with the classical masters. This places a potential 'Afghan return' not only after the reign of Timur Shah, but also after the later reigns of Shah Shujaʿ (r. 1803–9 and 1839–42) and Dust Muhammad Khan (r. 1826–39 and 1842–63) in the early to mid-nineteenth century.

The literary scholar Muhammad Zhubal notes that the shift away from the *ghazals* of the 'fresh' style to one more heavily focused on the lyrics and odes of Saʿdi, Hafiz, Anvari and others occurred in the late nineteenth century at the hands of several poets.⁶¹ Among those accorded a major role in this endeavour are those poets who flourished at the courts of Shir Ali Khan

(r. 1863–5 and 1868–79) and ʿAbd al-Rahman Khan (r. 1880–1901). Most prominent among those considered for having initiated a 'literary return' in Afghanistan is Ghulam Muhammad Tarzi (d. 1900), the father of the famed Afghan poet, intellectual and moderniser Mahmud Tarzi (d. 1933).[62] According to Zhubal, the elder Tarzi 're-instigated a new style and method in Afghan literature which was a return to the old styles', particularly the odes of the Khurasani style. Scores more poets supposedly followed.[63]

At the court of ʿAbd al-Rahman Khan, the 'Afghan return movement' is seen to have reached a new phase.[64] Continuing the trend of returning to the styles of the ancients were poets among the secretarial class, like Mirza Muhammad Nabi 'Vasil' Kabuli (d. 1891–2) and Sayyid Muhammad Muhsin 'Shamil' (d. 1891–2). They have both been depicted as promoting a return to the 'Iraqi style and, in particular, the poetry of Hafiz. Holding various positions at the Afghan court, and serving as a close companion to ʿAbd al-Rahman Khan, Vasil is held out as the paramount example of a poet shunning the so-called 'Indian Style' in favour of following the 'ancients'.[65] Other poets of the last quarter of the nineteenth century, such as Sharar Kabuli and Adib Pishavari, have also been regarded as instigating a 'literary return' in Afghanistan, albeit with less fanfare than Vasil.[66]

The idea of an 'Afghan return' has not been without its critics. The literary historian Muhammad Akbar Sana Ghaznavi, while reserving a slot for 'literary return' as one of the schools (*maktab*) in Afghan literary history, nonetheless notes that the poetry of Bidil and the 'fresh style' remained dominant throughout the nineteenth century. He posits that only a few poets sought to model their poetry on that of the ancients, but not enough to justify a widespread movement and displace other styles.[67] Equally sceptical of the idea that a recognisable 'literary return' occurred in nineteenth-century Afghanistan is the literary historian ʿAbd al-Qayyum Qavim. While noting that some poets wished to 'not let the light of knowledge and literature in their country be extinguished', he concludes that the period was primarily dominated by the weak lyrics of the moderns (*mutaʾakhkhirīn*) and odes of little value.[68] Others commenting on a 'literary return' in Afghanistan are more direct in their criticism, such as by declaring that there was never a self-conscious recognition of a 'literary return' project on the part of the participants. They contend that the imitation of the ancients' styles itself was not prevalent among a wide enough class of poets to amount to any sort of trend.[69] In other words, the activities of a few poets cannot be equated with a 'literary return' movement and the revival of the styles of old.[70] The entry in the 1950s state-affiliated *Aryana Encyclopedia* more or less reaches the same conclusion. Under the heading 'Literary Return and the Poets of Afghanistan', the entry details the rise of the 'return' movement in Iran and then notes the failed attempt by Afghan poets to initiate a return movement of its own. These poets were unable to succeed, the entry argues, because a few poets in Afghanistan were not capable enough to dislodge 'the primacy of the Indian style and imitation of the poetry of Bidil'.[71]

Did the practices of later nineteenth-century Afghan poets, such as Vasil, Shamil and Tarzi, constitute a 'return' movement towards the ancients or simply comprise isolated incidents of poetic practice? The answer largely hinges on one's definition of what constitutes 'literary return'. Since the idea of 'literary return' has been formulated as an exclusionary movement pertaining to Iran, most literary historians contend that any assessment of the Afghan case must adhere to the established Iranian model. Accordingly, an Afghan 'literary return' must presumably be assessed by two criteria understood as shaping the movement during its heyday under the Qajar state. First, it must be a self-conscious movement seeking to imitate the classical masters. Second, it must be a movement that promotes a style in imitation of the classical masters at the expense of other styles across state and society. Since these criteria are considered the two major attributes of the Iranian 'literary return' movement, any similarly inclined Afghan movement must pass this test of eligibility.[72]

In order to match the model of the 'literary return' experience as supported by the Qajar state in Tehran, historians have looked to the Afghan state as a naturally equivalent location to explore the existence of any 'Afghan return'. The courts of Shir Ali Khan and 'Abd al-Rahman Khan, two venues where a close cohort of state-sponsored poets convened, have led to a focus on such figures as Vasil, Shamil and Tarzi. The poetry and activities of these figures are then assessed to determine the overall viability of an 'Afghan return' in comparison to the Iranian model.

The problem with relying on such a framework of 'literary return' is twofold. First, it overlooks how the Iranian literary return movement at its inception in Isfahan was malleable and flexible prior to its institutionalisation in Tehran. Despite the attempts of later proponents to promote the movement according to its experience at the Qajar court, the emergence of the 'literary return' movement in Iran pertained to more than just poetics. The movement in its gestational phase, as detailed in the following chapter, was guided by the poets' social and cultural experiences and the desire to re-establish the position of the poet in post-Safavid Isfahan. Only later did it become a self-conscious movement under the Qajar state in Tehran when poetics in imitation of the masters, and neo-classical sensibilities, superseded all else. Second, using the Iranian experience as a model does not allow for the exploration of any sustained engagement with the poetry of the classical canon beyond that by a close collective of like-minded poets. The Iranian experience of 'literary return', whether in the case of an informal network of poets in Isfahan or a more formal gathering in Tehran, views the element of poetic assembly as a necessity for assessing trends in poetic production. Any sustained engagement with the classical canon unconnected to a coherent assembly of poets cannot be considered to have achieved a 'return' to the masters according to this definition. In other words, individual poets must imitate an individual canonic poet in their poetry and do so in a collective, self-recognised format.

Instead of solely favouring imitative poetics by an assembly of poets as the definitional feature of 'literary return', there are great benefits to examining a more flexible engagement with the masters in the nineteenth century. Such an approach allows for expanding the applicability of 'literary return' beyond a small cohort of poets to explore transregional trends in literary production. More importantly, it allows for assessing engagement with the masters in the nineteenth century as a feature and function of textual production and circulation, rather than defining it more parochially by the poetics at a courtly centre.

The greatest sustained engagement with the poetry of the classical masters in nineteenth-century Afghanistan is not to be found in the poetry of a few court-sponsored poets, but rather in the series of war-ballads (*jangnāmas*) composed in the style of Firdawsi's *Book of Kings* (*Shahnama*) to narrate the events of the first Anglo-Afghan War (1839–42). For it is here, when the newly emergent Afghan state frayed through internecine fighting among

Timur Shah's progeny, that the ancients of Persian poetry were once again summoned on a wide-range scale to help articulate and memorialise local events and identities in the face of chaos. In a period of political transition and social uncertainty, not unlike what the early members of the 'return' movement encountered in Iran, poets in Afghanistan turned towards recording social and political experiences by drawing on the verse of the masters.

The war-ballads, which in the words of the historian Mir Ghulam Muhammed Ghubar helped enliven 'the epic and battle spirit' (*rūḥ-i ḥamāsī va razmī*) of Afghan oral culture, complicate the exclusivity of the category of 'literary return' and all it has come to symbolise.[73] These texts widen our gaze to larger societal trends in poetry that extends beyond the individual examples of verse composed by an exclusive assembly of Iranian (or Afghan) poets. The appearance of the Anglo-Afghan war-ballads, as contemporaneous texts memorialising a major political event in the style of a canonic 'master', is enough to undermine the claim that poets in Iran were the only group utilising the ancients to define their literary, social and political experiences in the nineteenth-century Persianate world.

But more than the mere appearance of the Anglo-Afghan war-ballads are the multiple environments of their production and circulation on a transregional basis. The emergence of the war-ballads incorporated such a vast array of authors, patrons and publics to fluidly operate across the mediums of oral, manuscript and print culture that it created a market-place of works in imitation of Firdawsi's *Book of Kings*, unique to the Persianate world of the time. Stretching across Afghanistan and South Asia, the war-ballad marketplace points to how sustained engagement with the masters was closer to a normative practice across the nineteenth-century Persianate world. The case demonstrates how poets from different locales (outside of Iran) sought guidance and fortitude in the Persian canon amid the stark political, social and cultural changes happening around them. Recognising how local engagements with the 'masters' not only persisted in the face of political chaos and cultural tenuousness in the nineteenth century, but in many ways may have been precipitated by it, recalibrates what has heretofore been understood as a 'literary return' movement defined according to imitative poetics and Iranian exclusivity.

South Asian Stagnation

The amnesia created by the interpolation of 'literary return' in Persian literary historiography has dovetailed rather well with the overall narrative of Persian's 'decline' in eighteenth- and nineteenth-century South Asian historiography. The narrative of 'decline' of Persian in South Asia is largely a by-product of Persian's association with political changes resulting from the downfall and break-up of the Mughal Empire (r. 1526–1857) after the death of the emperor Awrangzib (d. 1707).[74] More often than not, the strength of Persian literary culture in South Asia has been seen as inextricably tied to the withering political fortunes of the Mughals. As the Mughal Empire went, it has been argued, so too did Persian literary culture. The rich corpus of administrative norms and practices, modes of patronage, literary models and trends in poetry tied to the Persian language and nurtured over the centuries is seen to have reached its apogee and then died away completely when the Mughal Empire fractured.[75]

Scholarship reflecting on how Persian literary culture functioned in eighteenth- and nineteenth-century South Asia tends to do so by emphasising two major shifts occurring in post-Mughal times. Recasting the story of Persian literary culture within the framework of these two larger shifts deeply affects the manner in which Persian literary history in South Asia is written. The first is the language policies of the British as executed through their political and colonial endeavours. The second is the growing usage of Urdu as a means of literary expression. The cumulative impact of assessing the fortunes of Persian literary culture in post-Mughal South Asia through the prism of these two hegemonic historiographies – colonialism and Urdu – relegates Persian to a transitional role of declining prestige and usage.

Coupled with a narrative of 'stagnation' on account of the so-called 'Indian Style', Persian literary culture of the post-Mughal period becomes all but forgotten. If the Iranian-centric narrative of 'literary return' needed to erase non-Iranian developments in the Persianate world to construct a taut narrative of literary nationalism in Iran, then South Asian narratives focused on the overwhelming impact of colonialism and the spectacular rise of Urdu needed to do the same in articulating their own origin stories. To do so effectively, as in the Iranian case, the messier elements of Persian literary culture in eighteenth- and nineteenth-century South Asia needed to be marginalised and ultimately erased. In the following sections, the general historiographical narratives related to the transition to English under the British and the rise of Urdu are presented in turn. This is followed by an argument for reconceptualising the place of Persian literary culture in eighteenth- and nineteenth-century South Asia.

The 'New Munshi' and the transition to English

Persian, of course, did find itself in transition in the latter days of the Mughal Empire. The political shocks of the eighteenth century, such as Nadir Shah's sacking of Delhi in 1739, initiated a breakdown of complex patronage networks and a loosening of the rigid social system of the Mughals, causing literati to leave Delhi and placing Persian literary culture and production in a state of flux.[76] The arrival of the British on the Subcontinent also played a large part. The impact of the British on informational networks wedded to Persian language and administrative norms is well-known. The way in which the British used and manipulated aspects of Persianate literary culture and reconfigured existing networks to fit with their own political aspirations certainly represents a major turning point for Persianate culture in South Asia. In their quest to achieve economic and political inroads into the Subcontinent, the British relied on informants, administrators and secretaries versed in the Persian language and its cultural norms.[77] One of the many ways in which to capture the larger trends working against Persian's administrative dominance can be gleaned by looking at the figure of the secretary (*munshī*) and how the British relied on this ever-dependable class whose administrative and scribal skills derived from their placement within Mughal governmental structures.[78]

During the early rise of the East India Company (EIC), especially from the mid-eighteenth to the mid-nineteenth century, munshis were crucial in helping the British navigate the established set of cultural norms related to the use of the Persian language. These munshis, skilled in the Persian language and Mughal administrative technologies, 'were desperately needed by the British as they maneuvered their way through diplomatic exchanges and political intrigues in their rise to power'.[79] Before 1830 in particular, the EIC used munshis to 'manipulate the information systems of their Hindu and Muslim predecessors' to their political advantage.[80] Approaching the Persian language as a 'pragmatic vehicle of communication with Indian officials and rulers through which … they could express their requests, queries, and thoughts, and through which they could get things done', the munshi proved indispensable to British political and economic activity.[81]

The British tasked these individuals with a variety of roles, ranging from administrator and secretary to language instructor and author. They served as administrative and cultural interpreters between the EIC and Mughal successor states, accompanied British diplomatic missions abroad and composed works on various aspects of South Asian history and culture at the behest of their British employers. Though no comprehensive work exists on the variety of roles occupied by the munshi class, a variety of studies have been devoted to individual munshis and their role within British residencies and language-training colleges.[82]

The heyday of the munshi as Persian interlocutor was relatively short-lived. Between 1820 and 1850 a new type of munshi emerged, one whose ability to communicate and conduct business in English was equally as important as, if not more important than, their abilities grounded in Persian literary and cultural norms.[83] In 1835, following closely on the heels of Thomas Macaulay's famous minute on education and the idea that not 'a single shelf of a good European library was worth the whole native literature of India and Arabia', Persian was abolished as the singular administrative language.[84] Thus, from the 1830s onward, it was not enough to be versed in Mughal diplomatic norms and Persian. The EIC now expected that a munshi should also have a Western education or familiarity with Western office practices.[85] It was the 'new' munshis' command of English, rather than Persian, that allowed them to keep up 'traditional roles as cultural mediators for, and trusted assistants of, government officials'.[86] Individuals like Mohan Lal (d. 1877) and Shahamat Ali, both of whom were instructed in English at Delhi College, and served British colonial officials in various capacities and left behind accounts of their travels in English, best exemplify this trend.[87] Indeed, Lal and Ali were regarded by their British patrons as exemplars of what 'new munshis' could achieve as 'modernised' and 'anglicised' iterations of Persian secretaries from generations past. As C. E. Trevelyan put in his foreword to Mohan Lal's *Travels in Panjab, Afghanistan & Turkistan*:

> In the person of Mohan Lal we proved to the Mohammedan nations beyond the Indus our qualification for the great mission with which we have been intrusted [sic], of regenerating India. We convinced them that we are capable of producing a moral change infinitely more honourable to us than any victory we have achieved … What has given Mohan Lal so decided an advantage over the generality of his countrymen? … It is simply his knowledge of the English language … such knowledge as enables him to read and understand English books, and to converse intelligently with English gentlemen on ordinary subjects. This is the simple cause of Mohan Lal's elevation of character.[88]

The transition from the British reliance on munshis skilled in Persian literary and cultural norms to 'new munshis' with English language skills offers an example of the shifting position of Persian in the nineteenth century. The prevalence and practice of Persian administrative norms were slowly being phased out, as the British sought to tailor the language politics of a South Asian ecumene to its own evolving colonial policy. It is a story of 'out with the old and in with the new'.

Language competition and the rise of Urdu

The increasing relevance of Urdu has been identified as the other main reason for Persian's outright decline during the eighteenth and nineteenth centuries. The rise of Urdu impacted literary culture, poetic expression and patronage practices associated with Persian, marginalising its social and literary value in certain venues and complementing it in others. The often linear presentation of the growth of Urdu in eighteenth- and nineteenth-century South Asia, however, favours the displacement of Persian as abrupt and complete, giving the impression that Persian literary culture declined and disappeared without a trace remaining. Such a view wishes to see the complex interplay between multiple languages in a shared literary environment as necessarily arcing towards the replacement of one by the other. It is a conception modelled on the romantic view of nationalism where monolingualism is an established feature of the modern nation-state.[89] As Francesca Orsini reminds us, careful attention must be paid to the particular configurations of multilingual practices and uses among different groups, places and genres in eighteenth- and nineteenth-century India, rather than that we fall into the trap of generalisations, such as the phenomenon of vernacularisation or a theory of language substitution.[90] The relationship between the register of Urdu and Persian literary tradition was indeed messy.

The origin and rise of Urdu, the circumstances and places where it developed and the genealogy of the name itself remain the subject of much controversy and debate.[91] Contrary to the linear narrative of its development, as nationalist and colonial constructions posit, the emergence of Urdu is the outgrowth of a long series of overlapping and cross-cutting histories. Urdu's emergence and use as a literary language can be related to far-flung phenomena spread across South Asia in the medieval and early modern periods, such as debates over its literary acceptability and new modes of patronage. Urdu's rise to prominence can best be seen as the cumulative impact of these many disparate factors, occurring in fits and starts in both the Subcontinent's north and south over several hundred years. Urdu's emergence is as much the result of Sufis in early fifteenth-century Gujarat using proto-Urdu to reach a wider audience, and the dual linguistic pattern of Persian and Dakhani under operation at various courts, as it is the outcome of debates among poets and literati concerning its merits as a replacement for Persian in later centuries.[92]

In the early eighteenth century, Rekhta – a mixture of Persian and Hindustani literary verse and a direct literary ancestor of Urdu – experienced its 'first great flowering', to borrow the words of Ralph Russell.[93] At this time, the language began to blossom as a court language, and later, more prominently, it began to blossom as a language of poetic expression.[94] Over the next two centuries, political developments, sociological processes and community desires all coalesced to initiate a greater utilisation of the Urdu vernacular as a growing medium of expression. Its emergence challenged Persian in certain settings, but remained coexistent with it elsewhere.

The break-up of the Mughal empire was a defining moment in this regard. The rise of various successor states in the wake of the empire's disintegration, along with new patronage opportunities at the court level and throughout society, had far-reaching impacts on Persian literary practice. A shift, however, had already been under way with regard to Urdu and Persian at the Mughal court. Beginning around the reign of Shah 'Alam II (r. 1759–1806), Rekhta (slowly coming to call itself 'Urdu') came to be used in the court of the Mughals. While Persian remained in place as the official language, the gentry in Delhi became less inclined to utilise it in their writings. They increasingly viewed Persian as a language most readily associated with the royal patronage practices of a strained imperial centre.

Outside of the imperial centre, cultures of newly emergent Mughal successor states began to take shape and, in time, impact patronage opportunities for Persian. Persian, of course, was already well-situated across the Subcontinent. The sprawling networks of Mughal bureaucracy and the significance accorded to the language as a marker of elite intellectual and literary status nurtured an active poetic culture in places like Lucknow, Agra and Lahore as well as other cities and provinces. As Purnima Dhavan notes, already by the early decades of the seventeenth century most Persian learners could be found 'not in the rarified inner circle of the imperial court, but in much more eclectic settings all over the province and cities of the emperor'.[95] Nonetheless, as Mughal central authority in the eighteenth century waned, the rise of regional powers witnessed the emergence of 'new cultural and institutional forms', allowing for Urdu, like other regional languages, to be enriched by the 'vocabulary and literary forms of Persian'.[96] In Awadh, for example, rulers beginning with Shuja' al-Dawla (r. 1753–75) – himself a Persianised Mughal and the grandson of a migrant from Iran – offered patronage opportunities for Urdu in addition to supporting the fine arts in general.[97] While the Nawabs of Awadh offered patronage to Persian poets on a lavish scale too, 'Persian poetry did not flourish here to any great extent … primarily because of the growing vogue for Urdu as a poetic medium'.[98] Sceptical and wary of the old Mughal elite, rulers such as Shuja' al-Dawla relied on local non-Persianised groups and imported others, like Shaykhzadas, Telingana Rajputs and Gosain mercenaries, who were more inclined to offer patronage to Urdu poets rather than Persian.[99]

Alongside the shift in political tides and patronage practices stemming from the break-up of the Mughal Empire, Urdu was simultaneously emerging as a more readily acceptable medium of literary and poetic expression in competition with Persian. Crucial to this shift in perception was the work of 'Vali' Dakhani (c.1667–1707), who elevated the status of Rekhta[100] by demonstrating that its poetry 'could rival, if not surpass, Indo-Persian poetry in sophistication of imagery, complexity and abstractness of metaphor'.[101]

This shift in perception led to the growth of poets choosing to write in Rekhta instead of Persian in the early 1700s. This would soon be followed by persistent efforts to compose poetry in Urdu.

Along with the increased attention to Urdu poetic composition came the need for poets to find instructors to teach them, the rise of poetic assemblies to share verses and hone skills, and the blossoming of master–student (*ustād–shāgird*) relationships.[102] The new world of Urdu poetics and poetic community put a premium on identifying with a master or lineage, association with a readily identified *ustād* being viewed as a major necessity. The new class of Urdu poets emerging in the eighteenth and nineteenth centuries would be more likely to identify themselves with a local and accessible *ustād* for easier affiliation than with an individual further afield or a historical poet that they could emulate, tightening the social network around Urdu composition.[103] Such an approach can perhaps best be seen in the Mughal court and the shifting terrain upon which the relationship between the courtier-poet and patron-ruler was now founded. Opposed to past practices in which rulers sought poets to offer panegyrics in their praise and celebrate special occasions, rulers such as Shah 'Alam II and Bahadur Shah II (r. 1837–57) sought out poets to serve as their own teachers with greater frequency.[104] The result was a new configuration of poetic community for those composing in Urdu. With the growth of master–student relationships, a whole new literary culture began to emerge, one in which poetic genealogy, status, codes and poetic gatherings for Urdu poets rose in importance. This was accompanied by various feuds, loyalties and competitions over patronage, either among royal patrons or among sought-after instructors in poetry. 'What began as a need', the literary scholar Shamsur Rahman Faruqi writes, 'soon became fashion, and then a minor industry and source of patronage.'[105]

On a more popular level, the assemblies (sing: *mushā'ira*) in the nineteenth century 'enjoyed mass popularity as a most favourite form of cultural recreation among all strata of educated urban dwellers', catering to different levels of poetic taste and literary connoisseurship.[106] Much of the desire for increased Urdu composition was foregrounded by an insistence on nurturing aspects of cultural identity more attentive to local circumstances than regnal ones. Daniela Bredi frames this shift in terms of writers of Urdu wishing to 'no longer address an international audience, but an Indian one'.[107] Especially following the 1857 rebellion, poets, storytellers and novelists 'reworked literary traditions and introduced new genres and modes of expression in their mission to reform and mobilise community'.[108] There is little doubt that this represented a conscious choice of opting for Urdu over Persian as the most appropriate linguistic medium in which to express the zeitgeist of the times. Fritz Lehmann situates this process in the latter days of a still-centralised Mughal authority when authors in Delhi began to turn their attention to writing in Urdu, pivoting more directly to a local, rather than a royal, audience.[109] Such a shift, he argues, helped foster the growth in Urdu of *shahr-āshūb* (city-disturber) literature, a genre allowing writers to comment on local conditions in a more easily understood medium for a larger audience.[110] As the *shahr-āshūb* genre pre-dates this period and flowered in Persian under the Mughals, often in relation to 'urban-topographical' themes, it would be inaccurate to tie the destiny of the genre to its appearance in Urdu or post-Mughal political turmoil.[111] Nonetheless, the shift in how the *shahr-āshūb* genre was differentially represented in Persian and Urdu does highlight how at least one poetic topos was being reconfigured across a complex linguistic terrain. As Sunil Sharma notes, 'during the early decades of the eighteenth century, historical and political changes led poets to redefine the function of the city poem: the exuberant city poem of Persian with *shahrashub* elements became the *shahrashob* (the disturbed city), a lament for the declining city in classical Urdu poetry'.[112] While the division between a local Urdu register and a global Persian one is no doubt an oversimplification, which among other things discounts for trends in how Urdu emerged as a lingua franca operating across the Indian Ocean and even perhaps into Africa, the groundswell around a vernacular equipped to harness the emotive thrust of local circumstances appears a defining feature of this period.[113]

If the eighteenth century witnessed the 'great flowering' of Urdu, then the nineteenth century witnessed its consolidation as a literary language. The community, popular appeal and networks among Urdu poets were growing stronger, reified in descriptions of lineages and assemblies as told in such biographical anthologies of Urdu poets as Mir Taqi Mir (d. 1810)'s *Points of Poets* (*Niqat al-shuʿara*) and Saʿadat Khan Nasir (d. c.1857–71)'s *An Elegant Encounter* (*Khush maʿraka ziba*). Perhaps indicative of the shifting tide in textual production, at least with regard to biographical anthologies, was the language of composition of each of the aforementioned works: Mir Taqi Mir composed his in Persian, while Saʿadat Khan Nasir composed his biographical anthology in Urdu. By the 1840s, as Frances Pritchett notes, the grip of Persian prose was broken: over half of the biographical anthologies of Urdu poets produced in that decade were composed in a language other than Persian, a far cry from the first four decades of the century when the situation was entirely reversed.[114] The literary career of the biographical anthologist Ghulam 'Mushafi' Hamdani (d. *c.*1824–5) illustrates such a trend at work: he wrote a Persian-language biographical anthology of Persian poets in 1784–5, then a Persian-language biographical anthology on Rekhta/Urdu poets ten years later, and finally a biographical anthology on both Urdu and Persian poets in 1820–1 almost completely in Urdu.[115]

It was also during this time that various individuals emerged as major exponents of Urdu literary theory and history and others as the 'great poets' of the time. It was the time of individuals like Muhammad Husayn Azad (1830–1910) and Altaf Husayn Hali (1837–1914), along with such poets as Zawq (1789–1854) and Ghalib (d. 1869).[116] While the former two authors delineated the parameters of Urdu poetic composition, literary history and its development, the latter two would soon be recognised as its greatest practitioners in prose and poetry.[117] In the realm of Islamic religious literature, Urdu began to achieve a more prominent role too. Beginning with the translation of the Quran into Urdu by Shah Rafiʿ al-Din (1749–1817), son of the renowned reformer Shah Waliullah, Urdu became an important medium for articulating religious thought and transmitting ideas with regard to tafsir, fiqh and hadith, which would help solidify its use by other Muslims sects and sub-groups later in the nineteenth century.[118]

The British played their own part in actively promoting Urdu, as evidenced by their educational activities at the College of Fort William in Calcutta in the early part of the nineteenth century. While Persian still remained relevant, as it did for many successor states, the British began to transition their educational and instructional activities from Persian to not just English but Urdu as well. Persian instructors continued to be hired both in Calcutta and at colleges in the UK, but the transition to Urdu was on its way. Starting in 1800, the EIC began hiring various writers at Fort William College to translate many popular Persian books into simple Urdu prose.[119]

Persian still remained popular among students; indeed, Fort William College displayed a great deal of continuity with literary culture of the previous century.[120] But Urdu was more than keeping pace with regard to enrolment, course offerings and publications.[121]

But multilingualism fades slowly, and the continued presence and prestige of Persian would not so quickly wash away: neither from the formal colonial apparatus, nor at the societal level, nor in genres of a high-register literary mould, nor from lesser, semi-literate attempts at creating Persianised Urdu in a hemstitch here or there. Indeed, even fifty years after Persian's supposed death knell was sounded in 1835, the British could still complain that Urdu munshis were writing in Persian, save for the replacing of the final Persian verb 'ast' with the Urdu verb 'he'. Classical Persian texts served as important sources in still-active Persian neighbourhood schools, to instruct both in the language and in its cultural and literary tradition. The British continued to invest resources in compiling and distributing Persian textbooks for instruction in the language, even if they now wished to promote Persian as a 'foreign' language disconnected from its local roots and traditions. As Amanda Lanzillo notes, 'Persian literacy offered access to an extra-colonial identity marker and extra-colonial forms of employment and patronage' well into the late nineteenth century in North India.[122] Indeed, even with the advent of lithography in North India and the rise of printed materials in English and vernacular languages, Persian was able to attract a new readership and sustain many of its modes of authority, at least until the 1860s.[123]

Despite such countervailing factors, Urdu's rise to prominence in eighteenth- and nineteenth-century South Asia tends towards a linear narrative of sudden dominance standing on the shoulders of Persian's irrelevance and 'decline'. Perhaps best encapsulating such a narrative is the introduction to *The Last Musha'irah of Delhi* by Farhatullah Bayg, itself a fictionalised account of a historical assembly that occurred in Delhi in 1845 at the court of the last Mughal ruler Bahadur Shah II. In introducing the work, Akhtar Qamber writes:

> It is now time to say that the language, that had a humble birth in Delhi, that was nurtured in the Deccan and refined, chiseled and enriched in Delhi and Lucknow, could by the time of Karim-ud-Din's musha'irah

vie with Persian in all respects. In fact, the reversal of the fates of Persian and Urdu is brought dramatically at Karim-ud-Din's musha'irah when the one and only ghazal read in Persian had failed to interest or move the audience. Very few now took delight in the once popular king's language of the Mughal court. Karim-ud-Din's musha'irah recorded a high point in the story of the Urdu language as will be seen in the quality of the ghazals recited on this occasion. It also marks a high point in the Mughal temper, mood and culture of an era fast approaching its close.[124]

The position of Persian, whether with regard to administrative practices, educational instruction or poetic expression, was clearly undergoing a significant transition in the eighteenth and nineteenth centuries. The rise of the 'new munshi' as initiated under the British and the increase in Urdu as a language for poetic expression helped displace Persian from its political, cultural and literary perch. But narratives founded upon Persian's displacement can only be part of the story. This is not to diminish studies devoted to explaining the shift towards English, Urdu and the resultant impact on Persian literary culture; rather, it is to note that such studies maintain different historiographical aims, which have promoted narratives requiring the expunging of Persian literary trends and relegating Persian to the dustbin of 'decline'.

Recent scholarship around the increased usage of Urdu in the eighteenth and nineteenth centuries has begun questioning the linearity of its growth, in terms both of how the language itself developed and its relationship with Persian. Investigation into debates over the promotion of Urdu as the language of primary instruction at Osmania University in Hyderabad during the early twentieth century reveals inherent tensions in attempts to formalise the language into a worldly vernacular and disagreements about the roots of its authority.[125] The proto-nationalist lens used to explain the growth of Urdu in the latter days of the Mughal Empire has likewise been questioned by exploring the channels of exchange and complex fluidity nurturing the language's rise in poetry.[126] Even a journal like *Avadh Akhbar*, which was consequential in promoting modern Urdu literature and which serialised one of the most famous Urdu novels, continued to promote Persian literature by announcing the publication of Ghalib's Persian works, pointing to a multilingual readership.[127]

Contrary to the narrative promoting Urdu's linear development, communities maintained varying degrees of literacy in Urdu and Persian, unbounded by the closed worlds of a romantic 'one people, one language' nationalism that leaves little room for a multilingual ethos. Walter Hakala has admirably dispelled the myth of Urdu's linear advancement and monolingual supremacy by demonstrating how lexicographical texts in Persian, Urdu and English operated in a multilingual and cross-cultural world of intertextuality, utilising shared methods of organisation and conceptual outlays.[128] Likewise, the activities of Delhi College, which served as a crucial venue for Urdu instruction, point to the way in which the language mediated knowledge through multiple traditions, including Persian, and did not understand the rise of Urdu in zero-sum terms vis-à-vis other languages.[129] Such occurrences serve as reminders of the coexistence of overlapping Urdu and Persian literary spheres, as do other examples cognisant of the active role of Persian literary norms amid the emergence of new linguistic and cultural modes in the nineteenth century.[130]

These studies certainly elucidate the multi-faceted linguistic and social role played by Persian in leading to Urdu supremacy, but they do not necessarily address trends in Persian literary culture beyond its service in explaining that emergent phenomenon. Dislodging Persian from the grander narrative of 'stagnation' and 'decline' in the eighteenth and nineteenth centuries demands extricating it from the world of language policies and preferences for English and Urdu, where one language is merely swapped for another.

Persian still had a place in the gatherings devoted to the recitation of Urdu verse well into the twentieth century, where Persian poetry could be recited 'without the audience or the poet feeling any incongruity'.[131] Even within the realm of language policies, both the British and members of Indian society continued debating the role of Persian and its shifting position within various institutions after 1835.[132] As the literary scholar Arthur Dudney points out, those anecdotally invoking the decline narrative as a causal factor in literary 'failures of the imagination' in Persian both misconstrue aspects of the era's innovative techniques and overlook an actual increase in the volume and quality of Persian literary scholarship following the break-up of the Mughal empire.[133] Instead of understanding elements of Persian poetics in terms of 'decline' or retroactively reading the period as an era of 'stagnation', Dudney opts instead to focus on debates around poetic authority and issues of intertextuality.[134]

Persian literary culture with all its attendant features in eighteenth- and nineteenth-century South Asia constitutes more than a story of mere language usage; it concerns the manner in which the language operated as a continually viable medium connecting local, regional and global interlocutors around matters of literary, political and social import. Recovering elements of Persian literary culture in this way allows for a more in-depth exploration of the intersection of local developments, regional exchanges and global trends in the Persianate word. Printing technologies prevalent in nineteenth-century Bombay led to the production of Persian texts that would circulate transregionally and connect religious economies across the Indian Ocean.[135] Textual exchanges between the Parsi community of Bombay and their co-religionists in Iran, well into the twentieth century, created a Bombay–Tehran marketplace of books and readers. By leveraging new technologies of print, the wealthier Zoroastrian community of Bombay could impact social, scholarly and intellectual trends in Iran through what the historian Afshin Marashi terms 'textual philanthropy'.[136]

The advent of European Orientalism and the spread of English in South Asia did not cut off exchanges in Persian, or conversations between Iranian, Indians and others about Persianate literary culture and South Asia's place within it. 'If anything', as the historian Farzin Vejdani notes, 'English as a new lingua franca in India and beyond led to further exchanges on whether or not Persian constituted a cosmopolitan lingua franca given its historical transregional use.'[137] Through a shared Persianate discourse and transregional scholarly interchange, Iranians, Indians and European Orientalists could collectively engage in literary history projects endeavouring towards a shared entrée to literary modernity.[138] Buoyed by the technological advancements of steam and print, and equipped with English as a new lingua franca, conversations in and about Persian in South Asia continued well into the twentieth century, uneradicated by the totalising impacts of vernacularisation, colonialism or nationalism.

Back in the nineteenth century, when new linguistic mediums of exchange still appeared in their gestational phases, Persian textual production, spanning such topics as religious sciences, history, poetry, botany and medicine, continued.[139] Such a range of Persian literary activity reveals not a singular world of textual practice, but the many worlds of Persian production, connected to greater bodies of literary and scientific knowledge, Persianate or otherwise, at the local, national or international level. Many of these works fall directly into the category that Mohamad Tavakoli-Targhi refers to as the 'homeless' texts of Persianate modernity, as they are dislodged from national memory in India and unaccounted for in Iranian literary history.[140] Engagement with such texts can evoke linkages between different transformations seemingly worlds apart.

The position of Persian in eighteenth- and nineteenth-century South Asia is perhaps best understood as a series of re-articulations in a period of political and socio-linguistic transformation. Among the many re-articulations amid the messiness of Mughal decline, the rise of colonialism, emergence of Urdu and general political uncertainty of the time is the Persian poetic environment at the court of Muhammad Ghaws Khan Bahadur (d. 1855), the last Nawab of Arcot. An exploration of the practice of textual production at the Nawab's court demonstrates at least one way in which a local expression of Persian literary culture persisted, re-articulated itself and remained connected to the larger Persianate world in the nineteenth century. It shows how one community in post-Mughal South Asia, in the south of the Subcontinent no less, grappled with the Persian canon, the historical position of the 'masters' and what it meant to compose poetry on the edge of the Persianate world. It is but one instance that displays how Persian literary culture, far from being mired in a state of stagnation, overwhelmed by colonial policies or indelibly eradicated by Urdu's rise to prominence, refashioned itself within the heady local, colonial and Persianate environment of the time.

Notes

1. Amin, '*Mujassama-i bud mujassama-i nabud*', p. 348. These articles appeared in the journal *Armaghan* (Gift) and appear in Bahar, *Bahar va adab-i Farsi*, vol. 1, pp. 43–66.
2. Shafaq, *Tarikh-i adabiyat-i Iran*, p. 377.
3. For the role played by biographical anthologies in shaping the writing of literary histories see Jabbari, 'The Making of Modernity in Persianate Literary History'.

4. 'Khurasani' refers to the region of Khurasan located in today's eastern Iran and western Afghanistan, as well as parts of Turkmenistan and Uzbekistan. ''Iraqi' refers to 'Iraq-i 'Ajam in western Iran.
5. See e.g. Zarrinkub, *Naqd-i adabi*. Farshidvard, *Darbara-yi adabiyat va naqd-i adabi*, vol. 1.
6. For some commonly held views about the 'Indian Style' and its emergence in history, see Ahmad, *Studies in Islamic Culture*, pp. 223–34.
7. The terms '*sabk-i Hindī*' and 'Indian Style' have been the subject of much confusion, particularly on account of the use of the signifier 'Indian'. Wishing to de-emphasise the possible confusion of the term with Indian ethnicity or the geographic space of India, some scholars have opted for other names instead. Paul Losensky in *Welcoming Fighani*, for example, opts to define the poetry that accords with the 'Indian Style' period as 'Safavid–Mughal Poetry', as 'the adjective "Indian" gives a local designation to a movement that was international in scope'. However, it should be noted that Losensky does not view 'Safavid–Mughal Poetry' as an exact equivalent of the 'Indian Style', but rather views the 'Indian Style' as simply one style of poetry, albeit the dominant one, that existed during the Safavid–Mughal period. Losensky, *Welcoming Fighani*, p. 4. Some scholars, for their part, have opted for calling the poetry during this period 'Safavi' or 'Isfahani'; however, as Ehsan Yarshater and others have noted, scrapping the appellation 'Indian' in favour 'Safavi' or 'Isfahani' simply replaces one ill-equipped term with another, no less restrictive in its construction. See Yarshater, 'The Indian or Safavid Style', p. 252 and Farshidvard, *Darbara-yi adabiyat va naqd-i adabi*, vol. 1, p. 781. Rajeev Kinra advocates doing away with the term 'Indian Style' altogether, as it carries too heavy a connotation of a particular (Indian) geography and heritage, which, in Kinra's estimation, leads one to focus too heavily on the influence of the Indian realm upon the Persian language (e.g. from a philological perspective) and does little to define the style according to literary criteria or more historically-bounded phenomena present in the greater Persianate world. Kinra prefers the term *tāza-gūʾī* (fresh-speak) instead. See Kinra, 'Fresh Words for a Fresh World', p. 131. For a longer discussion by Kinra, see *Writing Self, Writing Empire*, pp. 201–39. For a critical discussion on how and why to use the term 'Indian Style' see Mikkelson, 'Of Parrots and Crows', pp. 522–3.
8. Schimmel, *Islamic Literatures of India*, p. 23.
9. Jan Rypka, *History of Iranian Literature*, p. 296.
10. Those who have questioned such a haphazard approach to understanding

the poetics of the style include Ahmad Karimi-Hakkak, Paul Losensky and Riccardo Zipoli. See Karimi-Hakkak, 'Pusht-i rang-ha-yi khazan'. Losensky, *Welcoming Fighani*. Zipoli, *Chira sabk-i Hindi*.

11. For example, with regard to the poetry of Bidil (d. 1721), who is considered the practitioner par excellence of the 'Indian Style', Shafi'i-Kadkani notes two major characteristics of the great South Asian poet that can also be found in other styles: 'paradoxes', found in the mystical poetry of the 'Iraqi style, and 'synesthesia' (ḥess-āmīzī), found in the 'new' poetry of the modern period. See Shafi'i-Kadkani, *Sha'ir-i ayina-ha*, pp. 40–1. For a comparison between Bidil and a modern Persian poet see Husayni, *Bidil, Sipihri, va sabk-i Hindi*.
12. Faruqi, 'A Stranger in the City'.
13. Keshavmurthy, *Persian Authorship and Canonicity*, p. 2.
14. There is a long-standing anecdote that for every Persian manuscript produced in Safavid domains during the early modern period, ten were produced in Mughal South Asia.
15. Quoted in Khatami, *Pizhuhishi dar nasr va nazm*, p. 199.
16. For information on Dunbuli's life and his time spent as a hostage at the court of Karim Khan Zand see Werner, 'Taming the Tribal Native'.
17. Quoted in Khatami, *Pizhuhishi dar nasr va nazm*, p. 199. This is a slightly different version appearing in Dunbuli, *Tajribat al-ahrar*, pp. 213–14, that is based on the London copy of Dunbuli's text. Shawkat, Sa'ib and Vahid are three poets who came to be associated heavily with the 'Indian Style' of poetry in literary history. Zamiri refers to Kamil al-Din Husayn 'Zamiri' Isfahani (d. 1566) and Naziri refers to Muhammad Husayn 'Naziri' Nishapuri (d. *c*.1612–14).
18. Garrusi, *Tazkira-yi anjuman-i Khaqan*, pp. 606–7.
19. Khatami, *Pizhuhishi dar nasr va nazm*, p. 294. For Mushtaq's society also see Shams-Langarudi, *Maktab-i bazgasht*, pp. 48–51.
20. Khatami, *Pizhuhishi dar nasr va nazm*, p. 294.
21. Shahrukhi, introduction to Hatif, *Divan-i Hatif*, p. 20.
22. Ibid.
23. See Amanat, 'Legend, Legitimacy and Making a National Narrative'.
24. For information on how Hidayat was able to access and leverage recent textual production in Qajar Iran for the composition of *Assembly of the Eloquent* see Schwartz, 'A Transregional Persianate Library'.
25. Hidayat, *Majma' al-fusaha'*, vol. 1, pp. 9–10.
26. Hidayat's entry on Mushtaq is short and written in straightforward prose. He

simply notes Mushtaq's preference for 'follow[ing] the clear-speaking style of the eloquent ancients' and having 'departed from the method [used by] the modern poets of the Safavid state and those like them'. Hidayat, *Majma' al-fusaha'*, vol. 2, p. 928.

27. For a brief account of Naziri and his poetry see Kinra, *Writing Self, Writing Empire*, p. 212. For further information see Ghani, *A History of Persian Language and Literature*, vol. 3. For information on Zamiri see Gulchin-i Ma'ani, *Maktab-i vuqu'*, pp. 296–315.
28. André Lefevere, *Translation, Rewriting, and the Manipulation of Literary Fame*, p. 85.
29. Ibid.
30. Shafaq, *Tarikh-i adabiyat-i Iran*, p. 451.
31. Aryanpur, *Az Saba ta Nima*, pp. 16–19. Shams-Langarudi, *Maktab-i bazgasht*, pp. 48–51.
32. Aryanpur, *Az Saba ta Nima*, pp. 16–19.
33. Khatami, *Pizhuhishi dar nasr va nazm*, pp. 201–2.
34. Abe, 'The Politics of Poetics in Early Qajar Iran', pp. 133–7.
35. Akhavan-Sales, 'Nima mardi bud mardistan'. Quoted in Aryanpur, *Az Saba ta Nima*, p. 19.
36. Khatami, *Pizhuhishi dar nasr va nazm*, pp. 201–2.
37. Sadat-Nasiri, 'Bazgasht-e adabi', p. 430.
38. Ibid., p. 429.
39. See e.g. Tabataba'i, introduction to Dunbuli, *Tajribat al-ahrar*, p. 13.
40. On the use of classical modes of poetry during the pre-Constitutional and Constitutional period in Iran and their impact, see Karimi-Hakkak, *Recasting Persian Poetry*. For the Afghan case see Ahmadi, *Modern Persian Literature in Afghanistan*.
41. It is worth noting that while Mahmud Tarzi wrote only in Persian, he was an early exponent of 'zabān-i Afghānī' ('the Afghani language', i.e. Pashto). Later on, especially since the 1920s, the promotion of Pashto as the 'national' language of Afghanistan became of paramount importance to the state. The country is now officially a bilingual state. Prior to the 1920s, and throughout history, Persian was the only official language of Afghanistan, even if the Sadduzai and Muhammadzai rulers were of Pashtun ethnic origin.
42. Zhubal, *Tarikh-i adabiyat-i Afghanistan*, pp. 246–8. Shah Shuja' wrote only in Persian.
43. Ghubar, *Afghanistan dar masir-i tarikh*, pp. 377–8.

44. Na'il, *Sayri dar adabiyat*, pp. 8–9.
45. For the involvement of the Afghan state in the promotion and memorialisation of Bidil in the twentieth century see Schwartz, 'The Local Lives of a Transregional Poet', pp. 91–2.
46. Na'il, *Sayri dar adabiyat*, p. 146.
47. Ibid., p. 73.
48. Ghaznavi, *Tarikh-i adabiyat-i Dari*, pp. 271–2.
49. Ibid., pp. 243–7.
50. Shahbaz, 'Guftugu ba ustad-i Vasif Bakhtari', p. 16.
51. Mawla'i, 'Bazgasht-i adabi dar Afghanistan', p. 61. On the nature of poetic assemblies at Bidil's graveside in eighteenth-century Delhi see Tabor, 'Heartless Acts'.
52. The impact of Bidil's verse on Mir Hutak can clearly be seen in regard to word choice, rhyme and structure. See Na'il, *Sayri dar adabiyat*, pp. 58–9. Ghaznavi, *Tarikh-i adabiyat-i Dari*, p. 258.
53. Ghaznavi, *Tarikh-i adabiyat-i Dari*, pp. 261 and 263. Other poets who took part in such gatherings and court life at the time were La'l Mohammed 'Ajiz, Mirza Qaland Rizat and Mirza Ahmad Khan Ahmad. See Na'il, *Sayri dar adabiyat*, p. 62.
54. Ghaznavi, *Tarikh-i adabiyat-i Dari*, p. 265.
55. Ibid., p. 273.
56. This occurred during the reign of Habibullah Khan (r. 1901–19); however, this was not the advent of printing in Afghanistan. The first lithograph machine was brought to Afghanistan (from South Asia) by the ruler Shir Ali Khan, followed by the opening of printing houses and the first published periodical, *Shams al-nahar* in 1873. See Zhubal, *Tarikh-i adabiyat-i Afghanistan*, p. 257.
57. Ghaznavi, *Tarikh-i adabiyat-i Dari*, p. 265.
58. On the life and poetry of Vasfi, see Na'il, *Sayri dar adabiyat*, pp. 88–107.
59. Na'il, *Sayri dar adabiyat*, p. 104.
60. Ibid.
61. Zhubal, *Tarikh-i adabiyat-i Afghanistan*, p. 272.
62. On the life and impact of Mahmud Tarzi see Wali Ahmadi, *Modern Persian Literature in Afghanistan*.
63. These poets include Mirza Muhammad Salik, Adib Pishavari and Muhammad Hasan 'Imza'. Zhubal, *Tarikh-i adabiyat-i Afghanistan*, p. 272.
64. For a list see Qavim, *Mururi bar adabiyat*, p. 7.

65. Vasil begins his collected work of poetry, for example, by welcoming Hafiz. Na'il, *Sayri dar adabiyat*, pp. 149–51.
66. Mawla'i, 'Bazgasht-i adabi dar Afghanistan', p. 63.
67. Ghaznavi, *Tarikh-i adabiyat-i Dari*, pp. 255–6. Among those poets listed by Ghaznavi are Vasil, Shamil and Ghulam Muhammad Tarzi.
68. Qavim, *Mururi bar adabiyat*, pp. 7–14.
69. Nazimi, 'Darbara-yi bazgasht-i adabi Afghanistan'. Quoted in Na'il, *Sayri dar adabiyat*, pp. 148–9.
70. Barchaluyi and Shafaq, 'Bazgasht-i adabi dar shi'r-i Farsi-i Afghanistan', p. 54.
71. *Aryana's Da'irat al-ma'arif*, p. 605.
72. For how an understanding of an 'Afghan literary return' must necessarily compare with how the movement is purported to have evolved in Iran see Barchaluyi and Shafaq, 'Bazgasht-i adabi dar shi'r-i Farsi-i Afghanistan'.
73. Ghubar, 'Jangnama nuskha khati', p. 2.
74. The causes for the disintegration of the Mughal Empire have long been the subject of debate. For debates and correctives concerning the notion of 'Mughal decline' and its historiography, see Alam, *The Crisis of Empire in Mughal North India*. Bayly, *Indian Society*.
75. For an overview of Persian literary culture in South Asia see Alam, 'The Culture and Politics of Persian in Precolonial Hindustan'.
76. Sharma, 'Fā'iz Dihlavī's Female-Centered Poems', p. 169.
77. This was, of course, only one aspect of British engagement with the Persian language and Indo-Persian culture. As Michael H. Fisher notes, 'the Persian language and Indo-Persian culture conveyed conflicting meanings to various individuals and classes of Indian and British people in India and Britain'. Fisher, 'Conflicting Meanings of Persianate Culture', p. 225.
78. For information on the role of the munshi during Mughal times, their education and general place within the nexus of Persian administrative practices at the Mughal court and beyond see Kinra, *Writing Self, Writing Empire*; Alam and Subrahmanyam, 'The Making of the Munshi'; Zilli, 'Development of *Insha* Literature'; Alam, 'The Pursuit of Persian: Language in Mughal Politics'; Mohiuddin, *The Chancellery and Persian Epistolography under the Mughals*.
79. Zastoupil and Moir, *The Great Indian Education Debate*, p. 2.
80. Bayly, *Empire and Information*, p. 8.
81. Cohn, *Colonialism and its Forms of Knowledge*, p. 18.
82. See e.g. Digby, 'Travels in Ladakh, 1820–1821'. Digby, 'An Eighteenth Century Narrative of a Journey from Bengal to England'. For information on

the munshi as administrator and employee in the British residencies see Fisher, *Indirect Rule in India*. For information on the munshi as language tutor and instructor see Das, *Sahibs and Munshis*.
83. The term 'new munshi' comes from Bayly, *Empire and Information*, p. 229.
84. Macaulay, 'Minute on Education', 2 February 1835.
85. Fisher, *Indirect Rule in India*, pp. 339–40 and p. 439.
86. Zastoupil and Moir, *The Great Indian Education Debate*, pp. 18–19.
87. For information on how Mohan Lal and Shahamat Ali fit into British informational and educational networks see Fisher, *Counterflows to Colonialism*, pp. 351–67. Bayly, *Empire and Information*, pp. 229–35.
88. Lal, *Travels in the Panjab, Afghanistan & Turkistan*, pp. xiv and xix–xx.
89. Dudney, 'Testing the Limits of Comparatism'.
90. Orsini, 'Between *Qasbas* and Cities', pp. 69 and 71.
91. See e.g. Faruqi, 'A Long History of Urdu Literary Culture, Part 1'. Syed, 'How Could Urdu be the Envy of Persian'.
92. Such courts being the Bahmani Sultans (r. 1347–1528) and Qutb Shahis (r. 1490–1686).
93. Russell, *The Pursuit of Urdu Literature*, p. 21.
94. Syed, 'How Could Urdu Be the Envy of Persian', p. 297.
95. Dhavan, 'Marking Boundaries and Building Bridges', p. 171.
96. Metcalf, 'Urdu in India in the 21st Century', p. 30.
97. Qamber, introduction to Bayg, *The Last Musha'irah of Delhi*, p. 15.
98. Trivedi, *The Making of Awadh Culture*, p. 91.
99. Syed, 'How Could Urdu Be the Envy of Persian', p. 299.
100. Or, as it may have been called, recognised and practised at the time, Hindvi/Dakhani/Hindustani.
101. Faruqi, 'A Long History of Urdu Literary Culture, Part 1', p. 848. On the crucial importance of Vali Dakhani to the creation narrative of Urdu and the manner in which he came to be mythologised see Dhavan and Pauwels, 'Controversies Surrounding the Reception of Valī "Dakhanī" (1665?–1707?)'.
102. Faruqi, 'A Long History of Urdu Literary Culture, Part 1', p. 848.
103. Pritchett, 'A Long History of Urdu Literary Culture, Part 2', p. 886.
104. Naim, 'Mughal and English Patronage of Urdu Poetry', p. 263.
105. Faruqi, 'A Long History of Urdu Literary Culture, Part 1', p. 850.
106. Vasilyeva, 'The Indian Mushairah', p. 9.
107. Bredi, 'Remarks on *Ara'ish-e Mahfil* by Mir Sher 'Ali Afsos', p. 39.
108. Oesterheld, 'Campaigning for a Community', p. 44.

109. Lehmann, 'Urdu Literature and Mughal Decline', p. 126.
110. Ibid., pp. 127–30.
111. See Sharma, *Mughal Arcadia*, pp. 90–5.
112. Sharma, 'The City of Beauties in Indo-Persian Poetic Landscape', p. 77.
113. For how Urdu operated in the nineteenth and twentieth centuries beyond the confines of South Asia and served as a lingua franca for South Asian Muslims, Hindus and Sikhs in Africa, see Green, 'Urdu as an African Language: A Survey of Source Literature'.
114. Pritchett, 'A Long History of Urdu Literary Culture, Part 2', p. 881.
115. Storey, *Persian Literature* 1.2, p. 876.
116. Ghalib also wrote prolifically in Persian, both in poetry and prose. While he himself claimed that his best poetry was in Persian, he was forced to write mostly in Urdu for patronage purposes. For a brief overview of his life and works, see Rahman, 'Galeb'. Russell, *The Oxford India Ghalib*.
117. For the impact of Azad on the construction of Urdu literary theory and history, see Faruqi, 'Constructing a Literary History'. Pritchett, 'A Long History of Urdu Literary Culture, Part 2', pp. 902–3.
118. Rahman, 'Urdu as an Islamic Language', p. 105. Equally beneficial to this process, as Rahman notes, was the advent of modern techniques, such as the printing press and formal school chains. See Ibid., p. 104.
119. Naim, 'Mughal and English Patronage of Urdu Poetry', p. 270. On the intriguing occurrence of Persian instructors being hired at colleges in the UK in the late eighteenth and early nineteenth centuries, see Fisher, 'Teaching Persian as an Imperial Language'.
120. Orsini, 'Between *Qasbas* and Cities' pp. 74–5.
121. For the comparative statistics of Persian and Urdu see the charts in Das, *Sahibs and Munshis*, pp. 46–7, 69, 71 and 75.
122. Lanzillo, 'The Politics of Persian Language Education in Colonial India'.
123. Shah, 'Sustaining Authority in Persian Lithographed Books'.
124. Qamber, introduction to Bayg, *The Last Musha'irah of Delhi*, p. 17.
125. Datla, 'A Worldly Vernacular'.
126. Pauwels, 'Literary Moments of Exchange in the 18th Century'.
127. Stark, 'Politics, Public Issues and the Promotion of Urdu Literature', pp. 69–70.
128. Hakala, *Negotiating Languages*.
129. Minault, 'Delhi College and Urdu'.
130. For example, on the transitional role of Persian from newsletters (*akhbārāt*) to English newspapers see Pernau, 'The *Delhi Urdu* Akhbar'. For a similar

role played by the office of the news-writer (*akhbār-navīs*) see Fisher, 'The Office of Akhbar Nawis'. For the impact of Persian historical writing on British understandings of India see Chatterjee, *The Cultures of History in Early Modern India*.

131. Faruqi, *Early Urdu Literary Culture and History*. Quoted in Vasilyeva, 'The Indian Mushairah', p. 8.
132. Rahman, 'Decline of Persian in British India'.
133. See Dudney, 'Metaphorical Language as a Battleground'. Pauwels also questions the association of political and literary decline in speaking about the development of Rekhta/Urdu, noting 'while politically the Mughal Empire was disintegrating, culturally it was going through a phase of intense creative expression'. Pauwels, 'Literary Moments of Exchange in the 18th Century', p. 65.
134. Dudney, 'Sabk-e Hendi and the Crisis of Authority'.
135. Green, *Bombay Islam*.
136. Marashi, 'Parsi Textual Philanthropy'.
137. Vejdani, 'Indo-Iranian Linguistic, Literary, and Religious Entanglements', p. 445.
138. Jabbari, 'The Making of Modernity in Persianate Literary History'.
139. The scope of Persian textual production in the nineteenth century can be gleaned from even the most cursory glance at Hadi, *Dictionary of Indo-Persian Literature*.
140. Tavakoli-Targhi, *Refashioning Iran*.

2

Reformation and Reconstruction of Poetic Networks: Isfahan c.1722–1801

> Isfahan is the garden, and your munificence is the rain
> Isfahan is the body, and your command is the soul!¹
>
> – Azar

The poet and anthologist Azar Baygdili (d. 1781) must have written the above lines with a sense of relief. Isfahan in 1770 was no longer the seat of splendour it had once been under the Safavids (r. 1501–1722), but neither was it the constant target of raids and attacks by various parties in search of political or material fortunes, at least for the time being. The reign of Karim Khan Zand (r. 1751–79) brought relative stability to Iran, as did his mayoral appointee for Isfahan, Mirza ʿAbd al-Wahhab (d. 1770–1).

Azar was born into a family of officials who dutifully served the Safavids. His birth in Isfahan in 1722 nearly coincided with the city's fall. His first decade of life was spent travelling with his father, who went in search of employment opportunities amid the shifting political tides of the day. This sojourn would later be replicated by Azar himself as he moved in search of his own employment at the hands of various factions and aspirant rulers. His early life reflected the socially chaotic and politically fluid times. No wonder he rejoiced at the stability of Isfahan in 1770. The dust of destruction and uncertainty had settled. Isfahan under the rule of Mirza ʿAbd al-Wahhab, whose 'command' Azar praised as the 'soul' of Isfahan, could be recast anew. Azar's tribute continues throughout the ode (*qaṣīda*) in which the above lines appear, portraying the presence and rule of Mirza ʿAbd al-Wahhab as the source of Isfahan's re-emergence as an 'abode of happiness and security' and 'envy of the garden of paradise'.[2]

Azar's enthusiasm for the mayor's leadership and the city's revival is not the first association made with the poet. First and foremost, Azar is the author of one of the most famous biographical anthologies (*tadhkira*) of Persian literary history. His *Firetemple* (*Atishkada*) served as the template for many later anthologists in Iran and elsewhere, and has been equally valued by modern authors who codify classes of poets and trends in poetry. Yet little attention has been paid to the circumstances under which this text was written. As Mana Kia notes, 'the context of Azar's composition is the ruin of Iran, a perception that undergirds the *Atashkadah* as a whole and is an essential part of the rhetorical labor of the text'.[3] Kia's statement reminds us that influential texts cannot fully be understood apart from the circumstances that inspire their composition. A similar statement applies to the formation of the 'literary return' (*bāzgasht-i adabī*) movement of which this text and Azar are a part.

Despite this caveat, histories of the emergence of the 'literary return' movement continue to be constructed according to its attributes as a category in the unfolding of Persian literary history. Less attention is granted to the larger social, political and literary environments nurturing its growth. As a category within the four-school development of Persian literary history (see Chapter 1), 'literary return' is naturally positioned and defined by its relationship to the other three schools. As part of an evolutionary and chronological schematic devoted to explaining Persian literary history, 'literary return' is distinguished especially by its relationship to the previous category, the so-called 'Indian Style'. In this context, 'literary return' is presented as inspiring the dismissal of 'Indian Style' poetics in favour of its own.

Other factors related to the formation of the 'literary return' movement are treated as an afterthought or dismissed as non-factors altogether. Effectively, this approach presumes that the 'literary return' poets were detached from the social concerns of the existent world and instead entirely preoccupied with the blind imitation of previous classical styles.[4] What, then, to make of Azar and his clear celebration of the garden that is Isfahan and the presence of Mirza 'Abd al-Wahhab? Were he and other 'literary return' poets inattentive to their immediate environment and immune to their surroundings, save for the way they reacted to a particular 'Indian Style' of poetry, swirling in their midst and directing their every move? The stylistic opposition posited between the 'Indian Style' and 'literary return' is by no means unfounded. Biographical anthologies from the Zand and Qajar eras plant the seeds for this genesis narrative of 'literary return' as a conceptual category, as the previous chapter highlighted. It is an impression that has been crucial for later authors in their defining of the movement's primary characteristics and process of becoming. These texts note the existence of a group of eighteenth- and nineteenth-century poets who sought to 'return' Persian poetry to the style of the ancients. Indeed, evidence from the poetic verses profiled below demonstrates the insistence of eighteenth- and nineteenth-century Iranian poets on imitating the styles of various masters.

But many of these same biographical anthologies and the verse of the 'literary return' poets themselves contain other impressions of the external environments shaping the movement's early founding. These impressions reach back in history and expand beyond the notion of the poets' mere distaste for a particular style of poetry. They reference Isfahan's political, literary and social environment. Their absence undermines our understanding not only of the movement's appearance but also of the nature of early modern Persian poetic culture in Iran and its place within the Persianate world.

The social and political context of Azar's poetic experience, such as Mirza ʿAbd al-Wahhab's role in providing patronage to an early Isfahani Circle of poets, is a crucial factor in the 'literary return' movement's development. The patronage Mirza ʿAbd al-Wahhab provided to the Isfahani Circle of poets is one of several social and political elements affecting the emergence of the 'literary return' movement found in Zand and early Qajar sources. But this type of information has been elided by later Qajar-era authors and, more recently, by modern ones.

The aim of this chapter is to recover many of the forgotten or ignored circumstances under which the 'literary return' movement emerged and reframe its genesis and formation. Through close readings of Zand and early Qajar anthologies and the poetry of the 'literary return' poets, this chapter offers evidence that the driving force behind the emergence of the movement was not a group of poets' disdain for a particular poetic style, but rather the more robust social, political and literary circumstances of Isfahan in Safavid and post-Safavid times.

The poets' distaste for the so-called 'Indian Style' of poetry was not altogether absent from the movement's emergence, but it may best be described as a proximate cause. More significant for the movement's rise was the sociopolitical and intellectual climate of Isfahan before and after its fall in 1722. For this reason, the term 'Isfahani Circle' will at times be preferred in describing the collective of early poets that would be known to history as the 'literary return' movement, as it more accurately captures the spirit and circumstances of the movement at its inception.

The chapter is divided into three sections. Each part attempts to answer one fundamental question about the 'literary return' movement at its inception. Collectively they will serve to reframe the movement's emergence as a whole. 'Disruptions and Continuities' answers the 'where and when' of 'literary return' by reviewing the impact of the destruction of the Safavid capital of Isfahan on the city's social and literary culture. While recognising the political rupture created by the city's fall in 1722, this section highlights the continuities in social and literary culture between the Safavid and post-Safavid period. Understanding such continuities undercuts the argument that the 'literary return' movement emerged like a phoenix from the ashes – devoid of any discernible context beyond a void of darkness – to rescue Persian poetry. The poetic affiliations, gatherings and styles cultivated by the 'literary return' poets display remarkable similarities to what had existed previously. In other words, it was no coincidence that such a movement was able to emerge in Isfahan.

'Connections and Networks' answers the 'how' of 'literary return' by reconstructing the connections and social bonds among the group's affiliates through the use of Zand and Qajar biographical anthologies and the poetry of three major literary figures: Azar Baygdili (d. 1781), Sayyid Ahmad 'Hatif' Isfahani (d. 1784) and Sulayman 'Sabahi' Bidguli (d. 1793). These materials reveal how the poets' praise of one another, often expressed through an imitation of the classical masters' style, created an inclusive poetic community. Deprived of a larger poetic community and patronage opportunities to shelter them, these poets directed their talents towards one another, acting as both patron and poet, supporting one another through their work. This practice continued throughout the gestational phase of the 'literary return' movement and served as one of the key features in their consolidation as a community of poets.

'Patronage and Formation' answers the 'why' of 'literary return' by focusing on the role of Mirza ʿAbd al-Wahhab, mayor of Isfahan and patron of poetry. The support of Mirza ʿAbd al-Wahhab allowed the Isfahani Circle to transition from a community centred solely on poets and self-praise to one attached to a benefactor. Returning once again to the poetry of Azar, Hatif and Sabahi, this section explains why the 'literary return' movement was not simply determined to shift poetic styles, but, more importantly, dedicated to re-establishing a literary climate and role for the poet in future generations by looking to the past as a model.

Disruptions and Continuities

In many ways, Isfahan in the late eighteenth century was the perfect place for the 'literary return' movement to take shape, and in other ways it was not so advantageous. From the fall of the Safavids in 1722 until the early nineteenth century, Isfahan was a city in flux, ravaged by turmoil, natural disasters, famine and sieges by different political factions. Isfahan was both geographically and figuratively at the crossroads of political actors competing for control during a transitional time in its history.

The turmoil of the times, especially following the termination of the Safavid Empire, is often presented as evidence that a definitive historical break occurred in Iranian history not to be resumed until the rise of the Qajars. With the end of the Safavids the slate in Iran was wiped clean, so it goes, and any societal trends – literary or otherwise – that existed before and after were necessarily deemed disconnected from one another. Depicting the fall of the Safavids in such a way significantly abets conventional misreadings of the emergence of what would become known as the 'literary return' movement. Siphoning off Safavid times from what occurred afterwards excludes the recognition of any possible continuity in literary and cultural developments between the two periods. The result is an abstraction of the 'literary return' movement, removed from any previously established social or literary context. Moreover, the correlating belief that the general turmoil of post-Safavid Iran militated against any discernible environment whereby poets could effectively engage with coterminous social and political structures paves the way for a conceptualisation of 'literary return' as a singularly focused movement attendant to rekindling a classical poetic style. Effectively removing any semblance of non-literary factors from the equation, either during Safavid or post-Safavid times means that no other explanation of the emergence of the 'literary return' movement remains possible. According to such a rationale, it surely must have been a desire to 'return' to the style of the classical masters and expel any last vestige of the so-called 'Indian Style'. The impact of social and political disruption certainly had a role in shaping the emergence of the 'literary return' movement, but, as will be seen below, it neither entirely supplanted literary and social continuities between Safavid and post-Safavid times nor disallowed for the 'literary return' poets being attentive to their social surroundings.

During the mid-to-late eighteenth century, a changing cast of rulers and aspirants continually sought to control Isfahan. Not surprisingly, the city witnessed major periods of political instability, following its initial sacking by Afghan invaders in 1722. The number of groups attempting to gain control of Isfahan and the chaos and oppression ensuing from this jockeying for power are striking.[5] The policies of rulers and mayors did not help. For example, a drought in 1740–1 was exacerbated by Nadir Shah (r. 1736–47)'s policies, which both adversely affected planting and led to problems for residents in procuring food.[6] The situation following the death of Nadir Shah in 1747 was by all accounts disastrous. Attacks, sieges, pillaging and raiding by invading armies followed.

A slight respite from this mayhem resulted from Karim Khan Zand's rule (1751–79), which according to one observer appeared like 'an island of relative calm and stability in an otherwise destructive period'.[7] Even so, the Zand period did not protect Isfahan entirely from bouts of turbulence. During the oppressive rule of Hajji Muhammad Ranani, explored further below, the city also faced a severe famine in 1775 and an earthquake in 1778.[8] Following the death of Karim Khan Zand, a serious power vacuum ensued, and jockeying for dominance began anew. The situation in Isfahan devolved into anarchy. Battles between the Zands and Qajars followed.

Michael Axworthy sums up the tumultuous situation in Isfahan from its sack in 1722 until the turn of the century, when upheaval and destruction ruled the day. He writes:

By mid-century most of the built-up area of Isfahan, the former capital, was deserted; inhabited only by owls and wild animals. In the last years of the Safavids, it had been a thriving city of 550,000 people, one of the largest cities in the world; a similar size to London at the time, or bigger. By the end of the siege of 1722 only 100,000 people were left, and although many citizens returned thereafter the number fell yet again during the Afghan occupation and later so that by 1736 there were only 50,000 left. It has been estimated that the overall total population of Persia fell from around nine million at the beginning of the century to perhaps six million or less by mid-century through war, disease and emigration; and that the population levels did not begin to rise significantly again until after 1800.[9]

On the heels of the Afghan invasion, the fall of the Safavids, Nadir Shah's rule and the manoeuvring for power between the Afshars, Zands and Qajars, the rise of a coherent literary movement in Isfahan seems hard to fathom.

The attention paid to Isfahan by factions contending for power in post-Safavid Iran demonstrates the way in which the city continued to be viewed as one of the pre-eminent seats for establishing political power and legitimacy. The city remained central in the political consciousness of the time. As John Perry notes, the continued presence of Safavid pretenders and aspirants to the throne after that dynasty's fall is an indication of the persistence of Safavid-centred preconceptions among the populace, even in the face of an ever-shifting political landscape.[10] For Perry, this fact undermines the notion that the period between the Safavids and the Qajars is devoid of continuities and therefore represents a clean break in Iran's history, an important intervention for understanding the emergence of the 'literary return' movement in its proper context. Cultural continuities did exist, grounded in the city's image and historical place as the centre of literary culture in Iran. The literary historian Jan Rypka, for example, credited Isfahan with cradling the nascent 'literary return' movement precisely for this reason. On account of its recent history under the Safavids, Isfahan retained its reputation as the centre of cultural production among littérateurs and poets in post-Safavid Iran as well, making it the natural locus for the emergence of a literary movement after the Safavids' fall, political and social turmoil aside.[11] The literary historian Saʿid Nafisi expresses a similar sentiment: despite all the 'unpleasant events' occurring in post-Safavid Iran, it was a near certainty that if any such 'return' movement were to arise, then it would most certainly do so in the city that served as Iran's cultural and artistic heart during Safavid times.[12]

Isfahan during Karim Khan Zand's rule is often credited with providing amenable conditions for nurturing the rise of the 'literary return' movement beginning with the emergence of a literary society organised by the poet Sayyid Ali Mushtaq Isfahani. Few details are known of Mushtaq's life outside of his perceived contributions to the nascent 'literary return' movement and his role as mentor and teacher to other poets of the period. He was born in Isfahan around 1690 and appears to have spent his entire life in that city.

Zand- and Qajar-era authors are effusive in praising Mushtaq as the head of a literary society that sought a 'return' to classical modes of Persian poetry. Azar noted his role in rebuilding 'the structure of eloquent poetry of the old masters', while the historian Dunbuli declared that his poetry 'adorned the melodies of Barbad-like minstrels'.[13] As Matthew Smith has observed, the 'perpetuation of the image of Mushtaq as a revolutionary force in Persian poetry stems as much from the widespread influence of Azar's *Atishkada* as from an appreciation of Mushtaq's poetry itself'.[14] By the time Ahmad Bayg 'Akhtar' Garrusi composed his biographical anthology at the court of Fath Ali Shah in the early nineteenth century, Musthaq's reputation was well-established. Surpassing the praise heaped upon Mushtaq by his contemporaries, Garrusi recognises him as 'the lord of the poets and master of men of letters', noting that 'the renewal of the poetic methods of the ancient poets came from his perfection of taste'.[15]

If the establishment of Karim Khan's rule in 1751 allowed Mushtaq's literary society to take shape, then conditions must have come together rather quickly. Mushtaq most likely died in 1757–8 (though perhaps as early as 1751 or 1753) leaving him with a mere six or seven years to convene his literary society, attract a cohort of poets, gain the reputation of his students and stand out as the unequivocal voice leading a 'return' to the masters. Contemporary observers, such as Azar and Dunbuli, are quick to note that the arrival of Karim Khan Zand created an environment for poetry to be produced and appreciated again. Such attitudes give the impression that it was necessarily such conditions that allowed Mushtaq's society to convene and flourish. As will be seen further below, there is some truth to these observations. But the notion that Karim Khan's rule represented a clean break with the past removes the need to situate the emergence of Mushtaq's society and the germination of the 'literary return' movement in any developed social or literary context prior to 1751. The insistence of authors like Azar and Dunbuli on using the arrival of Karim Khan Zand to indicate a clean break with the poetic culture of the past – much as later authors will do with the fall of Isfahan in 1722 – feeds the narrative that the 'literary return' movement simply emerged in a vacuum intact.

This perspective overlooks significant affinities between Mushtaq's literary circle and the social and literary landscape of Safavid Isfahan. As Shams-Langarudi argues, Mushtaq's literary society was building upon the work of the 'realist school' (*maktab-i vuqūʿ*) and the poetry of individuals like Zamiri Isfahani (d. 1566) and Naziri Nishapuri (d. *c.*1612–14), who began imitating the masters' style during the Safavid period. Dunbuli too confirms the association of Mushtaq with Zamiri and Naziri, providing a near contemporary source recognising the stylistic affiliation. The link provides an avenue for exploring the continuities of poetic practice connecting the periods before and after the fall of Isfahan.

Founded in the first quarter of the sixteenth century, the 'realist school' is a poetic style examining 'anew the amatory origins of the *ghazal*', and one that reduced 'the idealization of the beloved in the interest of depicting the full range of psychological negotiations of mundane love'.[16] Stylistically, it sought to express love and the lover in 'a simple unvarnished poetry, absent of flowery language and hyperbole'.[17] The style situates the topics of love, lovers and amorous relationships in more earthly, rather than ethereal, contexts. In this regard, poets sought to portray the relationships between 'all-too-human lovers' and their 'mood swings, tantrums, evasions and elations'.[18] Shams-Langarudi aptly refers to the style as the 'bazaarisation' of the 'Iraqi style. In Safavid Isfahan it became a favoured style of the urban classes of poets populating the coffee houses.[19] The recognition that some poets of Safavid Isfahan were producing a simpler poetic style, by imitating classical masters like Saʿdi and Hafiz, should give pause to the argument that the 'literary return' movement suddenly arose in post-Safavid times.

The argument that the 'literary return' movement emerged with a new-found laser focus on imitating the stylistics of the 'masters' is further undercut by the diverse forms of poetry produced by its early members, including many participants of Mushtaq's literary society. Beyond producing lyrics and odes in imitation of classical styles, they offered praise for religious figures and rulers as well as poetry in commemoration of architectural achievements. Mushtaq's oeuvre contains odes for various rulers during the Afsharid period (including Nadir Shah), poems on the occasion of a ruler's coronation, elegies for historical figures, works in commemoration of victories in Qandahar and India and the history of architectural works.[20] Other early 'literary return' poets composed equally diverse types of verse.[21] This variation in their poetry points to a literary circle in its infancy still searching for its footing, rather than one invariably wedded to a particular poetic form and style. As Matthew Smith has recently shown, early 'return' poets like Azar, Hatif and Sabahi could equally 'draw inspiration from forms and genres popularized under the Safavids and Mughals ... rather than from the earlier poets whom they are accused of imitating'.[22]

Isfahan may have been severely destroyed and ravaged in the early-to-mid eighteenth century, but it was by no means forgotten. In keeping with Isfahan's literary centrality during Safavid times, members of the early Isfahani Circle flocked from elsewhere to partake in its literary life. Azar made his way back to Isfahan, the place of his birth, after much travel around the country. The poet and calligrapher 'Abd al-Majid Darvish (d. 1771–2), another member of this early cohort, came to Isfahan from nearby in search of science and learning.[23] Moreover, he most certainly arrived in Isfahan prior to the establishment of Karim Khan Zand's rule. Even during this difficult period in the early-to-mid eighteenth century, poets made their way to Isfahan, once again reaffirming that the city maintained its identity as a cultural centre.

Although political conditions changed after the fall of Isfahan, the make-up of the early 'literary return' movement as expressed through Mushtaq's literary society and the larger Isfahani Circle displayed many social and poetic continuities with the late Safavid period. Contrary to later impressions of how and why the 'literary return' movement emerged, it was neither disconnected from earlier poetic trends of Safavid Isfahan nor wedded to one particular style of poetry.

Connections and Networks

Biographical anthologies from the eighteenth to the late nineteenth centuries provide evidence for establishing the connections among individual poets that would later become known as the founders of the 'literary return' movement. In writing about a Central Asian biographical anthology from the Safavid period, Robert McChesney commented that, while the goal of *tadhkira*s is often 'to explain in a formal and conventional way individual creativity rather than social relations of individuals and groups', they nonetheless offer a great deal of information regarding the social, cultural and economic circumstances of the time. 'In the attempt to convey the creative factors and impulses of the individual's life', he continues, 'his relations with others and the part he may have played in society had necessarily to be accounted for.'[24]

The biographical anthologies of the Zand and Qajar periods do just that, identifying the relationships and connections among poets later known as the founders of the 'literary return' movement. They provide a roster of the poets associated with Mushtaq's literary society, the affiliations among poets after Mushtaq's death, the diverse class backgrounds of participants and the lineages of student–instructor relationships that stretch from the movement's early days in the mid-to-late eighteenth century to poets located at the Qajar court of Fath Ali Shah later on.

There are several categories of affiliations that define the social network among the 'literary return' movement from its early gestational form in Mushtaq's literary society to the movement's more formal institutionalisation at the Qajar court of Fath Ali Shah: instructional relationships between teachers and students, bonds of friendship, and family and professional relationships. The existence of these multiple, and often overlapping, lines of association helps to delineate the diverse ways in which the poets of a nascent 'literary return' movement were connected with one another.

Mushtaq's student Azar delineates many of the poets affiliated with Mushtaq's literary society. Azar cites in particular his friendships with Sahba (d. 1777), who, like him, was one of Mushtaq's early disciples, and with Hatif (d. 1784).[25] The three poets together would later organise Mushtaq's poetry into a collection (*dīvān*) after his death.[26] Also among this early circle of associates was Aqa Muhammad ''Ashiq' Isfahani (d. *c.*1767), a tailor by profession, and Rafiq Isfahani (d. 1811), a vegetable seller.[27] Their participation too points to the humble professions of some of the circle's members and the continued practice from Safavid times of poetic production among Isfahan's urban professionals.

Poets not definitely tied to Mushtaq's literary society, either as participant or student, also form a part of this larger network, such as Sulayman 'Sabahi' Bidguli (d. 1793). Either in Isfahan or in his birthplace of Kashan, Sabahi met Azar and Hatif, leading the three to embark on lifelong friendship.[28] Indeed, the triumvirate of Azar, Hatif and Sabahi has been heralded by the historian Dunbuli as Mushtaq's heirs in overthrowing the method of poetry whose meanings had become 'frigid and tasteless'.[29] The strong bonds of friendship and close companionship between Azar, Hatif and Sabahi are well-recorded, both in biographical anthologies and in their poetry.[30] Their poems, often in conversation with each other, offer some of the best evidence of how these poets viewed themselves and their surroundings, as will be seen further below.[31]

The network among the early 'literary return' poets in some cases cut across professional lines as well. Mirza Muhammad Nasir 'Tabib' Isfahani (d. 1771), who accompanied Karim Khan Zand from Isfahan to Shiraz to become the ruler's special physician, instructed the aforementioned Hatif in medicine and philosophy in Isfahan.[32] Azar displayed his admiration for Nasir 'Tabib' in several poems, praising his exceptional knowledge of poetry, philosophy and medicine. One of the poems is written in the same metre and rhyme scheme as Rudaki's famous poem in praise of Bukhara, pointing to an early example of an Isfahani Circle poet modelling his verse according to the specific form and style of a classical master.[33] One modern critic even credits 'Tabib' with being one of the crucial founders of the early 'return' movement, alongside Mushtaq.[34]

The presence of another 'Tabib' among this early grouping of 'literary return' poets demonstrates how the greater network incorporated familial connections as well. Mirza 'Abd al-Baqi 'Tabib' Isfahani (d. 1758–9), a one-time mayor of Isfahan and Nadir's Shah physician, became affiliated to the Isfahani Circle.[35] He was also the elder brother of Mirza 'Abd al-Wahhab, who played a crucial role in the 'return' movement after Mushtaq's literary society disbanded, and a relation of Nashat Isfahani (d. 1828–9), the major figure in the later 'literary return' movement at the Qajar court in Tehran.[36] The role of this particular family was indeed central to nurturing the activity of the 'return' movement during its early stages in Isfahan. Nashat Isfahani, for example, first came to prominence by convening a literary society in Isfahan dedicated to imitating the style of the ancients in early Qajar times. Having attracted the notice of Fath Ali Shah, he followed the future monarch to Tehran and rose to the position of chief letter writer and served the court in a variety of other functionary roles.[37] At the Qajar court he continued to be an avid supporter of the Qajar ruler's promotion of 'literary return' poets. In his own poetry he imitated the style of Hafiz and wrote the introduction to Fath Ali Khan 'Saba' Kashani's (d. 1822–3) famous *Book of Kings* (*Shahanshahnama*).[38]

Relational threads connecting members of the early 'literary return' poets in Isfahan to like-minded poets in Qajar Tehran extend beyond the above case of family connection. While the nature of the 'literary return' movement at the Qajar court falls outside the scope of this study, it bears mention that instructor–student relationships developed between several poets active in late eighteenth-century Isfahan and in early nineteenth-century Tehran.[39] Of particular note is Sabahi's tutelage of Saba, who would later become the poet laureate of the Qajar monarch Fath Ali Shah and champion the Shah's royal lineage and achievements in an imitation of Firdawsi's famous epic the *Book of Kings*.[40] Saba's work has been regarded as the apogee of the 'literary return' style at the Qajar court, even if it represents 'a telling example of anachronistic and … misplaced glorification of Fath Ali Shah on the model of ancient legends'.[41]

In exploring the relational connections among poets, one must be cautious about relying too heavily on biographical anthologies written by one member of a poetic cohort for information on that cohort's other members. Anthologists often bestowed upon their friends and companions an undue amount of prestige by memorialising them in a particular work. Matthew Smith's observation about how *tadhkira* authors use their works to insert their comrades into the canon of Persian poetry cannot be discounted.[42] Authors like Azar and Dunbuli, from whom much of the above information derives, were intimate with many of the poets they recorded in their works. At least some element of biased promotion within their works exist, as they often elevate the poetical status of their friends and uncritically compare them to the great 'masters' of Persian poetry. Dunbuli, for example, compares the poet Saba to many of the classical masters of old, such as Anvari (d. *c.*1180) and Khaqani (d. *c.*1190), in an effort to carve out a place for him in the Persian literary canon.[43] Nonetheless, *tadhkiras*' ability to delineate communities and establish connections between individuals is of crucial value for understanding poetic community, even if an element of biased promotion is present.

Outside of authors like Azar and Dunbuli, who were members of the communities they sought to remember and memorialise, other accounts exist that recognise the members of the Isfahani Circle as a connected cohort of poets. Mir 'Abd al-Latif Khan Shushtari's *Gift of the World and Commentary on Curiosities* (*Tuhfat al-'alam va dhayl al-tuhfah*) is a near-contemporary source detailing the poetic activity and works of the Isfahani Circle, though not produced by a member of the cohort itself. *Gift of the World* chronicles Shushtari's travels and observations in the Persian Gulf and South Asia. It also contains information on the contemporary poetic scene in Iran, offering a perspective from southern Iran on poets roughly contemporary with the author. In his brief section 'In Remembrance of the Famous Poets of 'Iraq-i 'Ajam who were the Imams of Art and Lords of Poetry', Shushtari lists a mere eight poets.[44] One may only speculate whether he organised these poets, recorded neither in alphabetical order nor according to geography, according to perceived talent, fame, or otherwise. Among the eight poets listed, Shushtari lists seven prominent names associated with the Isfahani Circle: Mushtaq, Azar, 'Ashiq, Rafiq, Sabahi, Sahba and Hatif. Shushtari's opinions, in other words, closely parallel those of other anthologies of the times. South Asian biographical anthologies of the late eighteenth and early nineteenth centuries also recorded the lives of various poets of the Isfahani Circle as well as referencing some of the connections and relationships among them.[45]

The attitudes and perceptions of anthologists should not be accepted as the sole source of information on poets' lives and associations. The poetry written by members of the Isfahani Circle, under-explored in scholarship, complements information found in biographical anthologies. Unlike *tadhkiras*, which are fundamental expressions placing poets within a particular historical or literary class, the poetry presented below is more private in content and intent. It includes notices written for a deceased friend or letters between companions. Such poetry presents intimate portrayals of friendship, expressions of esteem and commentary on poetic talent. Moreover, this poetry demonstrates how, absent a larger poetic community and patronage opportunities, these poets directed their talents towards supporting one another. They acted as both patron and poet, often in imitation of a precedent set by one of the classical masters. By praising one another, rather than a patron, they helped create and sustain a poetic community, one founded upon both deep social bonds and heartfelt praise.

The poetry of Azar, Hatif and Sabahi serves as a prism through which to view the strong social bonds, friendship and poetical affinity connecting members of the Isfahani Circle of poets. Their poems reveal how members of this nascent community were applauded for their exceptional talent, or perceived as masters or teachers of poetry, or how their deaths were mourned as a loss for the world of poetry.

In one of the many elegies Sabahi composed for his companion Azar, one glimpses how the poet viewed the loss of Azar for the greater world of poetry. Azar is the 'bird of clear speech' with whose death 'the heavens of poetry became concealed underground'. With his death, 'probity and eloquence fell away from the river of excellence'. The world is a cruel, unfortunate and inexplicable place, Sabahi writes, for how else can one explain the silencing of a poet whose 'proof of poetry is in the clarity of speech', from whom 'caravans of poetry' flowed forth, 'day and night, in both East and West'? He continues:

> How full of sorrow that the tradition of poetry became abrogated in this world,
> What use is poetry? When the arbiter of poetry has left.[46]

The esteem with which Hatif viewed Azar, his poetic talents and his critical skill as a master of poetry closely cohere with the words of Sabahi. In an ode that begins with the arrival of a heart-ravishing and heavenly breeze, carrying the scents of musk, amber and the beloved (soon discovered to be emanating from Azar himself rather than the gardens of paradise), Hatif comments on Azar's incisive knowledge of poetry. 'Toward incorrect speech, the blade of your tongue acts like the sword of Haydar toward non-belief', he writes.[47] Later, commenting more specifically on Azar's own ability to compose poetry, not simply his opposition to 'incorrect speech', he notes that 'each one of your ruby-like poetic verses, is a star shining more bright than Venus'.[48]

Another instructive example of this poetic community's emotional bonds is seen when members separate from one another, as with Azar's departure from his comrades in Kashan for Qum. Chief among those touched was his close friend Sabahi, who composed a thirty-four-line poem describing the pangs of separation he felt on his friend's departure.[49] The geographical separation of the two poets did not prevent them from exchanging a series of poems. The poems exchanged represent another example via which to chart the strong bonds flowing through the early 'literary return' movement poets.

Sabahi wrote two odes to his friend, while Azar responded in kind with one poem. In the earlier ode, Sabahi compares himself to a nightingale in a cage, barred from the world of beauty and unaware of the surrounding garden and all it has to offer. Only with the assistance of Azar, the sweet-singing nightingale with freedom of movement, does Sabahi become educated about the world beyond the confines of the cage. In the latter ode, Sabahi portrays himself as the unaware poet yearning for the companion so crucial to his own poetic development. The work expresses the emptiness and loneliness resulting from Azar's departure. But that does not prevent Sabahi from once again heaping praise upon the poetic prowess and skill of his friend Azar, whom he calls one of the pre-eminent poets of his day. Staying true to the poetics of imitating the classical masters, he writes this poem in the same metre and rhyme scheme as the classical poet Anvari (d. *c.*1180), who wrote his ode in honour of Hajib Nasir al-Din. Azar maintained the same rhyme scheme and metre in his response.

The lines presented below illustrate the mutual esteem and respect in which the two poets held each other, all the while staying true in replicating the style and metre of a classical master. Of note is Azar's method of responding to the praise of Sabahi with the same imagery and language that was accorded to him. First, Sabahi:

> Oh you, before whom the teacher of knowledge
>   kneels in deference to learning.

> From your poetry, the Pleiades undid the knot of its arrangement,
>> From your hand, the Red Sea spilled its water.
> The sun, which is the source of life,
>> performs ablutions with the dust of your door.[50]

And Azar in his response:

> Your poetry is the knob opening the Pleiades,
>> Your prose is the river stealing the [Red] Sea.
> It appears that Anvari wrote this *qaṣīda*,
>> but I see him planting barley, while yours is like grain!
> In your company, poetry from others
>> means no more than dry ablution by the banks of the Tigris.[51]

These brief selections serve as a prism through which one can see the manner in which some of the Isfahani Circle of poets perceived themselves and their relationships with one another. The praise and deference they display is indicative of their camaraderie and strong bonds of friendship. Notably, they directed their praise to their comrades, focusing on each other's poetic talents rather than the accomplishments or character of a particular ruler or patron, which were lacking at the time. Oftentimes, these praise poems either employed the models of specific poems from the classical masters, as in the case above, or sought to relate a poet's talent by comparing him to one classical master or another, thereby inserting him alongside the masters in the classical canon. Sabahi, in particular, was fond of the latter approach, beckoning the poets Saʿdi and Nizami (d. 1209) to come forth and offer praise for Azar's talents.[52] In another poem, he refers to Azar as 'the Saʿdi of the time, the Anvari of the age and Firdawsi of the era'.[53]

Sabahi, having outlived most of Mushtaq's literary circle, records the death of many of the Isfahani Circle of poets. At times, such elegies express not only personal sorrow but also a sense of hopelessness for how the larger poetic world can cope with the companion's loss. During this transitional time, when the Isfahani Circle turned 'literary return' movement was in its nascent stages, there was no doubt anxiety over a loss of a member or even a separation between members. Azar, in a short poem in the form of letter, likely to Hatif, asks the recipient to pass along his heartfelt words of separation to

Sabahi. Tell him, he writes, that 'the domain of Paradise, without you, would be like hell to me; the pure water of Kawthar, without you, would be like scalding water'.[54] Elsewhere, Azar reflected on his heartfelt companionship with Sabahi amid their separation by noting 'Azar spent happy times there with Sabahi / May the memory of those good times live on'.[55]

Displays of admiration can also be found in the many praise poems written by Azar for Nasir Tabib, including one written in the same metre and rhyme scheme as Rudaki's famous poem in praise of Bukhara. He was not alone. The practice of the Isfahani Circle poets in offering praise for each other is one of the major features of their collective experience. Their continued insistence on uplifting one another, even while composing other types of poetry, helped solidify their bonds and sense of community, absent the traditional support of patrons. This practice also reveals their anxiety at being separated (by relocation or death) and thus not able to carry out their poetic activities together, hinting at a shared sense of mission. Again, this practice remained a key feature of their shared poetic experience and outlook, especially before and after their receipt of patronage from Mirza 'Abd al-Wahhab, as discussed below.

These works certainly reflect the poets' mutual commitment to following a classical Persian poet, as was the case in the letters exchanged between Azar and Sabahi and their desire to follow Anvari in rhyme scheme and metre. However, the methods, attitudes and perceptions found in their poetry take us beyond defining the 'literary return' movement as simply a commitment to a particular style of poetry, rather than a network and community of poets germinating around social-literary bonds. As will be seen below, the poetry of Azar, Hatif and Sabahi speaks not only to their relationships, favoured poetic style, and attempts at sustaining a tight-knit poetic community, but also to how they viewed their surrounding social conditions and the role of the poet within that milieu.

Patronage and Formation

Crucial to the formation and coherence of the early 'literary return' movement is the patronage many of the early poets received from one of Isfahan's mayors during the Zand period – Mirza 'Abd al-Wahhab Musavi Isfahani. That the Isfahani Circle of poets had a patron, let alone the mayor of Isfahan, sheds a different light on the formation of the 'literary return' movement, especially since Mirza ʿAbd al-Wahhab's involvement occurred after the passing of the movement's putative founder Mushtaq. It is unclear when Mirza ʿAbd al-Wahhab was first appointed to rule Isfahan. It is possible that he served as mayor in 1759, but, if so, it was only for a short time.[56] Known with more certainty is that he did serve as mayor of Isfahan from 1767 to 1770–1, the year of his death.

Mirza ʿAbd al-Wahhab hailed from a family that settled in Isfahan (from Fars) and provided medical services to the Safavid kings for several generations.[57] As mayor of Isfahan, he was well-respected for the nature of his rule and management of affairs. Being from a respected Isfahani family with a pedigree of government service certainly would have been beneficial, especially in the context of years of uncertainty and tumult. His pedigree and knowledge of Isfahan no doubt helped maintain the relative calm and stability associated with the period of Karim Khan Zand's rule. Dunbuli notes that Mirza ʿAbd al-Wahhab 'rose to the office of mayor (*kalāntar*) in the government of Isfahan, out of distinction, purity, generosity, intelligence, good taste and unrivaled genius'.[58] In the preceding period, from 1732 to 1759, more than twenty people had served as mayor of Isfahan, but few were natives of the city.[59] For almost the entire twenty-year period from 1759 to 1779, corresponding to Karim Khan Zand's suzerainty over Isfahan, the city was ruled by two individuals, both members of respected and reputable Isfahani families: Mirza ʿAbd al-Wahhab and Aqa Muhammad Marbini.[60] These two mayors' tenures stand in contrast to the tenures of those active under Nadir Shah, who sought to limit the power of the mayor of Isfahan by both appointing non-Isfahani natives and frequently dismissing them.[61]

According to the historian Dunbuli, the general populace during the Zand period was 'overwhelmed in joy and happiness', and 'calamitous misfortune was distant from the face of time'.[62] The relative calm and stability in Isfahan no doubt helped create the conditions for increased literary activities and productivity. An added benefit for those writers and poets in Isfahan was having a ruler receptive to poetic activities, who maintained an interest in the arts and served as a patron of writing and poetry.[63] Mirza ʿAbd al-Wahhab, in addition to being mayor, was also a student of the renowned calligrapher and poet 'Abd al-Majid Darvish, who was affiliated with the Isfahani Circle of poets, as noted above.[64]

Under Mirza 'Abd al-Wahhab Isfahan continued to expand the image of its recent glories. Dunbuli referred to Isfahan under Mirza 'Abd al-Wahhab's rule as a place experiencing the gathering of 'poets, geniuses, first-rate minds of every type and masters of verse [who] every day upon the branches of poetry ... were constructing lyrics and choice lines'.[65] During his tenure as mayor, Mirza 'Abd al-Wahhab remained well-connected to the Isfahani Circle of poets:

> Truly, during that time, the good fortune of esteemed masters arose from a deep sleep and the desire of people of learning was adorned with favors of various kinds. The realm of Isfahan in great blessings, easiness, and repose from grief was established as a piece of paradise – 'Of the (city of) Iram, with lofty pillars, the like of which were not produced in [other] cities' [Quran, *Surat al-fajr*, 7–8]. The Iram-like glory of its poetry was adorned with the presence of wise men, scholars, miraculous rhetoric and poets. Every day its joyful gathering, which included Darvish 'Abd al-Majid, 'Ashiq, Azar, Sahba, Safi, Hatif, Ghayrat, Nasib, Niyazi and Rafiq, was the envy of holy gardens and the world of spiritual ones.[66]

Rarely is Mirza 'Abd al-Wahhab's role as patron of poetry after Mushtaq's death referenced in relation to the rise of the 'literary return' movement.[67] As Dunbuli's statement makes clear, under Mirza 'Abd al-Wahhab's patronage the Isfahani Circle of poets appears to have expanded by adding several poets not earlier associated with Mushtaq's literary society. The community of poets first started by Mushtaq was accruing members and gaining steam.

Figures 2.1 and 2.2 visualise the Isfahani Circle as it existed before and after the arrival of Mirza 'Abd al-Wahhab in Isfahan. Figure 2.1 represents the modest community of poets that can be definitively tied to Mushtaq's literary society. (While other poets were known to be affiliated with Mushtaq and some of his students during this time, as noted above, their presence in the actual society itself is not confirmed.) Figure 2.2 depicts the community of poets receiving patronage from Mirza 'Abd al-Wahhab, alongside the poets associated with Mushtaq's literary society. What should be clear is that not only did the presence of Mirza 'Abd al-Wahhab lead to an expansion of the

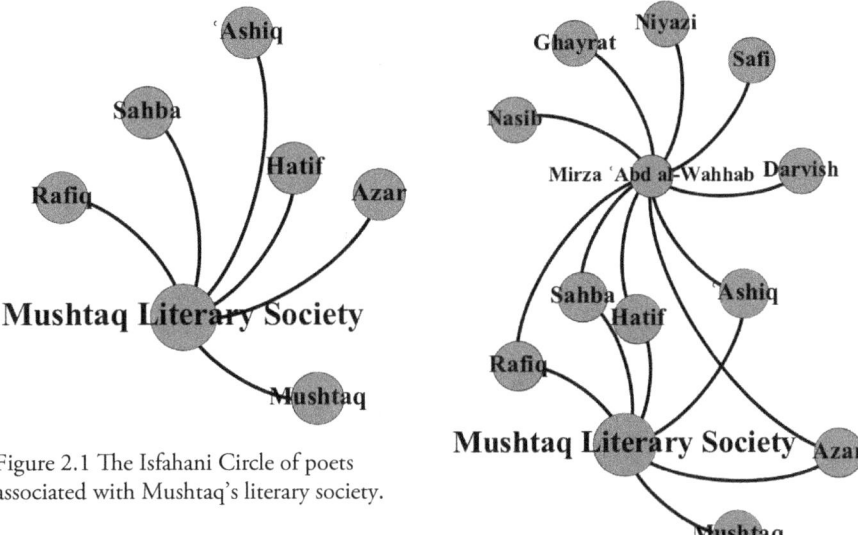

Figure 2.1 The Isfahani Circle of poets associated with Mushtaq's literary society.

Figure 2.2 Expansion of the Isfahani Circle of poets under the patronage of Mirza ʿAbd al-Wahhab.

Isfahani Circle of poets, but also, those poets once affiliated with Mushtaq's now-defunct literary society were able to maintain their existence as a literary community with Mirza ʿAbd al-Wahhab's arrival.

The significance of Mirza ʿAbd al-Wahhab's rule, and his positive impact on the poetic community, are evident in a poem composed in his honour by Azar. In an ode spanning nearly sixty lines, Azar celebrates the mayor of Isfahan for restoring that city to its former place of glory and harmony. Finding himself in the midst of a garden resembling paradise with trees 'bejeweled like the standard of Faridun', Azar seeks out the gardener to enquire about the nature of the paradisiacal place he has stumbled upon.[68] He soon discovers that this garden 'filled with huris and denizens graced with eternal life is not Paradise, nor Khusraw's palace', but instead 'the sacred garden of the world's master, the auspicious slave of the Justice Giver, Wahhab, who is the master of the abode of Isfahan'.[69] Azar then goes on to praise the magnanimity, justice and wisdom of Mirza ʿAbd al-Wahhab. He compares the mayor's attitude towards his subjects with that of a shepherd guarding his flock. Under his trusteeship Isfahan is safe, secure and prosperous. 'From his temperament, it is as though Isfahan is the abode of happiness', Azar writes; 'from his justice it is as though Isfahan is the abode of security.'[70] No one under his rule will be at a loss or down on their luck, for Mirza 'Abd al-Wahhab will be there to protect them:

> Isfahan is the garden, and your munificence is the rain
> Isfahan is the body, and your command is the soul![71]

In Isfahan under the rule of Mirza 'Abd al-Wahhab, all is well and in order. All, that is, but the certainty of Azar's recompense from his patron for composing such a wonderful ode. As the ode draws to close, Azar deftly reminds Mirza 'Abd al-Wahhab of his position as a poet and notes that in such auspicious and fortunate times the debt owed to the poet should not be forgotten. It is a subtle reminder by Azar of the professional role and institution of the poet in service to a patron. The ode, too, may be understood as indicative of an effort by Azar to bring greater formality to Mirza 'Abd al-Wahhab's patronage, beyond that of a 'joyful gathering'.

Requesting recompense from a patron at the end of an ode, after the obligatory praise, is certainly not atypical of the genre. But it is worth recognising the social and political environment during which Azar's ode was written. Azar's experiences and understanding of the times certainly shaped his attitudes towards the professional role of the poet and patronage. Azar would have been in an excellent position to recognise a shift in his fortune (and those of poets in general) resulting from the renewed poetic environment in Isfahan and a more peaceful Iran. He would know to strike when the iron was hot, so to speak.

Azar was born into an Isfahani family that included officials who reached high positions under the Safavids. His birth in 1722, however, occurred nearly simultaneously with the Afghan invasion of Isfahan, leading the entirety of his family to flee to Qum. Before he eventually returned to Isfahan his travels took him to Bandar Abbas (where his father was appointed to a position by Nadir Shah), 'Iraq-i 'Ajam, Fars, Sham, Mecca, Mashad and Azerbaijan. After the assassination of Nadir Shah (d. 1747) he served various rulers: the Afsharids 'Adil Shah and Ibrahim Shah, and the Safavids Isma'il III and Sulayman III.[72] In short, he experienced at first hand the vagaries of a chaotic time in Iran's history and was cognisant of the consequences that years of political upheaval and turmoil could have for family and professional prospects. Azar's keen awareness of the shifting fortunes of Isfahan and his utmost admiration for that city can be seen elsewhere in his poetry.[73] In his introduction to the section dealing with the poetry of his contemporaries in his *Firetemple*, Azar's understanding of the effect of Iran's chaotic recent history upon literary activities is on full display:

> For many years, on account of the revolution of the time, at once the customs of poetic compositions are nullified and poets, from great anguish, are changed. The resolve of poets is corrupted. The scattering of easy circumstances and state of confusion are such that no one is in the state of reading or composing poetry.[74]

Azar notes that for fifty years the condition of his contemporaries (*mu'āsirīn*) was defined by the tyranny, oppression and evil that reigned over all parts of Iran, once the paragon of the garden of heavens. During this torturous time Iran saw its 'wealth plundered – her daughters massacred, or sold to bondage – and the denizens of the once-smiling gardens ... exiled and wandering in a foreign clime'.[75] Azar is adamant not only in detailing the sorry state of affairs in eighteenth-century Iran, but also in justifying the poetry and position of his contemporaries, which must be viewed with consideration of these debilitating social and economic conditions. He juxtaposes the amicable social conditions of the ancient poets with the tumultuous times of his contemporaries, thereby indicating that any comparison between the two would not be fair. The ancient poets were 'nurtured in the cradle of prosperity and peace, and obtaining every want and wish beneath the shadow of the protection of the monarchs of the age'.[76] Contemporary poets, on the other hand, were left at the mercy and whim of oppression and misfortune, heavily restricting their ability to compose poetry.

As Azar describes the arrival of Karim Khan Zand, he references the beneficial conditions more amenable to literary production, as witnessed in the case of Mirza 'Abd al-Wahhab. But this did not mean Azar or his contemporary cohort were to be entirely immune from the social and political vicissitudes during the time of Karim Khan Zand's rule, nor necessarily able to cope with the loss of their patron Mirza 'Abd al-Wahhab. With the death of Mirza 'Abd al-Wahhab, patronage for the Isfahani Circle was disrupted and fractured. Faced with uncertainly following the loss of their patron, many of the formative members of this literary circle travelled elsewhere in Iran in an effort to seek new opportunities.

This interregnum between Mirza 'Abd al-Wahhab's death in 1770–1 and the establishment of Fath Ali Shah's literary society (*anjuman-i Khāqān*) in Tehran, when the 'literary return' style achieved supremacy, is a crucial period for understanding how the early movement developed. During this period one gains a better insight into the understandings and perceptions of the 'literary return' movement, the social conditions of which it was a part and the manner in which the poets viewed themselves. Several rich poetic sources from this time, including letters and elegies, capture some of the attitudes of the Isfahani Circle during a period when the formative stage of their movement ended and a new stage was to begin.

Figure 2.3 offers a final visualisation of the Isfahani Circle of poets as it existed in the mid-to-late eighteenth century by elucidating the ways this nascent poetic community was connected through poetic output. This network can be thought of as the final stage in the formation of poetic community beginning with participation in Mushtaq's literary society (Fig. 2.1) and expanded upon through the patronage from Mirza 'Abd al-Wahhab (Fig. 2.2). In Figure 2.3, black lines once again indicate attachment to Mushtaq's literary society or the patronage of Mirza 'Abd al-Wahhab; grey lines indicate a poetic connection between two individuals, no matter the type – praise poem, elegy or letter. The thicker lines connecting Azar, Hatif and Sabahi are a consequence of their multiple exchanges and visualise their significant friendship, which in many ways encapsulates the social and literary bonds among this community of poets. Some of these poems connect members of the Isfahani Circle to one another before Mirza 'Abd al-Wahhab came on the scene, while most were produced after the latter's death when the community of poets was thrown into flux. Without a society or patron to speak of, the bond of poetry increased in importance.

Once again Dunbuli serves as the keen observer of this transformation by describing the break-up of the Isfahani Circle after Mirza 'Abd al-Wahhab's death and the arrival of the new mayor Hajji Muhammad Ranani Isfahani. He writes:

ISFAHAN c. 1722–1801 | 105

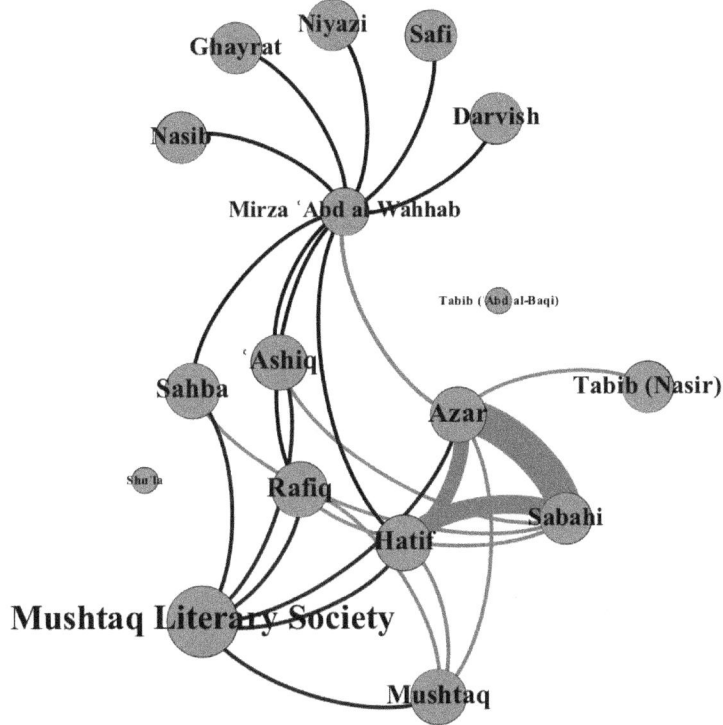

Figure 2.3 Literary bonds among the Isfahani Circle of poets.

Mirza 'Abd al-Wahhab died and in his place Hajji Muhammad Ranani Isfahani became mayor. He raised taxes for Karim Khan and increased [them] upon the population of Isfahan. He had no interest in poetry and poetical composition, refinement or perfection. He was barren, avaricious, evil thinking and badly behaved … He destroyed houses, manifested unusual measures, kept the poor wretched and collected riches. He forced the general populace and especially the wise men of Isfahan to emigrate and become homeless. He made matters so difficult on nobles and commoners that the pen cannot express it clearly. The elite and the masses were averse to that greedy wolf … The days of his government continued as oppressive days. Great fear and terror befell the population … In the year 1775, the grandees and nobles of Isfahan, from chief, vizier, plebian, noble, district magistrates, people of trade and commerce, using the excuse of putting-their-accounts-in-order, and with hearts full of grief, came to Shiraz. They became humbled under the shadow of the wall of abasement and complained to the court. Poets and geniuses emigrated from the heart of the capital and, like [disparate] lines of odes, were dispersed [in various] regions of Iraq. Azar, Hatif and some of the elegant ones traveled from Isfahan to the corners of Qum and Kashan [i.e. places of seclusion]. Aqa Muhammad Taqi Sahba and Mawlana Husayn Rafiq came to Shiraz.[77]

Azar was equally attuned to the changing fortune of Isfahan. He wrote several poems deriding the rule of Ranani. In one ode, addressed to Karim Khan Zand, Azar describes the conditions in Iran as peaceful and secure. He declares that all of Iran, 'from the edge of Kirman to the Tigris of Baghdad, from the shore of Oman to the edge of Darband', is enveloped in light from the justice of Karim Khan Zand.[78] In such a harmonious place, only Isfahan suffers on account of the 'wolf' Ranani, as Azar reminds Karim Khan in the final two lines:

> Helpless Isfahan that a wolf there
>   became the shepherd – this year was the equivalent of ten.
> Beware! Don't entrust a single caravan to a treacherous thief,
>   Beware! Don't allow the pain of the flock by the crooked wolf.[79]

Azar's reaction to the arrival and rule of Ranani in Isfahan demonstrates how attuned the early 'literary return' poets were to their surrounding social conditions. It was a political change in Isfahan that caused the break-up of their post-Mushtaq literary society and affected their understanding of the times. Ranani's arrival caused the 'literary return' poets' separation from one another and the movement's reconstitution elsewhere. Azar's awareness of and engagement with such an important social and political development was in no way unusual for the Isfahani Circle of poets, even if such examples have been severely overlooked by critics and historians parochially understanding their verse through the lens of stylistics and as detached from the surrounding world. As Matthew Smith has observed in relation to poetry composed by Azar, Hatif and Sabahi in response to the deadly earthquake that rocked the city of Kashan in 1778, these poets could act 'as agents of social order during times of calamity as well as celebration, explaining to their audience the historical events in which they were caught up'.[80] The narratives they constructed around this event – and presumably others – provided 'shelter in a literary and metaphorical sense', with the poets themselves serving as both 'witness and guide' to explain to the population at large how to cope with such tragedy and suffering.[81]

What then does it mean that the death of Mirza ʿAbd al-Wahhab led the major poets of the early 'literary return' movement to leave Isfahan for elsewhere? If the primary event defining the formation of the 'literary return' movement was the imitation of classical Persian poets in response to the so-called 'Indian Style', then why were these poets so dismayed by Mirza ʿAbd al-Wahhab's replacement by Ranani? Why not just stay in Isfahan and continue the tradition of Mushtaq's literary society? After all, Mushtaq's literary society convened at a time of instability in Isfahan after its fall to the Afghans. For the poets who left Isfahan, was it solely a matter of convening and composing poetry in amicable social conditions or gaining a more professional role as poets dependent on patronage? To answer many of these questions, one must return to the poetry of Azar, Hatif and Sabahi.[82]

A roughly 120-line poem by Azar from this time serves as one of the richest sources recording the perceptions of the early 'literary return' poets. It shows, for example, how they earnestly grappled with their place in an uncertain literary climate and conceived their relationship to the Persian canon. In the poem, Azar details a conversation on poetry with his two friends, Sabahi and Hatif. The poem begins with the poets discussing a collection of lyrics (*ghazals*), under the shade of a tree in a garden square, when suddenly Sabahi reveals from under his arm another collection of poetry. Intrigued by its appearance, Azar takes the book from his companion, 'its pages falling like the leaves of winter, scattered, diffusing an odor from an old smell'.[83] But 'like paradise', he writes, 'the roses grown in it are abundant, where a single thorn harms the hand of no one'.[84] He soon discovers that the collection of poetry is the work of Muʿizzi (d. 1147–8), a classical poet from the Seljuk period (1040–1157) known as the 'Amir of Samarkand'.[85] Having made the discovery of the author's identity, Azar proceeds to extol the poet's eloquence while at once recognising the difficulty undertaken in creating such a pleasant yet heart-rending work. Providing an opening for Azar's companions to respond, the oeuvre of Muʿizzi sets in motion an intriguing conversation on the current state and appreciation of poetry, the role of the poet in society, and the poetry, impact and conditions of the classical masters.

Sabahi is the first to respond to Azar, declaring that in all the gatherings of which he was a part, no one prior to Azar enquired about this collection of Muʿizzi. He laments the lack of curiosity about Muʿizzi's verse, bemoaning his contemporary poets and the current poetic atmosphere in which they live and work. He declares that the poets of today who 'gain fame from claiming the dominions of poetry are adversaries [of the true path of poetry]'. 'They don't know the difference between sugar and colocynth, they don't know who the Amir of Samarkand is!', he writes. Nonetheless, whoever composes poetry or strings two lines together 'raises his head to the heavens in astonishment', believing he has created dazzling verses. Sabahi then turns his attention to the poetic climate of Iran, expressing despair that any good poetry could actually be appreciated in such a state of hopelessness. His admonishments about the market for poetry in Iran, the lack of an audience and the absence of any willing patrons are striking. It is a theme that Sabahi will dwell upon elsewhere. He says to Azar:

> Don't you see how the sacred Huma in this land and country,
>   is worth less than the owl of misfortune?!
> There is no buyer of gems in this domain,
>   the seller makes no profit from selling goods.
> After this may you too not suffer senseless pain,
>   don't deliver a fine speech for anyone.
> What's the use to put yourself through such trouble,
>   just to put a few lines into verse?
> When you begin to recite it
>   they will signal with their fingers on the lips to stop.
> And if you prepare something from pen and paper,
>   they'll value it as nothing, just like this book.[86]

After a short interlude by Azar, Hatif picks up the thread of Sabahi's thoughts. His comments are the longest in the poem, some seventy lines. Hatif weaves his way through a variety of topics: the current state of poetry in Iran, the beneficial role of the poet in society, the glory of the old masters and praise for Azar's role in preserving the masters' legacy. These verses offer a nuanced insight into the early 'literary return' poets' view of their surroundings and their role within it. Hatif, like Sabahi, bemoans the forlorn state of poetry. He declares the time 'when it was only his [Muʿizzi's] name and nothing else' over:

> Since he left, no one took his place
> > no speaker, poet and intelligent ones remained.[87]

For Hatif, like Sabahi, the classical poet Muʿizzi is a synecdoche for the classical masters and their style of poetry. The manner in which the poet and his verse have been forgotten represents the greater amnesia shrouding perceptions of the classical masters during this time. But Hatif is more optimistic about the future of poetry than Sabahi. Relying on imagery from Iran's mytho-historical past made famous in Firdawsi's *Book of Kings*, Hatif assures his companions that just as the 'standard of Faridun' and the 'portico of Jam' re-emerged after a thousand years of Zahhak's tyranny and oppression, so too will poetry rise again.[88] Much like the classical poet Rudaki, who 'strung the pearls of Dari from childhood' and allowed 'eloquent speakers' to step from nothingness into 'the banquet of knowledge', so too will poetry return and renew the world of listeners. The necessity for the poet in this renewed state of affairs is unquestionable. The poet reveals the world's mysteries and makes the garden bloom. Hatif outlines the need that life itself has for poets by comparing a life without them to one in which they reign freely. As bad as the situation may be, spring will come again and restore poets and poetry to their rightful place in the world. Hatif reminds his companions:

> If the universe, one day, measures for Zayd and ʿAmr[89]
> > a little rice wine instead of grape wine
> The seed of the vine will not be dry
> > and the same smell of musk will flow from the wine house.
> If now no poet remains in the world,
> > then no flower blossoms across the garden.
> If there is no sign of the nightingale in the rose garden,
> > then Hindustan is empty of parrots.
> If the garden crows will not let out their crooked cry,
> > then they will not seek the smell of flowers and taste of sugar.

> If winter emptied the meadow of trefoils,
>> then branches and canes will be emptied of flowers and sugar.
> Don't be sad: it is tomorrow that spring
>> will lift the parasol of clouds from the mountainous land.
> The Zephyr will bud a flower on the edge of the branch,
>> to the cane will come an open collar for sugar.
> The nightingale will let out its cry in the rose garden,
>> the parrot will sip sugar in its beak.
> Poets will make their way to the garden,
>> in one hand a book, and in the other a goblet.
> Flowers will gladly remove the veil from their cheeks,
>> and nightingales will gleefully cry out in song.[90]

Hatif clarifies his comments about the re-emergence of the poet in contemporary society by advising Azar specifically on his role and contribution as a poet. Azar himself, according to Hatif, will play no small part in poetry's revival by following the path of the classical masters. In Hatif's comments one finally finds a hint of the commitment that the early 'return' movement poets had to the imitation of the classical masters:

> You too, praise be to God, are today
>> in the fortress of poetry, mighty like Muʿizzi.
> Both he and other poets of yore,
>> were attuned to the work of poetry.
> On account of you, their name will become alive in this world
>> even though they are at rest in the earth.
> From your efforts, their efforts will not be in vain,
>> since you bring out gems from their treasure.[91]

Hatif's comments on the role of the poet in society and, specifically, the role of Azar in a renewed poetic environment – dedicated to rekindling the masters' prestige – do not end here. Nor are they solely couched in terms of praise. He also offers Azar some stern advice, displaying a particular view of what his societal role (and that of the poet in general) should be. Adding to an understanding of the attitudes of the early 'literary return' poets, Hatif advises:

> Don't praise kings when they do not deserve it
> > for inevitably you'll end up writing him a satire.
> What's the point of you coming like Firdawsi from Tus
> > to Ghaznin to kiss the Shah's foot?!
> You'll uselessly suffer for thirty or forty years
> > so that the Shah can scatter some treasure upon your hem?!
> From a life of thinking you'll receive a slap,
> > you'll not see fidelity from its promise.
> Why like Nizami will you intentionally
> > praise the Shah of Ganja day and night out of sincerity?!
> In order to become the leader of those who offer praise,
> > [how long] will you sit aside from the corner of contentment?
> What do you want with offering praise?
> > Like Anvari they'll put a chain around your head like a women's scarf!
> Out of jealousy, they'll make you ride a donkey in Balkh
> > you'll be sweating and crying!
> If from the tree of wisdom you must have fruit,
> > you must pass through the rose-garden of Sa'di.
> Where every type of flower you want has blossomed,
> > for Shaykh [Sa'di] had something to say on everything.[92]

On the surface, Hatif's advice to Azar seems clear: follow the masters of Persian poetry and spread their style, but do not praise kings. His choice, however, to cite Firdawsi, Nizami and Anvari, three classical masters of Persian poetry, as examples of why kings should not be praised seems to undercut his argument. How should one strive to follow the masters, but at the same time avoid being like Firdawsi, Nizami and Anvari? Were they not great 'masters' worthy of imitation? As evidenced by voluminous examples in the eighteenth and nineteenth centuries, to say nothing of previous eras, these three poets were greatly sought after as models. Hatif even praised Sabahi in a letter by comparing the luminosity of his wisdom to that of Anvari.[93]

Hatif's references to Firdawsi, Nizami and Anvari, rather, are directed towards the social circumstances surrounding their poetry, and the manner in which they were treated, not the poetry itself. Firdawsi's disappointment at receiving what he considered to be inadequate recompense from Mahmud of Ghazna for his labour on the *Book of Kings* (*Shahnama*) is well-known. Anvari's misfortune, one of several of his life, stems from an accusation that a book or several verses satirising the people of Balkh was written by him. He was paraded in the streets of Balkh by an outraged mob, while wearing a woman's headdress.[94]

In Hatif's estimation, the 'wolf' Ranani's treatment of poets and lack of concern for poetic affairs as mayor of Isfahan must have seemed no different from the treatment these three masters received from their patrons. A poet should not praise kings or strive to be like Anvari, Firdawsi and Nizami, because in the eighteenth century no adequate audience or patron exists for a poet to establish himself in society. In such unfortunate times, better to be like Sa'di, who according to Hatif presumably did not concern himself with ungrateful patrons or an uninterested audience. Hatif's disavowal of praising kings constitutes a voice among the early 'literary return' poets interested in more than the simple promotion of poetry through patronage. Poetry can speak for itself through a more quietist approach and does not require patronage to serve as its intermediary. This attitude counters the view that the 'literary return' poets were solely interested in promoting their poetry and that of their friends in the most earnest way possible through the composition of anthologies by their companions.

Hatif's words further emphasise the interplay of social circumstances with poetic production and the interest of one's audience. His comments, along with those of Sabahi, illustrate the early 'literary return' poets' understanding of their social surroundings and the role of the poet within them. They are as concerned with the non-existence of an adequate environment for poetic production as they are with the proliferation of unskilled poets and the poetic style of the classical masters. Azar dramatises the situation well in a letter to Sabahi: 'I am a mute and my listeners are deaf, from mute speech, what benefit comes to the deaf?'[95]

The views of Azar, Hatif and Sabahi on these topics, however, are not monolithic. Instead, they present diverging opinions, as evidenced by Azar's response to Hatif's advice.[96] After praising Hatif for his wisdom and understanding, Azar responds to this advice directly:

> I am one who collects treasures
> > and doesn't sell it to the bazaar merchants for free.
> I choose pearls and rubies and gems
> > in order to adorn the horseshoe of Khusraw's horse.[97]

Azar's opinion is perhaps not exactly what Hatif wanted to hear. But since he spent his early years in the service of various rulers, and is clearly appreciative of his relationship with Mirza ʿAbd al-Wahhab, patronage was fundamental to his view of the poet's rank. Affording himself the final say in the manner, as the author of the poem, Azar tells Hatif that earning money for his poetry is exactly the path he will follow.

Other poems by Hatif, Sabahi and Azar corroborate many of the ideas and opinions found in the above poem. These other poems, whether letters or elegies, continually reflect the poets' awareness of their social surroundings and concern for the role of the poet in society, while directly implicating the classical masters or replicating their style. Following Azar's death in 1781, Hatif and Sabahi exchanged letters sharing their grief. While bemoaning the heavens and the fate of their friend, they soon shift their conversation to the latest state of poetic affairs in Iran. Hatif and Sabahi together portray a composite picture of the poetic environment facing them: the 'decline of the times', the under-appreciation of their art and the prevalence of less-than-skilled poets. Under such circumstances, they question their labour of poetry and whether it is worth all the trouble. With the loss of their esteemed companion Azar and his contributions to poetry as the backdrop, their remarks are tinged with anger, hopelessness and despair – anger resulting from the poetic climate of the times and despair because their poetry may be in vain. They go on to express the derision they feel for 'the base people of the bazaar', blaming them for much of what is wrong.[98] Together they contend that such an unappreciative audience is unaware of good poetry when they hear it. For Hatif, such people end up mocking the land where poetry should reign free:

> The heavens made me deal in my helplessness
> > with base people of the bazaar.
> Sometimes from their curses
> > affliction comes to me and sometimes heart-rending.
> Damn the land where the crow of the plain

> makes fun of the mountain dove.
> I, with this base labor and such partners,
>> accepted it all in helplessness.
> What is my profit from this lowly work, do you know?
>> – to bear the burden of misery from dear ones.[99]

Sabahi depicts the 'base people of the bazaar' in even more vitriolic terms. Worse than even their bad taste in poetry is that they believe themselves to be connoisseurs of art. Once again, Sabahi leads the charge in chastising individuals unwilling to recognise, or incapable of recognising, adequate poetry, which to him means being in lock-step with the classical tradition:

> If a group of the base people of the bazaar,
>> boast as if they're equal to you,
> They may be conspicuous in striped cloaks but,
>> they're naked of the ornament of art.
> They argue with Jesus,[100]
>> but not even the donkey of the antichrist would accept them as a veterinarian.
> They are hostile like Qipchaqi[101] warriors,
>> coquettish like Farkharian[102] idols
> They have no crown on their head but [are] tax collectors nonetheless,
>> no blade in the palm but [are] bloodthirsty nonetheless.[103]

Hatif and Sabahi continue by fretting over their place as poets among such distasteful listeners. Hatif, who was trained as a physician, couches his role as a poet in medical terminology, as helping 'sick' patients.[104] But he sees little reason for hope. As much as he tries to cure his 'patients', feeling one hundred pangs of sorrow in his attempts to cure just one of them, they may be considered dead nonetheless. Sabahi, for his part, has lost all taste for poetry. To his ear 'the sound of the starling and the melody of the turtledove' are one and the same as the 'lament of the owl'.[105] His pen has forgotten both 'shameless insults and pleasant-speaking'.[106] During this time of despair, in a world full of poetic know-nothings and one deprived of his companion Azar, Sabahi sees little value in maintaining an interest in composing poetry.

The example of Azar's poem and the letters between Hatif and Sabahi should not be taken to mean that the early 'literary return' poets remained unconcerned with poetic style, but rather that such concerns were subsumed under more general attitudes about the role of the poet and poetry in society more generally. As seen above, Hatif advises Azar to follow the path of poetry as delineated by the masters in an effort to re-establish the role of the poet in forsaken lands.

Sabahi strikes a similar chord in a letter to Rafiq by complaining about his fellow poets' lack of knowledge, bad composition and vanity. This letter confirms that members of the Isfahani Circle of poets did express disdain for those poets who may have resisted the shift in style to one of imitating the classical masters.[107] Sabahi words his letter of complaint against his contemporaries in explicit terms, lodging four charges against them: disrespect for their elders, lack of clarity, lack of knowledge in poetic composition, and misuse of terms. He then bitingly describes his contemporaries as follows:

> They didn't pursue the path of the right way, but stood there pointing the direction,
> They didn't find the way to truth, but sat there [pretending] to investigate it.
> They trumpet their learning all the way to the sky, but don't know,
> Suhayl from Suha and neighing from braying.[108]
> They cursed Khizr and it is they who wander lost in the desert,
> They laughed at Noah and it is they who are drowning at sea.
> They curse the old masters,
> when even two of their lines are of the highest order.[109]

Sabahi then goes on to reassure his companion Rafiq: 'Our path was in following the masters (*iqtifā-yi ustādān*), the masters of the way will not be harmed by nonsense.'[110] The establishment of Fath Ali Shah's royal literary society at the Qajar court in Tehran, where the 'return' style of poetry was heavily promoted, testifies to the fact that Sabahi's words were not made in vain.

Conclusion

This chapter has provided an alternative understanding of the emergence of the Isfahani Circle of poets, historically known as the founders of the 'literary return' movement. This understanding builds on the biographical anthologies (*tadhkiras*) of the Zand and early Qajar period to recover some of the social, political and literary circumstances leading to the formation of this poetic circle. These factors are often overlooked by later Qajar and modern critics. The poetry of the Isfahani Circle of poets serves as another resource, adding to an understanding of the social connections among poets, the formation of their poetic community and their self-perception as artists in an uncertain time. If the biographical anthologies of the period assist in reconstructing the social and political environment of the time, then the poetry of the Isfahani Circle helps situate its members within it.

The environment of post-Safavid Iran displays important continuities with Safavid times despite the deteriorating social and political situation that divides them. Mushtaq's literary society demonstrates remarkably similar traits to those of literary societies in Safavid Iran. Poets continued to come to Isfahan and connected with like-minded artists and littérateurs. They shared ideas and honed their skills, even without the benefit of coffee houses, which were the centre of poetic activities in Safavid Isfahan. Several members of Mushtaq's early literary circle came from humble beginnings and had 'day jobs' just like the poets of the 'urban classes', who occupied the Safavid poetic landscape. The 'realist style' utilised by poets of Safavid times and the poetry of the early 'literary return' poets display similarities with one another. This can be seen through the equal attention both groups of poets devoted to modelling their verse on that of the classical masters and the Isfahani Circle's familiarity with the work of the poets Naziri and Zamiri.

The poetry of Azar, Hatif and Sabahi serves as a window into the perceptions and attitudes of the early 'literary return' Isfahani Circle. Their poetry demonstrates that as much as they concerned themselves with the promotion a particular style of poetry, they were primarily concerned with and consciously aware of the role of the poet in society. Early on, in the absence of patronage, they praised one another through the composition of odes, often relying on the models of the classical masters. By doing so, they helped create a poetic community of like-minded poets who turned to one another for support. Their actions, along with those of other early 'literary return' poets, demonstrate the manner in which they sought to re-establish the role of the poet – their roles as poets – in a fluid, fast-changing time. They soon benefited from the patronage of Mirza 'Abd al-Wahhab, giving them a first taste of official patronage and beginning the process of re-institutionalising the practice of deference to a patron. When Mirza ʿAbd al-Wahhab died, these poets moved elsewhere. Having had the experience of a renewed and re-invigorated role for poetry, they would not let the chance easily slip away.

The Zand- and Qajar-era biographical anthologies no doubt contain an element of self-promotion through their over-emphasis on certain poets' importance and consequent insertion in the Persian literary canon. These works likely also oversold some of the deleterious effects of social conditions in post-Safavid Iran on the general poetic environment. The more post-Safavid Isfahan could be shown to be tumultuous and hopeless, the better could it be juxtaposed with the peace and stability of Zand (and later Qajar) Iran. Doing so could assist in presenting a more powerful creation narrative of the 'literary return' movement as arising from the ashes of destruction. But such attitudes of the 'literary return' movement's emergence only supersede other elements of its formation if one views anthologies as no more than sources meant to solidify literary canons (and a poet's place within the canon), rather than accounts of poetic networks and communities.

Scattered throughout this chapter are examples of different poets engaging with the poetry of one classical master or another in different ways and contexts. While 'literary return' poets may have been concerned with the use of a particular style, both their actions and their poetry demonstrate that they shared other concerns, in particular re-establishing the role of the poet in society. Thinking through what it meant to be a poet in late eighteenth- and early nineteenth-century Iran and how to reassert their roles as poets was for them an important first step in the formative process of the 'literary return' movement. This process involved, first, establishing their poetic community based solely on their own membership and social connections. Only after this could they attach themselves to a mayor in Isfahan, Mirza ʿAbd al-Wahhab. When he died, some of these poets went to Shiraz to reconvene at the Zand court, initiating a process that would culminate with the 'literary return' style's full institutionalisation later in Tehran at the Qajar court of Fath Ali Shah.

By seeking to re-establish their role as poets in an official capacity, the 'literary return' poets not only gained stylistic dominance in nineteenth-century Iran, but also inspired the late-Qajar anthologists of the nineteenth century to promote their tale as one of the utmost importance and necessity: the breaking of the so-called 'Indian Style' and re-establishment of the role of the eloquent ancients. But before such a story could be told, the 'literary return' poets needed to resurrect the poet's central role and secure the necessary patronage to be in a position to promote a particular style. As the poetry of Azar, Hatif and Sabahi demonstrates, they were well aware of the task in hand.

Notes

1. 'Azar', *Divan-i Azar*, p. 23.
2. 'bayt al-surūr va dār al-amān' and 'rashk-i gulzār-i jinān'. Ibid., pp. 22–3.
3. Kia, 'Contours of Persianate Community', p. 105. For an in-depth discussion of *Atishkada* and the way its author conceptualised geography during an uncertain time in the Persianate world see Kia, 'Imaging Iran before Nationalism'.
4. See e.g. Aryanpur, *Az Saba ta Nima*, pp. 16–19. Shams-Langarudi, *Maktab-i bazgasht*, 48–51.
5. See Perry, *Karim Khan Zand*.
6. Shirzadfar, *Isfahan dar dawran-i Afshar va Zand*, p. 51.
7. Axworthy, *Empire of the Mind*, p. 168.
8. Perry, *Karim Khan Zand*, pp. 126–7.
9. Axworthy, *Empire of the Mind*, pp. 168–9.
10. Perry, 'The Last Safavids'.
11. Rypka, *History of Iranian Literature*, p. 307.
12. Nafisi, introduction to 'Ashiq, *Divan-i 'Ashiq Isfahani*, p. 6.
13. Azar, *Atishkada* (1958 edn), p. 416. Dunbuli, *Tajribat al-ahrar*, p. 214.
14. Smith, 'Literary Connections', p. 205. Smith singles out the *Atishkada* of Azar as crucial in codifying the contribution of Mushtaq to the 'return' movement beyond his poetry.
15. Akhtar, *Tazkira-yi Akhtar*, p. 168. For the general importance accorded to Mushtaq by nineteenth- and twentieth-century writers see the introduction by Husayn Makki to Mushtaq, *Divan-i ghazaliyyat*, pp. 1–10.
16. Losensky, 'Vahshi Bafqi'.
17. Gulchin-i Ma'ani, *Maktab-i vuqu'*, p. 1.
18. Losensky, 'Poetic and Eros in Early Modern Persia', p. 749.
19. For the important role played by coffee houses in the cultural urban landscape of Safavid times see Matthee, 'Coffee in Safavid Iran'. Falsafi, 'Tarikh-i qahva va qahva-khana'. Pahlavan-Zada, 'Qahva-khana-ha-yi 'asr-i Safavi'.

20. Mushtaq, *Divan-i ghazaliyat*, pp. 158–76.
21. For example, the poet Sabahi composed elegies for renowned figures, and poems in praise of collective enterprises such as schools, a bazaar and a mausoleum. The poet Hatif composed verse in praise of the establishment of a mosque, a fountain and gardens. See Sabahi, *Divan-i Sabahi* (1987 edn). Hatif, *Divan-i Hatif*.
22. Smith, 'Betrayed by Earth and Sky', p. 177.
23. Shirzadfar, *Isfahan dar dawran-i Afshar va Zand*, p. 192.
24. McChesney, 'The Anthology of Poets', p. 58.
25. Azar, *Atishkada* (1958 ed.), pp. 402 and 423. Dunbuli also mentions the relationship between Sahba and Azar. See Dunbuli, *Tajribat al-ahrar*, p. 424.
26. Hidayat, *Majmaʿ al-fusahaʾ*, vol. 2, p. 699.
27. For ʿAshiq see Azar, *Atishkada* (1958 ed.), p. 404. Dunbuli, *Tajribat al-ahrar*, pp. 239–47. For information on Rafiq see Dunbuli, *Nigaristan-i dara*, p. 196. Dunbuli, *Tajribat al-ahrar*, p. 440. Hidayat, *Majmaʿ al-fusahaʾ*, vol. 2, p. 320.
28. Azar mentions the vast amount of time spent in Sabahi's company. Sabahi also credits Azar with providing his pen name. Azar, *Atishkada* (1958 ed.), p. 388.
29. Dunbuli, *Hadaʾiq al-udabaʾ*. Quoted in Gulchin Maʿani, *Tarikh-i tazkira-ha-yi Farsi*, vol. 2, p. 596.
30. Also see Hatif, *Divan-i Hatif*, p. 21.
31. Following the deaths of Azar, Hatif and Sahba, Dunbuli wrote that it became Sabahi's turn to rise to prominence, noting that among the 'noble poets of the period he [Sabahi] seized the ball with the polo-stick of eloquent rare speech'. Dunbuli, *Tajribat al-ahrar*, p. 373. Sabahi, having survived the longest among this group of poets, wrote numerous elegies for many of his companions, including Azar, Hatif, ʿAshiq and Sahba. Sabahi also is credited with establishing a literary society in Shiraz, frequented by members of Mushtaq's literary society, such as Rafiq and Sahba, during the last quarter of the eighteenth century, but the veracity of this claim is questionable. See Imdad, *Anjuman-ha-yi adabi-i Shiraz*, p. 47.
32. Imdad, *Anjuman-ha-yi adabi-i Shiraz*, p. 51.
33. Azar, *Divan-i Azar*, pp. 146–50.
34. See Hatif, *Divan-i Hatif*, p. 20.
35. Farahani, introduction to Tabib Isfahani, *Divan-i Tabib Isfahani*, p. 9.
36. Ibid., p. 11.

37. Khatami, *Pizhuhishi dar nasr va nazm*, pp. 23–4.
38. Aryanpur, *Az Saba ta Nima*, p. 29.
39. Nafisi, introduction to 'Ashiq, *Divan-i 'Ashiq Isfahani*, p. 7.
40. It was also Sabahi who provided Saba with his pen name. For an example of a poem by Saba in which he praises his teacher Sabahi see Bayza'i, introduction to Sabahi, *Divan-i Sabahi* (1959 edn), pp. 10–13.
41. Amanat, 'Iranian Identity Boundaries: A Historical Overview', p. 15.
42. See Smith 'Literary Connections'.
43. Dunbuli, *Nigaristan-i dara*, pp. 40–6.
44. Shushtari, *Tuhfat al-'alam va dhayl al-tuhfah*, pp. 192–237.
45. See Khalil, *Suhuf-i Ibrahim*, pp. 6, 74, 87–8 and 92. Qudrat, *Tadhkira-yi nata'ij al-afkar*, pp. 86 and 664. *Suhuf-i Ibrahim* was completed at Benares in 1790. *Nata'ij al-afkar* was completed at Arcot in 1842.
46. Sabahi, *Divan-i Sabahi* (1987 ed.), pp. 170–1.
47. Hatif, *Divan-i Hatif*, p. 136.
48. Ibid.
49. Sabahi, *Divan-i Sabahi* (1959 ed.), pp. 164–5.
50. Azar, *Divan-i Azar*, pp. 94–5 (of introduction). Sabahi, *Divan-i Sabahi* (1959 ed.), pp. 40–1.
51. Azar, *Divan-i Azar*, pp. 91–4. Dry ablution (*tayammum*) refers to the practice of making ablution with dust, a permissible act when water is unavailable, impure or hazardous to obtain.
52. Sabahi, *Divan-i Sabahi* (1959 ed.), p. 13.
53. Ibid., p. 48.
54. Dunbuli, *Tajribat al-ahrar*, p. 308. Kawthar is a spring in Paradise from which all other rivers derive.
55. Smith, 'Betrayed by Earth and Sky', p. 191. His translation.
56. Shirzadfar, *Isfahan dar dawran-i Afshar va Zand*, pp. 67–8.
57. Dunbuli, *Tajribat al-ahrar*, p. 437.
58. Ibid., p. 241.
59. Shirzadfar, *Isfahan dar dawran-i Afshar va Zand*, p. 78.
60. Ibid., p. 79.
61. Ibid., p. 50.
62. Dunbuli, *Tajribat al-ahrar*, p. 270.
63. Mahdavi, *Tadhkirat al-qubur*, p. 398. Shirzadfar, *Isfahan dar dawran-i Afshar va Zand*, p. 186.
64. Shirzadfar, *Isfahan dar dawran-i Afshar va Zand*, 193–4.

65. Dunbuli, *Tajribat al-ahrar*, p. 242.
66. Ibid., pp. 241–2.
67. The few references to the role of Mirza 'Abd al-Wahhab as patron of the society in Isfahan that became recognised as part of the 'return' can be found in Mahdavi, *Tadhkirat al-qubur*, p. 398. Shirzadfar, *Isfahan dar dawran-i Afshar va Zand*. Firuzkuhi, "'Asheq Esfahani'.
68. Azar, *Divan-i Azar*, p. 21.
69. Ibid., p. 22.
70. Ibid.
71. Ibid., p. 23.
72. Bland, 'Account of the Atesh Kedah', pp. 382–3. Also see Azar, *Atishkada* (1958 ed.), 433–4. Matini, 'Azar Bigdeli'.
73. For example, in his poem in praise of Nasir 'Tabib' Isfahani, Azar promotes the glory of Isfahan and its superiority in different respects over Baghdad, Sham, Greece and China, while at the same time recognising that it had not been long ago that destruction and ruin had dominated the city. Azar, *Divan-i Azar*, pp. 146–50.
74. Azar, *Atishkada* (1881–2 ed.), p. 1 of section 'dhikr-i ahval-i mu'asirin'.
75. N. Bland, 'Account of the Atesh Kedah', p. 372. His translation.
76. Ibid., pp. 374–5. His translation.
77. Dunbuli, *Tajribat al-ahrar*, pp. 270–2.
78. Ibid., p. 273.
79. Ibid.
80. Smith, 'Betrayed by Earth and Sky', p. 177.
81. Ibid., p. 194.
82. While some uncertainties remain over dating the poems explored below precisely, internal evidence suggests that they are likely to have been composed after the break-up of Mirza 'Abd al-Wahhab's literary society following his death.
83. Azar, *Divan-i Azar*, p. 418.
84. Ibid.
85. Amir Mu'izzi was the Poet Laureate of the Seljuk ruler Sanjar. He died when the latter shot him with an arrow while practising archery. Browne, *Literary History of Persia*, vol. 2, pp. 327–30.
86. Azar, *Divan-i Azar*, p. 419.
87. Ibid., 421.
88. The portico of Jam refers to that element of the palatial structure at Persepolis.

Zahhak was the mythical ruler who reigned tyrannously for 1,000 years. Faridun was the hero who eventually defeated Zahhak, thereby restoring justice and order.

89. In Islamic philosophy and mysticism, Zayd and 'Amr are often the names used when referring to individuals in hypothetical situations or in presenting a proof.
90. Azar, *Divan-i Azar*, pp. 420–1.
91. Ibid., p. 421.
92. Ibid., p. 422.
93. Dunbuli, *Tajribat al-ahrar*, p. 352.
94. Browne, *Literary History of Persia*, vol. 2, p. 382.
95. Azar, *Divan-i Azar*, p. 94.
96. There is an interesting poem by Azar, addressed to Hatif, in which there seems to have been a rift between the Sabahi and Hatif. In this poem Azar sides with Sabahi against Hatif, admonishing the latter to accept Sabahi's apology and put aside their differences. One can only speculate on what the particular rift was about. Azar, *Divan-i Azar*, pp. 298–9.
97. Azar, *Divan-i Azar*, p. 423.
98. The 'base people of the bazaar' are referred to as 'siflagān-i bāzārī' by Hatif and 'furūmāyigān-i bāzārī' by Sabahi.
99. Dunbuli, *Tajribat al-ahrar*, pp. 353–4.
100. The implication being that these poets are full of both ignorance and obstinacy if they are willing to argue with Jesus, known for accomplishing many miraculous cures.
101. The Qipchaq are nomadic people of Central Asia, to the north of the Caspian Sea, famed for their lightning raids.
102. Farkhar is a city in Central Asia, renowned for its idol temples.
103. Dunbuli, *Tajribat al-ahrar*, p. 356.
104. Ibid., p. 354.
105. Ibid., p. 356.
106. Ibid.
107. Sadat-Nasiri, 'Bazgasht-i adabi', p. 427.
108. The star Suhayl (also known as Canopus) is one of the brightest stars in the southern sky and was often used for navigation purposes and possibly also associated with wisdom. Suha (also known as Alcor), alternatively, is fainter in brightness, and one's ability to see it was often considered a test of good vision. It is perhaps for this reason that the two stars are juxtaposed here by Sabahi to

say that those whom he criticises cannot even observe the obvious distinction between the two in the night sky.
109. Sabahi, *Divan-i Sabahi* (1987 ed.), pp. 193–4.
110. Ibid., p. 194.

3

A Market for the Masters: Afghanistan c.1839–1842

Amid the historical works, diaries, journals and other depictions of the British invasion, occupation and eventual withdrawal from Afghanistan in the mid-nineteenth century is a series of Persian war-ballads (*jangnāma*s). These works narrate the various events of the first Anglo-Afghan War (1839–42), modelled on the *Book of Kings* (*Shahnama*) of Firdawsi (d. 1019 or 1025), and provide information on the war from an Afghan perspective.[1] Composed in the mid-nineteenth century in the years immediately following the war – at the same time as a 'literary return' was in full flower in Iran – these war-ballads occupy an intriguing place within Afghanistan's literary and national history. Located at the juncture of interpretations of war, Afghan nationalism and the legacy of the *Book of Kings* in Persianate societies, the war-ballads of the first Anglo-Afghan War highlight the dialogical process in which texts narrating Afghanistan's history emerged through engagement with geographically far-reaching genres, patronage networks and modalities of power.[2]

Multiple war-ballads in Persian of the first Anglo-Afghan War are known to exist, and still others may come to light.[3] The focus here is on the three texts that congealed in nationalist historiography as products meant to shape a sense of shared Afghan history and collective memory: the *War Ballad* (*Jangnama*, c.1843) of Muhammad Ghulam 'Ghulami' Kuhistani, *The Book of Akbar* (*Akbarnama*, 1844) of Hamid Allah Kashmiri and the variously titled *The Victory Book of Kabul* (*Zafarnama-yi Kabul*, c.1844–7) by Qasim Ali.

Like other texts recording elements of Afghan modern history, the war-ballads of the first Anglo-Afghan War 'can only be understood through the recognition of cross-border networks, dialogical developments and deep regional dynamics' governing their production, circulation and reception.[4] Understanding the war-ballads in this way recognises both how Afghan literary products were shaped by transregional processes and the manner in which engagement with the 'masters' remained a purposeful and productive endeavour outside of Iran in the nineteenth century. Before turning to such developments through a close appraisal of the texts, an account of their location and reception within Afghan nationalist historiography is in order.

The first two of these texts, *War Ballad* and *The Book of Akbar*, were brought to life for an Afghan audience in the mid-twentieth century and rendered as national accounts of 'the Afghan struggle for liberation from a colonial power as an image for the Afghan quest for self-determination'.[5] Each work first appeared serialised in the Kabul-based journal *Aryana* and was later published by the Historical Society of Afghanistan (*Anjuman-i Tarikh-i Afghanistan*) in a printed edition shortly thereafter.[6] Neither text remained dormant prior to its publication, but existed in archives, private collections and libraries, was passed from hand to hand, circulated orally, and partially existed in lithograph.

But it was only in the mid-twentieth century that these two war-ballads were 'recovered' to be distributed and serialised within the annals of Afghanistan's national history.[7] The intrepid scholar and historian Ali Ahmad Kuhzad wrote the introductions for the printed editions of both texts.[8] Kuhzad's interest in the *Book of Kings* and the text's relationship to Afghanistan extended to his other works as well. His *Afghanistan in the Book of Kings* (*Afghanistan dar Shahnama*) argued that the majority of places found in Firdawsi's classic work, often presumed to be parts of Iran, were actually located in modern-day Afghanistan.[9]

The eventual publication of *War Ballad* and *The Book of Akbar* under the auspices of the Historical Society (est. 1942) was in lock-step with the general scholastic environment of the times. Beginning in the 1930s, Afghanistan's past was being rapidly re-imagined and retold through the discovery of sources, translated works, archaeology and new historical methods.[10] The process largely unfolded under the protection of the state. As de facto government employees, Afghan scholars and intellectuals were tasked with

Figure 3.1 Cover of Hamid Allah Kashmiri's *Book of Akbar* (*Akbarnama*) published by the Historical Society of Afghanistan in 1951–2.

producing various projects that strengthened the state's legitimacy, ideology and Afghan national and cultural identity.[11]

The Historical Society, like the Kabul Literary Society (*Anjuman-i Adabi-i Kabul*) established a decade earlier, epitomised the manner in which state protection and intellectual production remained intertwined.[12] Located within the government's press department (*riyāsat-i maṭbū'āt*), the Historical Society was tasked with recording and disseminating information on various aspects of Afghanistan's history, heritage and culture.[13] Among its articles of association were directives for the 'compiling [of] a complete history of Afghanistan from the earliest times to the present' and for 'collecting and publishing sources of Afghanistan history', whether documents, treaties or manuscripts.[14] The Society's journal *Aryana*, a name referencing ancient Afghanistan, sought to publish materials of national interest in the fields of

Figure 3.2 Cover of *War Ballad* (*Jangnama*) by 'Ghulami' published by the Historical Society of Afghanistan in 1957.

history, ethnography, literature and archaeology.[15] While much work during this period remained devoted to relinking Afghanistan's national history to its pre-Islamic past, accounts of Afghanistan's more recent political and military history were no less privileged. As examples of 'heroic resistance to foreign domination', *War Ballad* and *The Book of Akbar* found a place alongside archaeological excavations in an environment meant to glorify Afghanistan's past in the most profound manner.[16]

The third text featured in this chapter, *The Victory Book of Kabul* by Qasim Ali, has met with a different, though no less important, fate in Afghan nationalist historiography. For if *War Ballad* and *The Book of Akbar* have been depicted as glorifying the Afghan people's success in defeating foreign invaders, then *The Victory Book of Kabul* is viewed as a work of foreign propaganda. Typical depictions of Qasim Ali understand him to be a

British 'lackey', who dutifully composed *The Victory Book of Kabul* at the British behest. The text was supposedly offered as British response to other previously-composed war-ballads like *The Book of Akbar*, that were spreading and circulating narratives of British defeat across Afghanistan and South Asia. Thus, the composition of *The Victory Book of Kabul* is regarded as an account of imperial subterfuge meant to undercut narratives depicting the valour and heroism of the Afghan resistance to foreign invasion. Criticising *The Victory Book of Kabul* and its author has become something of a tradition among Afghan scholars.[17]

The actual circumstances surrounding *The Victory Book of Kabul* are significantly more complex, however. *The Victory Book of Kabul* was less the product of a British propagandist, determined to carry out a foreign power's bidding, than the outgrowth of an author operating in the high-stakes world of transregional patronage, where Persianate poetic genres intersected with both British and non-British structures of power. *The Victory Book of Kabul*, after all, appeared in different renditions and formats with some less-than-glorifying depictions of the British role in Afghanistan. A close engagement with the many lives of this single text can help articulate how *The Victory Book of Kabul* could be 'embedded in a wider dynamic of prestige and space that transcended modern notions of centralization and boundedness', a process Noelle-Karimi recognises in her assessment of earlier Durrani histories of the eighteenth-century Indo-Persian world.[18] The many parts of what came to be *The Victory Book of Kabul*, tailor-made to match the proclivities of Afghan nationalist historiography, are undoubtedly greater than its sum.

Understanding the forgotten elements governing the production and circulation of *The Victory Book of Kabul*, like those of *War Ballad* and *The Book of Akbar*, open a space for us to understand the war-ballads of the first Anglo-Afghan War beyond their strict configurations as products of an immemorial Afghan nation. As the historian Nile Green notes, 'the languages, genres, narratives, and epistemologies through which Afghans have conceived and constructed their past were almost never uniquely Afghan … [but] belonged to the wider cultural and political arenas with which Afghans interacted'.[19] An exploration of the multitudinous social, literary and political environments guiding these texts' emergence reclaims the war-ballads as

Afghan literary products shaped by transnational characteristics.[20] Doing so assists in highlighting the transregional features crucial to the formation of the modern Afghan state and nation.

Attending to the circumstances of the war-ballads' composition, circulation and inter-relationships also highlights the lively space they created and occupied in nineteenth-century Afghanistan and South Asia. The emergent image is one of vigorous literary activity and productivity: a 'market-place' of texts engaging with the work of one of the canonic masters, spanning geographical regions and embracing oral, manuscript and print culture. Such a transnational market-place of texts not only runs counter to the category of 'literary return' as an exclusively Iranian practice of engaging with the style of the masters in the nineteenth century, but demonstrates the larger literary canvas on which engagement with the masters occurred. The phenomenon of the war-ballads, as well as other coeval texts modelled on the *Book of Kings*, indicates a corpus of norms and practices that promoted the production and circulation of texts and oral tales related to the poetry of the classical canon on a wider scale. Their very existence may point to an alternative model of what is meant by 'literary return', based not entirely on collective action and output by a group of poets, but on processes of textual production, circulation and reception as well. More importantly, they demonstrate that engagement with the masters in the nineteenth century cannot be restricted to imitative stylistics or neo-classical sensibilities alone.

This chapter begins with a brief overview of the historical epic and the war-ballad genre modelled after Firdawsi's *Book of Kings*. It argues that the war-ballads of the first Anglo-Afghan War constitute a unique example of the genre. The chapter then explores in detail the three war-ballads noted above and delineates the social, political and literary environments under which they were composed. In doing so, it offers insight into a complex set of factors often overlooked in nationalist readings. The composition and afterlife of these texts, the extent to which they circulated and the inter-relationship among them are all factors essential to a complete understanding of these works. These factors help extend the analysis of these texts beyond one simply founded upon replicating a model of the great ancients, as seen in Iranian literary history, or feeding a nationalist historiography, as seen in the Afghan case. The chapter concludes by arguing that the war-ballads of the first Anglo-Afghan War are best seen as having participated in a market-place of works engaging with a classical master, challenging the interpretation of 'literary return' in the nineteenth century as an exclusively Iranian category.

Preparing for Battle

The impact of Firdawsi's *Book of Kings* upon textual production in the Persian-speaking world has resulted in an outpouring of renditions, continuations and imitations throughout history. The *Book of Kings* has served as a model for authors seeking to retell the tales and triumphs of various personalities contained within it and as an inspiration to create stand-alone 'cyclical' or 'secondary' epics. It has also served as a repository of style, language and metaphor to be borrowed, incorporated and sprinkled across works of multiple genres, and has had its concepts of justice and kingship utilised for didactic purposes.[21] By the fifteenth century, as Julia Rubanovich notes, Firdawsi's work 'had taken its particular place in every stratum of the Persian literary system, and was to keep its singular position throughout the forthcoming centuries'.[22] Firdawsi's *Book of Kings*, it bears mention, was also part and parcel of a larger, multilingual literary universe that extended beyond Persian and commingled with like-minded epics represented in different languages.[23]

The focus here is on the *Book of Kings* as a model for authors to narrate events close to their own lifetimes, either contemporaneous with their own life or in the recent past. Texts that rely on an epic tradition of the *Book of Kings* to narrate historical events are what the literary historian Zabihullah Safa refers to as 'historical epics' (sing. *ḥamāsa-yi tārīkhī*). In his work on the Persian epic tradition, Safa cites the variety of historical epics composed in different geographical and political settings from the early thirteenth century to the early nineteenth century, many of which rely on the *Book of Kings* as a model.[24] It is within this tradition of epic poetry and imitation of the *Book of Kings* that the war-ballads of the first Anglo-Afghan War are best understood.

The first historical epic imitating the *Book of Kings* model and contemporaneous with the events it described is *Shahanshahnama-yi Payizi*, produced during the reign of Sultan 'Ala al-Din Muhammad Khwarazm Shah (r. 1200–20). It recounts the Sultan's various victories, and, like many such historical epics, was produced at the court of the patron it was praising.[25] The early-modern and modern periods also witnessed a proliferation of similar historical epics modelled on the *Book of Kings*. In some cases, these imitative texts were more heavily influenced by the particular style of Nizami's (d. 1209) *Book of Alexander* (*Iskandarnama*), itself a text focusing on one character from Firdawsi's epic.[26] Imitations of the *Book of Kings* predominated in Safavid and Ottomans domains, mainly but not exclusively at the court.

At the court of the Safavid monarch Tahmasp (r. 1524–76), who is often portrayed as shunning non-religious poetry, the poet Qasimi composed several historical epics in praise of various rulers. *Qasimi's Book of Kings* (*Shahnama-Qasimi*) included one part celebrating the deeds and victories of the Safavid founder Shah Isma'il (r. 1501–24) (entitled *Shahnama-yi mazi*) and a second part dedicated to the deeds of his son Shah Tahmasp (entitled *Shahnama-yi navab-i 'ali*).[27] Later, during the reign of Shah Abbas (r. 1588–1629), an unknown author produced two war-ballads, entitled *War-Ballad of Qishm* (*Jangnama-yi Qishm*) and *Book of Jarun* (*Jarunnama*), in imitation of Firdawsi's epic. These works describe battles between local forces and the Portuguese over various islands in the Persian Gulf in the early seventeenth century. The works highlight the heroic deeds of local actors, such as Imam Quli Khan of Shiraz, as well as the role played by the British East India Company (EIC).[28] In the eighteenth century, the poet Muhammad Ali Tusi, the self-proclaimed 'Second Firdawsi', composed a *Book of Kings*-inspired epic entitled *Shahnama-yi Nadiri* on the triumphs and heroics of the Iranian ruler Nadir Shah (r. 1736–47). According to Abbas Amanat, it is one of the first post-classical epics articulating proto-nationalist sentiments around Iranian territory and the first epic depicting a post-Safavid ruler according to 'symbolism that harks back to a mythical Iranian past'.[29] Such depictions would continue into the following century with the *Shahanshahnama* by the poet Saba, one of the last great court-sponsored imitations of the *Book of Kings* in Iran, produced at the court of the Qajar monarch Fath Ali Shah (r. 1797–1834).[30]

Further west in Ottoman domains, the *Book of Kings* also served as a model for recounting recent events. The Ottoman court collected various copies of the manuscript and translated it into Ottoman Turkish, inspiring the production of several imitations of the *Book of Kings* recounting the deeds of various sultans.[31] These works first appeared in Persian verse in the same metre and style as Firdawsi's text, but later began to be written in Turkish, sometimes in prose.³² The high-point for composing such works occurred during the reign of Shah Sulayman (r. 1520–66) when authors earned the rank of 'writer of *Book of Kings*' and received salaries for their efforts.³³ Several works focus on battles between the Ottomans and Safavids.³⁴ Although singing the praises and deeds of an Ottoman Sultan through a *Book of Kings* imitation served a quasi-propagandistic purpose, this objective appears to be secondary to the literary and cultural prestige the act of composing such a work entailed.³⁵

In South Asia, the *Book of Kings* served as model to be replicated for recounting the heroic deeds of Mughal rulers as well.³⁶ The court poets Kalim (d. 1651) and Qudsi (d. 1646), who both migrated to South Asia from Iran, composed long poems in the epic style of Firdawsi to narrate the events of Shah Jahan's reign (1628–58) and imperial realm. Their works appeared under various grandiose titles like *Book of Kings* (*Padshahnama*), *Book of Shah Jahan* (*Shahjahannama*) and *Victory Book of Shah Jahan* (*Zafarnama-yi Shahjahan*).³⁷ The practice of situating contemporary events according to the *Book of Kings*' model was accompanied by a general reverence for the work in South Asia, which, like elsewhere, included the production of exquisitely illuminated manuscripts and the appearance of court-sponsored '*Book of Kings*-reciters' (*Shāhnāma-khwāns*) as well as others outside the court who memorised the text.³⁸

The impact and proliferation of the *Book of Kings* model during Mughal times and after made the Subcontinent one of the more robust places for the re-imagination and circulation of the text. For example, *The Heart-Opening History, for Shamshir Khan* (*Tarikh-i dil-gusha-yi Shamshir-Khani*), a prose summary of the *Book of Kings* commissioned in Ghazni during Shahjahan's reign, circulated widely throughout the eighteenth and nineteenth centuries and elicited multiple illuminated manuscripts, both during the time of Shahjahan and as late as the nineteenth century.³⁹ Its massive circulation throughout South Asia caught the attention of British Orientalists: the Persianist James Atkinson regarded it as the best-known version of the *Book of Kings* in South Asia.⁴⁰ Such features of the impact and reception of the *Book of Kings* in South Asia explain the viability of the transregional and interconnected market of the war-ballads of the first Anglo-Afghan War in the nineteenth century.

Finally, in Afghanistan, several works drawing on the epic tradition of the *Book of Kings* pre-date the war-ballads of the first Anglo-Afghan War. The *Shahnama-yi Ahmadi* concerns the deeds of Ahmad Shah Durrani (r. 1747–72), celebrated as the founder of the modern Afghan state. Another work dedicated to many of Ahmad Shah's victories on the battlefield is simply titled *Book of Conquest* (*Fathnama*).[41]

A major feature of the texts listed above was that they were composed within the confines of a royal court. In couching their patron's glorious deeds (most notably on the battlefield) within the *Book of Kings* model, these poets honoured their patron's regal stature by linking it to monarchical prestige in a widely disseminated and respected epic tradition. One of the unique features of the war-ballads of the first Anglo-Afghan War is that praise for a particular individual patron did not appear to be of primary concern. As Noelle-Karimi has demonstrated, a strong and unified state structure did not truly exist in mid-nineteenth-century Afghanistan, deeply affecting prospects for patronage.[42] One finds heroes throughout these Anglo-Afghan war-ballads, but such heroes were not necessarily the patrons of poets, a practice quite atypical in the history of war-ballad production. While the Anglo-Afghan War ballads were not altogether disconnected from modes of patronage, as will be seen with *The Victory Book of Kabul*, they were more concerned with representing events and creating literary products than royal praise. The terms and circumstance of their production fell outside the strict confines of a particular court as they dedicated themselves to the narration of a recent event, not the deeds of a regal patron.

The three war-ballads under consideration tied a recent event of historical import to the long-established *Book of Kings* tradition in a unique manner, operating across a spectrum of dissemination and circulation via oral transmission, copied manuscripts and print in the nineteenth century. Contrary to the texts featured above, the war-ballads of the first Anglo-Afghan War represent an instance where several similarly styled works – all dedicated to the same event and representing it in the same form – appeared alongside one another. No other class of 'historical epics' can make such a claim, at least not those produced so close to the occurrence of the event itself. As a result, these texts represent a unique occurrence in the genre of *Book of Kings* imitation, warranting close examination alongside other concomitant trends of eighteenth- and nineteenth-century Persian literary culture where the 'masters' of Persian poetry loomed large.

Recounting the War: The *War Ballad* of 'Ghulami' and Oral Culture

Mawlana Mulla Muhammad Ghulam 'Ghulami' Kuhistani's *War Ballad*, the inaugural war-ballad detailing events of the first Anglo-Afghan War, was probably being composed while the war was still ongoing. It quite literally emerged from the debris of the war itself. Its recovery in manuscript form by the Historical Society of Afghanistan seems more redolent of national lore than reality. According to Kuhzad in his introduction to the printed edition, Mir Muhammad Hasan Khan, a relative of the famous fighter Mir Masjidi Khan, delivered the manuscript to the Historical Society in 1952–3. The manuscript was partially composed on official paper belonging to the offices of the British, evidenced by the fact that the first seventy-six pages of the 166-page manuscript contain ledgers of the names of British officials and officers on the reverse. On the tops of some of the pages, the heading 'Ludhiana Political Agent, Political Agent Shikarpur' with the years 1841–2 is discernible. Ludhiana, India, was the location of the exiled Shah Shuja' (r. 1803–9 and 1839–42) and his court before being returned to the throne by the British. Kuhzad concluded that the paper was recovered by an Afghan fighter amid the loot of battle sometime between November 1841 and January 1842, perhaps from Bala Hissar or another English fortress or encampment near Kabul. It was on this paper, Kuhzad notes with more than a hint of national pride, that Ghulami recorded the 'names of national brothers and high-minded fighters of the homeland in epic fashion'. The work itself was most likely completed around 1843, around the time Dust Muhammad Khan (r. 1826–39, 1842–63) returned to the throne in Kabul after being deposed by the British.[43]

The events detailed in Ghulami's work are presented in a straightforward chronology focused on Dust Muhammad Khan's defeat at the hands of Shah Shuja' and the former's subsequent flight.[44] Ghulami champions the deeds of men from Kuhistan and their role in the resistance to British occupation, having himself hailed from the village of Aftabchi in that region. Directing the narrative is Ghulami's conscious effort to compose his work in imitation of Firdawsi's *Book of Kings*. This choice appears to represent an instance in which Firdawsi's work was regarded as the appropriate model for recording current political events and highlighting the important personalities involved.

Ghulami's choice was not unique among Afghan authors relying on the *Book of Kings* model. As Shafiq Shamel notes, the stories of the *Book of Kings* have been recalled in Afghanistan 'as models to be emulated in order to overcome existential or socio-political difficulties and to restore the dignity of oneself, one's people or one's nation'.[45] Texts reliant on the *Book of Kings* model also appeared during the time of Ahmad Shah Durrani, the presumptive founder of the modern Afghan state, as noted above.

In his *War Ballad*, Ghulami replicates the metre of the *Book of Kings* and utilises language and stylistic choices found in the epic, such as referring to armies as 'rivers' and heroes as 'dragons'.[46] The practice was not uncommon for those looking to the *Book of Kings* for inspiration. The opening praise for Dust Muhammad Khan, prior to the narrative of the text, reveals the intention to follow the *Book of Kings* further. Dust Muhammad Khan and his actions are recontextualised alongside the heroes and ancient lore found in the great Persian epic:

> The Grand Amir, the head of regality,
> > the son of Payinda Khan [Dust Muhammad Khan]
> In manners, he is like Alexander, in magnificence like Jamshid,
> > Deserving of throne, crown and royal waist-band.
> His stock is Durrani, his land is Kabul
> > in strength, alas, he is the Rustam of Zabul!
> May every day of his days be like Nawruz,
> > may his nights be as splendid as the Night of Qadr.[47]

Later, Ghulami will seek to raise local personalities, like his Kuhistani kinsman Mir Masjidi Khan, to the status of heroes in a similar fashion. In this regard, he followed a practice Louis Dupree observed in Afghan folklore as late as the 1960s as the desire to 'reinforce pride in local heroes and groups'.[48] Kuhzad maintained that the only existent manuscript of Ghulami's *War Ballad* came to the Historical Society by one of Mir Masjidi Khan's progeny. It was likely guarded by the latter's Kuhistani family during the intervening period as a source of familial pride, in which a member of kin embodied highly valued virtues like bravery and sacrifice.

As a confirmed witness to the events of the first Anglo-Afghan War and as one writing while the war was still smouldering and fresh in people's hearts,

Ghulami through his choice to replicate the *Book of Kings* helped solidify the war's events into the domain of oral tales and legend.[49] The lack of additional manuscripts of *War Ballad* suggests that the text mostly circulated orally. By drawing upon a familiar and paradigmatic model to subordinate the temporality of the war's events to folkloric proportions, Ghulami provided a format for the personalities of the Afghan resistance to be elevated to the status of epic heroes for a listening audience.[50] The heroic status Ghulami accorded to individuals like Dust Muhammad Khan, Akbar Khan and Mir Masjidi Khan would not subside in Afghan society, as evidenced by their future treatment in literary and non-literary formats. To note two prominent examples: Akbar Khan's heroic deeds serve as the centrepiece for one of the first Afghan novels, *Akbar's Jihad* or *The Great Jihad* (*Jihad-i Akbar*), and have more recently been referenced in the poetry of the Taliban.[51] Likewise, the highest civilian honour awarded by the Afghan government today is named after Mir Masjidi Khan. Ghulami's depiction of the resistance fighters' deeds and the ability of his text to enter Afghan oral culture while the war was winding down solidified perceptions of these heroes in the Afghan imagination. But the interplay between oral and literary culture cut both ways.

Ghulami's work as much created new national heroes and legends by drawing on the epic model of the *Book of Kings* as it emerged from a larger discourse of epic tales and myth-making prevalent in Afghan history. He was giving voice, coherence and a narrative to the stories of heroism and valour likely already being circulated among the Afghan populace during the time, but not yet in the form of a concretised literary text.[52] Indeed, the first poetic reaction of the populace against the rule of Shah Shujaʿ and his British overlords was a verse known to have circulated only orally:

> Coins minted with silver and gold by Shah Shujaʿ,
> >   The pupil of the eyes of 'Lords' and [Alexander] 'Burnes',[53] the dirt
> >   under the feet of the 'Company'.[54]

Ghulami's *War Ballad* is representative of the work of other nineteenth-century authors seeking to explain events and dramatise uprisings against political authority through the war-ballad format and *Book of Kings* model. As the first known example from its time, Ghulami's account of the first Anglo-Afghan War stands at the forefront of works by other similarly inclined authors seeking to retell current events in a local context by emphasising heroic deeds from their own region. A host of other authors sought to place events of nineteenth-century Afghanistan, such as local rebellions or revolts against the Afghan ruler Amir ʿAbd al-Rahman Khan (r. 1880–1901), in a similar model.[55] Modelled after a prolific Persianate genre and articulating accounts of events specific to Afghanistan in the nineteenth century, *War Ballad* points to the 'dialogical character of Afghan historical consciousness', pairing local influences and transnational paradigms.[56]

Not long after Ghulami produced his work on the first Anglo-Afghan War, a Kashmiri poet was compiling the most famous of the period's war-ballads, *The Book of Akbar*, in honour of Dust Muhammad Khan's son Muhammad Akbar Khan. *The Book of Akbar*'s composition sets in motion events that display the full breadth and circulatory power of *Book of Kings*-like texts and tales of the first Anglo-Afghan War.

A Bazgashtian Tale? *The Book of Akbar* of Hamid Allah Kashmiri

The circumstances under which Hamid Allah Kashmiri composed *The Book of Akbar* differ significantly from those under which Ghulami's *War Ballad* was written. While Kashmiri did not bear witness to the war's events like his Kuhistani counterpart Ghulami, he nonetheless felt compelled to narrate the events of the war by using the *Book of Kings* model. Hamid Allah Kashmiri was born in the district (*pargana*) of Shahabad in Kashmir.[57] He was the son of Mawlavi Himayat Allah, a religious scholar of Kashmir, with whom he studied at an early age and from whom he most likely gained his first knowledge of the classical Persian canon.[58] While he is the author of several other works, it is his *Book of Akbar*, dedicated to the national hero Akbar Khan, on which his fame rests. The work has earned him appellations in later histories such as the 'Firdawsi of Kashmir' or 'the saz (*sāz*) of Kashmir'.[59]

Kashmiri composed *The Book of Akbar* in 1844, only one year after the composition of Ghulami's *War Ballad*. He died four years later in 1848. Indications in the text suggest that he was old and infirm while completing it and too weak to travel.[60] There is also no indication in the text that Hamid Kashmiri had any knowledge of Ghulami's *War Ballad*. While the lack of connection between the two texts on the surface runs counter to the notion that a market for texts existed in the aftermath of the first Anglo-Afghan

War, intertextual references and authorial awareness among the various texts are only one element of this story. On the contrary: the composition of Kashmiri's work without knowledge of Ghulami reinforces the significance of a shared model among nearly contemporaneous tales. Both texts conveyed their stories using Firdawsi's *Book of Kings* and tapped into reserves of circulating traditions prevalent in the Persianate sphere. One of the telling factors of the war-ballads of the first Anglo-Afghan War is that a single event could elicit several distinct instances of similarly structured texts.

Removed from the events of the war due to his location in Kashmir, Hamid Allah relied on oral accounts to compose his work, such as tales of heroism and valour in the war that likely flowed through the population.[61] In his epilogue, Kashmiri notes that he collected bits and pieces about the war's events from travellers and passers-by who were more than eager to share what they had heard or seen of the war. He composed *The Book of Akbar* from such oral information:

> I asked of wise people
>> who were inhabitants of that domain.
>
> In reports there were differences of words,
>> I brought them together in agreement and spoke [them] whole.
>
> I did nothing but adorn the battle itself,
>> I didn't add anything extra in this tale.
>
> If there remains confusion in the narrative
>> My professional declaimer (*rāvī-i man*) is responsible for it, not me.[62]

Kashmiri's reliance on contemporary oral reports is not the only instance of how the work's composition was influenced by the surrounding atmosphere. Complementing its relationship to the oral culture concurrent with the war's aftermath is *The Book of Akbar*'s relationship to the literary climate of the time, extending beyond the temporal confines of the war. If it was oral culture that allowed Kashmiri to access the raw material needed for him to compose the work, then it was his perception regarding the current state of Persian literary culture and poetics that instigated the project of writing. This aspect of *The Book of Akbar*'s composition, though not entirely overlooked, has not been given its fair due, especially in the context of nineteenth-century Persianate literary culture.[63]

The Book of Akbar's connection to nineteenth-century Persianate literary culture is at times forgotten amid the national acclaim garnered by the work and its place in a nationalist discourse about Afghanistan's resistance to foreigners. Indeed, Kashmiri's birth and poetic life in Kashmir does not preclude his work from being part of the national literature of Afghanistan.[64] Kashmir was long a centre of Persian literary output, especially during Mughal times. It attracted a throng of poets and rulers and kindled a literary imaginary of paradise on earth.[65] Kalim, the Poet Laureate of the Mughal ruler Shah Jahan, resided in Kashmir while completing his *Book of Kings*-inspired work on the events of his employer's reign.[66] In other words, Kashmir was well-integrated into the Persian literary ecumene and not as far from Afghanistan as it may seem today.

But where Kashmiri's work ended up is not where it began. He may have produced an Afghan national epic, but his intention was not necessarily to do so. Kashmiri was responding to trends and perceptions of his own literary climate that viewed the achievements of its poets and authors as devoid of the excellence once attained by the great classical masters. In this respect, the situation resembled perceptions of some of the Isfahani Circle and Qajar-era authors of biographical anthologies discussed in earlier chapters, even if Kashmiri did not display the latter writers' same neo-classical sensibilities.

Kashmiri tells his audience in the prologue that he composed the *Book of Akbar* as proof that the tradition of the esteemed masters of Persian literature was still relevant and that imitation of their styles was still possible. He relates the story of how he had a dream of spending an evening at a literary gathering (*anjuman*) among 'masters of bright dispositions' and the recitation of pleasant lyrics. These well-seasoned critics and poets were engaged in a conversation concerning the literary climate of the time. In such a setting, amid the reading of lyrics and masnavis by classical masters like Khaqani (d. *c.*1190), Rumi (d. 1273) and Saʿdi (d. 1291–2), the following occurred:

> In the end someone from amongst the assembly said:
>   'Alas, the people of speech have come to an end.
> I don't know what happened to those auspicious times
>   when such speech-cultivators were around.
> In these times, the urban and the village fools (*juhhāl*)
>   with meaningless, nonsense poems

speak emptily of the esteemed masters (*ustādān-i ʿālī*)
   and call themselves perfect practitioners.
They draw nothing from the elegant and intricate class of [past masters]
   except verse-stealing.'[67]

These critical remarks directed towards the members of the literary gathering, spoken by a person not further identified by Kashmiri, provide insight into the literary climate in which *The Book of Akbar* was produced. That this gathering appeared to Kashmiri in a dream, a common trope used by poets to relate the inspiration behind their work, should not detract from the content. It remains as much a reflection of Kashmiri's perceptions of his surrounding literary climate and position in it as if he had related the events of a 'real' literary gathering.

The unidentified speaker of the literary salon expresses ire and disappointment regarding the poetic climate of the time. He employs stock-and-trade phraseology to convey his concern. He uses phrases like 'nonsense poems' and addresses certain poets' misplaced self-designations as 'perfect practitioners' – terms with equivalents elsewhere in works of the nineteenth-century Persianate world. The nearly contemporaneous biographical anthologies from the Zand and early Qajar period employ equally dismissive language about certain classes of poets and bemoan the present dire state of poetic affairs in similarly scathing terms. One is reminded of the 'rose garden' conversations among members of the Isfahani Circle and the letter from Sabahi to Rafiq that reflected the same concerns and used similar language to do so. In the aforementioned cases and elsewhere, the general market for poetry and, in particular, the inept verse of certain classes of poets appear to be the objects of criticism. The language used by Kashmiri, in a work modelled upon Firdawsi's *Book of Kings*, suggests that the speaker of Kashmiri's creation was voicing concerns about those poets out of step with the tradition of the classical masters. Such language parallels commentaries by the Isfahani Circle of poets. Phrases such as 'the people of speech have come to an end' (*ahl-i sukhan khatm shud*) and other accusations mirror the language utilised by poets in Iran, such as Hatif and Sabahi. In other words, evaluating deleterious poetry unmoored from the classical tradition and its impact on poetic production was not the sole domain or concern of poets in nineteenth-century Iran.

The language of Kashmiri's speaker also resonates on a deeper level with discussions about the proper and authentic representation of the classical masters in contemporary verse. Kashmiri's interlocutor talks of poets who 'speak emptily of the esteemed masters and call themselves perfect practitioners'.[68] He also impugns those very same poets for knowing nothing but 'verse stealing' (*shi'r-duzdī*). Here, such criticisms are aimed not at those unwilling to engage with the classical tradition, but those feebly attempting to imitate the classical masters. The speaker displays disdain for those poets proclaiming perfection by borrowing the verses of the classical masters, which apparently is no better than 'verse-stealing'. This appears to express a general distaste for poets unsuccessfully imitating the classical masters, not for those who challenge such masters' poetic style per se. It bears remembering that the context for this discussion is not simply a literary gathering, but one where the poetry of Khaqani, Rumi and Sa'di was being recited. It begs the question: why would the speaker be so upset if the poetry of masters was already being recited among the participants of the literary gathering?

The criticism expressed by the unknown speaker and addressed to the members of the gathering elicited an impassioned response from Kashmiri. It sets in motion a challenge that would lead Kashmiri to pen his famous work. Indignant at the speaker's claim that the time of poets has passed, Kashmiri makes his position known with force. 'The flame of anger engulfed my mind', Kashmiri writes. 'I said to him: Oh friend, slow down and stop your foolish talk.'[69]

Kashmiri proceeds to correct the original speaker's perceptions of the current literary climate. He seeks to refute the argument that the time of the masters is over and to assert his own connection with them. Feeling personally slighted by the speaker's claims, Kashmiri defends his poetry to the gathering, challenging all present to 'scan the depths of my poetry line by line' and relate which verses have been stolen.[70] In other words, Kashmiri is challenging the members of the literary society to offer proof of his lack of poetic skill and any evidence that would place him in the category of poets unwilling to imitate, or incapable of imitating, the masters of classical tradition. When Kashmiri is finished with his impassioned response (thirty lines in all), the original speaker challenges him to back up his claims with action:

> 'Oh, from among all in poetry,
> > prepared for self-praise and claim
> You became angry for the sake of all,
> > you've been taken prisoner in place of all
> If you have a trace of truth-telling,
> > now is the time to prove your claim.
> And recite the tales of battle of that young lion,
> > the foreigner-breaking hero Akbar
> Who in the battle of Kabul, in the field of war,
> > was a lion-of-a-man scattering lions!
> Like his sword, make your language sharp in clarity
> > in his manliness, make your own manliness manifest
> Since you have made the claim, offer proof!
> > and, if not, then stop your idle talk!'[71]

While the exact nature of the exchange between the irritated member of the gathering and Kashmiri is not clear, it seems the latter was more than up for the challenge, either by imitating the masters in combatting a different *en vogue* style, potentially that of the 'fresh-speak' style, or by rising above contemporary poets who themselves were unproductively imitating the masters.

Buried in the *Book of Akbar*'s prologue, and rarely cited in connection with the text, is another understated aspect of Kashmiri's motivations in writing his work: the issue of patronage. Not unlike his Iranian counterparts, and nearly echoing the words of Azar Baygdili, Kashmiri references the issue of patronage and the plight of poets facing decreased opportunities. He beseeches all to refrain from claiming 'no poets exist in the world'. 'There are plenty of poets', he writes, 'but no patron.'[72] Introducing social and political realities which his interlocutor so casually brushed aside in favour of aesthetic judgements, Kashmiri is concerned with the role of poets, given the troubling lack of patronage opportunities. Kashmiri, again like Azar, is asking that the poets of his time not be judged according to the past experiences of the classical masters. The 'masters', as Azar said, were 'nurtured in the cradle of prosperity and peace, obtaining every want and wish beneath the shadow of the protection of the monarchs of the age' while 'the contemporaries' were not.[73]

It appears Kashmir was no kinder to Hamid Allah Kashmiri than post-Safavid Isfahan was to Azar Baygdili. The one-time literary paradise and 'Mughal Arcadia' remained socially chaotic and politically unsettled throughout Kashmiri's lifetime. Under Afghan (1753–1819) and later Sikh (1819–46) rule, Kashmir was dominated by times of political upheaval, intermittent attempts at revolt, oppressive rule and avaricious governors.[74] Kashmiri himself was no friend of the authorities. In his *Book of Injustice* (*Bibujnama*) he likened the rulers to wolves amid a population of sheep and bemoaned the depths of death and destruction into which Kashmir had fallen.[75] Again, the echoes of Azar resonate, as when the poet chastised Isfahan's new mayor as a 'crooked wolf' feeding off 'the pain of the flock'.

Kashmir's only respite from political and economic pressures during the period of Afghan and Sikh rule occurred during the rule of Sukh Jivan Mal (r. 1754–62), marked by a flowering of literary activity attached to patronage.[76] According to the anthologist Azad Bilgrami, Sukh Jivan Mal held weekly symposiums to which he invited all poets from the surrounding areas.[77] He also commissioned a group of poets to compose a history of Kashmir in the style of the *Book of Kings*. Bilgrami notes that the undertaking was carried out by five poets, each of whom had ten assistants; the entire process was led by a chief poet who had to approve each draft.[78] Kashmiri in all likelihood would have known of Sukh Jivan Mal's earlier project and would have regarded it as a stark change from his prospects for patronage some eighty years later.

The *Book of Akbar* offers compelling evidence for reconsidering what was involved in engaging with the Persian masters in the nineteenth century and the prospects for a 'literary return' outside of Iran. Kashmiri's poetic experience, such as bemoaning the poet's role, a lack of patronage and the desire to compose poetry in the style of the masters, closely mirrors the experience of the Isfahani Circle. The internal evidence of the *Book of Akbar* only strengthens this claim: a gathering in which the poetry of certain classical masters was recited; a lamentation for current poetic affairs; a decrying of the loss of patronage, and false claims of 'masterhood'. These tropes are taken for granted in the case of explaining 'literary return' in Iran, but cast aside when viewed outside of Iran's territory and captured in a demonstrably

'Afghan' literary product, composed in Kashmir, no less. But taken together, these contextual elements of the *Book of Akbar*'s composition contribute to a larger Persianate literary discourse of the time. The case for seeing a multi-regional engagement with the canonic masters outside of Iran is becoming more thinkable. Such a case is further augmented when the *Book of Akbar* enters the public domain.

Propaganda and Patronage: *The Victory Book of Kabul* by Qasim Ali

When *The Book of Akbar* entered the public domain it became part of the oral and literary landscape that helped bring it to life. Kashmiri anticipated that his work would be famously received in Kabul and elsewhere, writing in his epilogue:

> Now it travels the domain of the world,
> > adorning banquets of grandees.
> It travels to Kabul in every society,
> > like a spring breeze, from meadow to meadow
> Wise elders and enlightened minds
> > sit in the private banquet of the Amir [Dust Muhamamd Khan]
> Drinking my sweet speech,
> > imbibing my colourful poetry.[79]

While there is no hard evidence detailing the extent to which *The Book of Akbar* circulated, it is presumed that it was distributed widely at the time. Scholars investigating the topic conclude that copies of the work passed from hand to hand or that it was recited in various societies, not only among the population of Afghanistan but also in South Asia.[80] As evidenced by the manuscripts utilised in bringing *The Book of Akbar* to publication in the twentieth century, different manuscripts of the text were widely available, both in libraries and private collections.[81] The present-day location of various nineteenth-century manuscripts, in places like Bombay, Calcutta and Hyderabad, testify to its prevalence.[82] Chiriqani-Barchaluyi and Shafaq note the work's impact even further in writing that the 'spiritual influence the work had on the people of Hindustan (who were under British colonialism) and the nation of Afghanistan is unprecedented and unique', but this cannot be known with certainty.[83] In any case, it is likely that copies of *The Book of*

Akbar circulated in South Asia, passing from hand to hand and being recited in various societies.

The circulation of *The Book of Akbar* in Afghanistan and South Asia appears to have inspired the third war-ballad in imitation of Firdawsi's *Book of Kings* featured here: *The Victory Book of Kabul* by Qasim Ali. The circumstances associated with this work involve one of the more intriguing and confusing stories about the textual production of war-ballads in the aftermath of the first Anglo-Afghan War and pursuit by the British of their regional aims.

The confusion stems not least from the lack of unanimity as to the name of the author, the title of the text and its date of completion. C. A. Storey, for example, lists the author as Qasim Ali 'Qasim' Akbarabadi and the work as *The Battle of Kabul* (*Muharaba-yi Kabul*). Here he is following the information provided on the title page of an apparent lithograph edition that first appeared in Agra in 1855–6.[84] Other manuscript catalogues provide a range of names, titles and years of completion, such as: *The Victory Book of Akbar* (*Zafarnama-yi Akbari*) by Qasim of Agra completed in 1844–5;[85] *The Victory Book of Kabul* (*Zafarnama-yi Kabul*) by Khwaja Qasim Dihlavi completed in 1848;[86] and simply *The Book of Akbar* (*Akbarnama*), not to be confused with the text of Hamid Kashmiri discussed above.[87] Charles Rieu in *Catalogue of the Persian Manuscripts in the British Museum* refers to the work as *The Victory Book of Kabul*, with no author listed, completed in 1844–5.[88] Since this is the only manuscript I have been able to access, I will refer to the text as *The Victory Book of Kabul* with the most widely accepted author name of Qasim Ali.

The confusion over the author and title of the *The Victory Book of Kabul* is matched by the intrigue surrounding its composition. It is typically assumed that Qasim Ali did not simply compose the work in response to Kashmiri's *Book of Akbar*, but did so at the behest of the British. Unhappy with the circulation of *The Book of Akbar* and the manner in which it portrayed British defeat at the hands of the Afghans, the British evidently commissioned Qasim Ali to pen an alternative version of events. Accordingly, scholars have tended to view the work as a propaganda piece that was quickly lithographed and disseminated by the British to combat unsavoury depictions of their failings in Afghanistan. While *The Book of Akbar* has been viewed as 'the national and free history of Afghanistan'[89] and awakened 'the feelings of the people',⁹⁰ *The Victory Book of Kabul* is seen as having achieved little success or support among the general populace. As the author of such a presumed piece of propaganda, Qasim Ali has alternatively been described as a merchant or trader recruited by the English, a companion of Shah Shuja', or, more colourfully, 'a foreigner worshipper and fawner'.⁹¹

Qasim Ali's association with the British is clear. He was involved in political activities as an employee of Ross Bell, the political agent for Western Sindh, for whom he reportedly travelled to Baluchistan in 1840.⁹² One of the dedications in *The Victory Book of Kabul* is directed towards Queen Victoria, whom the author praises as the world-ruler and adorns with similar accolades.⁹³ It is primarily on these counts that Qasim Ali has been labelled a sycophant and apologist for the British. However, it is not certain to what extent the British actually sponsored *The Victory Book of Kabul*.

Criticism of Qasim Ali and scepticism towards his work have become somewhat of a tradition among Afghan scholars.⁹⁴ This nationalist approach has shrouded aspects of Qasim Ali's employment history and the socio-political context in which he was writing as well as having elided features of the work less in line with the anti-British narrative that has congealed in Afghan historiography. For example, while the praise for Queen Victoria appears in the first book of *The Victory Book of Kabul*, the work's second book opens with a dedication to Maharaja Savai Nani Singh, a member of the royal family of the Jaipur State in the mid-nineteenth century. Indeed, Qasim Ali boasts of his relationship to the Maharaja and implies that he composed this portion of the work after entering the Maharaja's service and leaving the employment of Ross Bell.⁹⁵

This incidence of multiple employers points to the ways in which Qasim Ali may have been less wedded to producing a British version of the first Anglo-Afghan War than to leveraging his work to receive patronage from whoever would be willing to grant it. Like many other administrators and secretaries of the nineteenth-century Persianate world, Qasim Ali was caught within the interstices of empires, where the transitioning of political authorities and the shift in language practices made the prospect of employment ephemeral. Searching for employment opportunities in this heady environment was of the utmost importance.

A closer inspection of the text reveals that Qasim Ali's work is not as pro-

British as presumed by its detractors. In describing the conditions under Shah Shujaʿ, which led to a general rebellion following his return to the throne by the British, Qasim Ali pulls few punches. He cites the 'intense tyranny and oppression of the Shah' as having created an atmosphere of general destitution and depravity. It was a situation in which the people of Afghanistan (especially women and children) were significantly worse off than in the time before the deposed ruler's return to the throne. Qasim Ali recounts:

> When a Shah diminishes the sustenance of the people
> > He will ruin the people and their households
> There is no patience for the hungry in pain,
> > he will make robbery, thievery and trickery.
> He will have no memory of honour and reputation,
> > and will sell his [own] women and children for naught.
> For each one who was previously destitute,
> > sixty women and children become orphans.
> All men and women will turn base and perverse,
> > in search of bread, they will turn impious and irreligious.
> In such intense tyranny and oppression of a Shah,
> > life and households will be destroyed.
> Death would be better than such a life
> > where one's women and children are destitute.[96]

The verse above is clearly not the work of someone who can simply be described as a lackey of the British or a companion of Shah Shujaʿ. His depiction of the travails of society following the arrival of Shah Shujaʿ and the British resounds with protest. The above selection portrays how societal norms of piety and religiosity were overturned and the traditional position of women and children undermined.[97]

Qasim Ali's depiction of the leader Akbar Khan, the nationalist hero at the centre of Afghan resistance to the British, is equally surprising in light of the work's supposed pro-British bent. He presents Akbar Khan as a man of valour and courage, not unlike the other war-ballads of the times. He celebrates, for example, Akbar Khan's killing of the British political agent William Macnaghten (d. 1841), who was negotiating the terms of the British army's withdrawal from Kabul.[98] Moreover, he depicts Akbar Khan as a leader in touch with the opinions of the people and in lock-step with the population's hostile attitude towards foreign occupation.[99] In this way, *The Victory Book of Kabul* is consistent in affirming Akbar Khan's honourable reception among the populace along with the other two war-ballads discussed here and in later historical works produced in twentieth-century Afghanistan.[100] Not as pro-British as it seems, *The Victory Book of Kabul* reflects more fully the social and political circumstances during which it was composed. The author's employment by the British, it seems, was only a part of the work's compilatory genesis.

Given its more balanced approach to the war's events and, at times, its anti-British interludes, it should be not surprising that *The Victory Book of Kabul* circulated more thoroughly than is often regarded. Its printing in Agra in 1855–6 may have garnered it few readers due to its likely association and distribution by the British, but the persistent idea that the work 'was quickly printed and soon disappeared' appears false. In fact, the first verified appearance of the text in a non-manuscript form was not in Agra, but in Lucknow in 1850–1. Selections from *The Victory Book of Kabul* appeared in a prose work by Munshi ʿAbd al-Karim entitled *The Battle of Kabul and Qandahar* (*Muharaba-yi Kabul va Qandahar*). Munshi ʿAbd al-Karim's work first appeared in Hindustani in 1847, but was later translated into Persian by ʿAbd al-Rahman Khan, the brother of the printer M. Mustafa Khan and owner of Mustafai Press which was responsible for the lithographed edition.[101]

ʿAbd al-Karim's work contains approximately two hundred lines penned by Qasim Ali. In the introduction, he refers to 'Munshi Qasim Jan's' *Book of Akbar* (!), stating that it was composed in 1847 – four years prior to its appearance in this work and nearly a decade before the Agra printing supposedly sponsored by the British. The inclusion of the poetry of 'Munshi Qasim' (Qasim Ali) in *The Battle of Kabul and Qandahar*, published years after its composition and a decade before its printing at Agra, further indicates the complicated and robust environment in which this war-ballad was produced, replicated and circulated.[102] Munshi ʿAbd al-Karim provides more clues to the text's provenance by noting that Munshi Qasim/Qasim Ali witnessed the events of the war himself and 'without deficiency, enthusiastically depicted the events of import and gallantry of both sides'.[103] Lauding his contemporary further, Munshi ʿAbd al-Karim continues:

Figure 3.3 Frontispiece of Munshi ʿAbd al-Karim's *Battle of Kabul and Qandahar* (*Muharaba-yi Kabul va Qandahar*), lithographed at Lucknow 1850–1.

> The truth is that the aforementioned author [Munshi Qasim/Qasim Ali] during this time, in which the market of poetry and prose is dull, eloquently stole for himself earlier speech from his contemporaries and equals.[104]

Once again one sees the well-established trope of a 'dull' 'market of poetry and prose' and the emergence of an author seeking to overcome it. The echoes of Azar and Hamid Kashmiri, who harboured similar sentiments, resound. For Munshi ʿAbd al-Karim, Munshi Qasim/Qasim Ali was not simply providing a service by narrating events of the first Anglo-Afghan War, but undertaking an unparalleled work in an otherwise dreary literary market lacking in talent. Perhaps this view is evidence of an author being gracious towards a colleague or attempting to depict the author on whose work he will rely in the most felicitous manner. But other evidence points to Qasim Ali's literary objectives as well, including his desire to imitate the work of Firdawsi and to have his work admirably received by his peers and by men of letters.[105] In the epilogue, with a sigh of relief for having completed his work, Qasim Ali looks to the heavens and thanks the 'noble Firdawsi [who] faced me from paradise (*firdaws*)'.[106]

Qasim Ali's coda to his *Book of Kings*-inspired work and overall desire to imitate one of the classical masters points to yet another of the many life forms a text like *The Victory Book of Kabul* can inhabit at once in the nineteenth-century Persianate world: a political tool in the eyes of the British, a means of employment for the author, and a source of inspiration and literary triumph in the eyes of the contemporary historian.

The War-ballad Market-place

There are clearly more to these three war-ballads of the first Anglo-Afghan War than the manner in which they have been condensed into Afghan nationalist or literary historiography. Assessing the reasons for their composition and the environment in which they emerged helps to better explain their place in nineteenth-century Persianate literary culture too. There is a fuller habitat that these war-ballads occupy, one that points to a very active space permeating society in oral, written and print culture during the nineteenth century. More than mere contemporaneous representations of the events of the first Anglo-Afghan War, constructed as war-ballads and based on the *Book of Kings* of Firdawsi, these texts were part and parcel of a free-flowing and interconnected market-place of Persian literary activity and culture in Afghanistan and South Asia in the nineteenth century.

All three of the texts featured here were products of primarily different, though not exclusive, discursive environments: *War Ballad*, the oral environment; *The Book of Akbar*, the literary environment; *The Victory Book of Kabul*, the social environment. Ghulami, as a witness to the war, sought to model his war-ballad in imitation of the *Book of Kings* in the first instance, reaching into the repository of epic literature and oral tales to find a narrative framework both appropriate for his task and recognisable by his audience. Kashmiri's *Book of Akbar*, produced a year later, likely benefited from the valiant and courageous tales of Afghan war heroes being shared among the populace, to which Ghulami's work contributed. Other authors narrating recent political events may, also, have benefited from the template established by Ghulami.

More than a nationalist tale of Afghan resistance to foreigners, Kashmiri's *Book of Akbar* connects with larger debates related to the composition of poetry imitating the masters at this time. In some respects, the *Book of Akbar* is a 'literary return' tale, written either in response to a scorned poetic style, possibly that of the 'fresh style' (*tāza-gūʾī*) of poetry, or to redress the ill-advised and poorly executed efforts of poets unable to imitate the ancients. The text reveals, albeit somewhat ambiguously, an engagement with debates and literary trends not usually associated with the output of poets from nineteenth-century Kashmir, or for that matter the non-Iranian Persianate world. What is clear, however, is that Kashmiri's prediction in his epilogue about the circulatory powers of his text proved correct.

The urge to circulate versions of the events of the war in imitation of the *Book of Kings* extended to the British, whose sponsorship of the third text, *The Victory Book of Kabul* by Qasim Ali, has been viewed as a piece of propaganda in Afghan nationalist historiography. But the text was more than a mere propaganda tool. Qasim Ali's employment history and criticism of Shah Shujaʿ (and by extension the British) makes it likely that he was more interested in the literary endeavour of the work itself and in securing patronage than in creating a tool of colonial propaganda. While the text at some point may have been sponsored by the British, most likely as a response to Kashmiri's *Book of Akbar*, it had multiple life forms, many preceding British involvement. The text itself was composed and in circulation between eight and eleven years prior to the printing at Agra in 1855 and its likely distribution under British sponsorship.

Collectively, the discursive environments of these three war-ballads offer a robust image of the ways in which the *Book of Kings*, the work of an undisputed 'ancient' in 'literary return' terminology, operated across a variety of planes and platforms in Afghan and South Asian society in the nineteenth century. Audiences existed for this type of poetic-political text; there were employers willing to sponsor their production and printers invested in their distribution. No wonder these texts circulated orally and in manuscript and print forms quite significantly.

The chronology and geography of war-ballad textual production help characterise this market-place. From the epicentre of the war in Kabul to Kashmir and finally to the cities of Lucknow and Agra, the market-place stretched over time from Afghanistan to South Asia while also appearing in new lithographic formats. The trajectory begins with Ghulami's *War Ballad*, a text composed while the war was still smouldering, the immediacy of its production evidenced not only by when it was written but by how it was looted from the scene of battle. Eastward in Kashmir, Hamid Kashmiri picked up the tales arriving in his domain from travellers moving east. This oral culture flowing into Kashmir made his work possible. Such travellers, like Kashmiri himself, may not have been directly aware of Ghulami's text, but they were participants in an oral environment that Ghulami helped foster and sustain. The fame of the *Book of Akbar* no doubt ventured back west into Afghanistan, either orally or through manuscript copies, buttressing the legendary status of its eponymous hero Muhammad Akbar Khan in Afghanistan. It validated Kashmiri's own boast that his tale would pass through the societies of Kabul 'like a spring breeze, from meadow to meadow'.

The Book of Akbar's movement eastward ushered the war-ballads into a jurisdiction beyond Afghanistan, to the world of British India and new technologies for distribution in places like Lucknow and Agra. The appearance of *The Victory Book of Kabul*, first in Munshi 'Abd al-Karim's work and later in a stand-alone format, confirms that the war-ballad texts related to events in Afghanistan were sought to be made accessible to a South Asian readership.

The exact role of the British in sponsoring, producing and potentially circulating a version of *The Victory Book of Kabul* in response to the prevalence of Kashmiri's *Book of Akbar* remains unknown. Known with more certainty is that the entry of *The Victory Book of Kabul* into the market-place initiated the dissemination of war-ballads on a transnational scale and in new forms of media. In a decade or less, these war-ballads went from being copied on looted paper in Kabul to being printed in major South Asian cities. No longer restricted to Afghanistan or solely the domain of oral and scribal culture, the war-ballads entered another realm. In the final analysis, the geography of these texts incorporated not only a variety of physical locations of production but also a constellation of different authorial intentions, modalities of distribution and methods of consumption.[107] Once again, one can see how the emergence and circulation of these texts points to the transregional dialogic character that has defined Afghan literary production. These texts remained part of a larger multilingual ecumene of cross-border exchange, where not only the epic tales but romances too continued to flow from Afghanistan to the Subcontinent. For example, the poet Niʿmat Allah, often referred to as the Firdawsi of Pashto, saw three of his romances printed in Delhi between the years 1883 and 1888.[108]

The phenomenon of texts seeking to record contemporary events in the style of the *Book of Kings* in the nineteenth-century Persianate world extends beyond the war-ballads of the Anglo-Afghan War. The desire to engage with the *Book of Kings* as a model for epic poetry *qua* history consumed a wide range of writers and patrons alike. This occurred most remarkably in South Asia, both for interfering foreign powers like the British and local South Asians – whether Hindus, Sikhs, Zoroastrians or Muslims.

Writing in the 1830s, the Persianist and British civil servant James Atkinson, in his introduction to an abridged translation of the *Book of Kings*, observed that 'in India … wherever the Persian language is understood and cultivated, the Shah Nameh is also highly prized'.[109] While the statement certainly applies to abridgements, translations, and the production of manuscripts and lithographs, it may equally extend to the continued practice of using the *Book of Kings* model to corral and explain contemporary events and recent history of the nineteenth century.

The *Book of George* (*Georgenama*), written by the Parsi Zoroastrian priest Mulla Firuz (d. 1830) and composed between 1811 and 1830 in Bombay, recounts the story of the British conquest in South Asia. Like the Anglo-Afghan war-ballads that would follow it, the text serves as yet another example of how the *Book of Kings* remained relevant in nineteenth-century South Asia, capable of blending older models of epic-history writing and sovereignty, on the one hand, with contemporary events and newly-arrived patrons, on the other. As Daniel Sheffield notes, 'the *Georgenama* provides a fascinating insight into the intellectual world of Persianate Bombay, a world in which poets actively sought the patronage of merchants and mercantile colonialists, and portrayed patrons' activities as continuations of ancient forms of sovereignty, establishing a Persianate literary basis for mercantilism and capitalism'.[110] As much a recounting of the British arrival in South Asia, the *Book of George* served to 'legitimize mercantile sovereignty in the context of Persian epic'.[111] It was the *Book of Kings* model that was relied upon for the execution of such a task, under the sponsorship of an East India Company officer, no less.

The *Book of George* was not the only *Book of Kings*-modelled text to be sponsored by the British in the nineteenth century. In the century's first decade, another non-Muslim, 'Shimbhu Brahman', recounted the exploits of the British in the *Book of Victory* (*Zafarnama*). The focus of the text is the military career and victories of General Gerard Lake (d. 1808), commander-in-chief of the British army in India under Marquis Wellesley.[112] British interest in sponsoring both the *Book of George* and the *Book of Victory* lends greater credence to British sponsorship of Qasim Ali's *The Victory Book of Kabul* following the first Anglo-Afghan War.

The role of the British in regional affairs, and military efforts to extend their influence, remained the theme par excellence in these texts. In 1855, while the Anglo-Afghan war-ballads continued to circulate, Raj Kunwar composed the *Book of Lahore* (*Lahurnamah*) in imitation of Firdawsi's famous work. The text detailed the wars between the British and Ranjit Singh (d. 1839) ending in the latter's defeat and the annexation of Punjab. It was dedicated to the Asaf Jahi ruler of Hyderabad.[113] Similar textual endeavours extended beyond the Persian language as well, in such languages as Balochi, Pashto, Punjabi and Urdu.

Figure 3.4 visualises the location of Persian texts produced in imitation of the *Book of Kings* and used to record contemporary events in nineteenth-century Afghanistan and South Asia. This map is not comprehensive as it does not include those texts without a reliable place of production, texts in languages other than Persian, or copies of known and unknown works awaiting discovery. Nonetheless, the market-place for texts modelled on Firdawsi's *Book of Kings* and appearing outside of Iran in the nineteenth century, as visualised in Figure 3.4, was in no way inconsequential. Incorporating oral, manuscript and print culture, these texts weaved together a transregional network of patrons, poets and printers. The power and currency of the *Book of Kings* model inspired a poet in Kashmir, a Zoroastrian priest in Bombay and a printer in Lucknow as much as British, Sikh and Muslim patrons located in courtly centres and elsewhere.

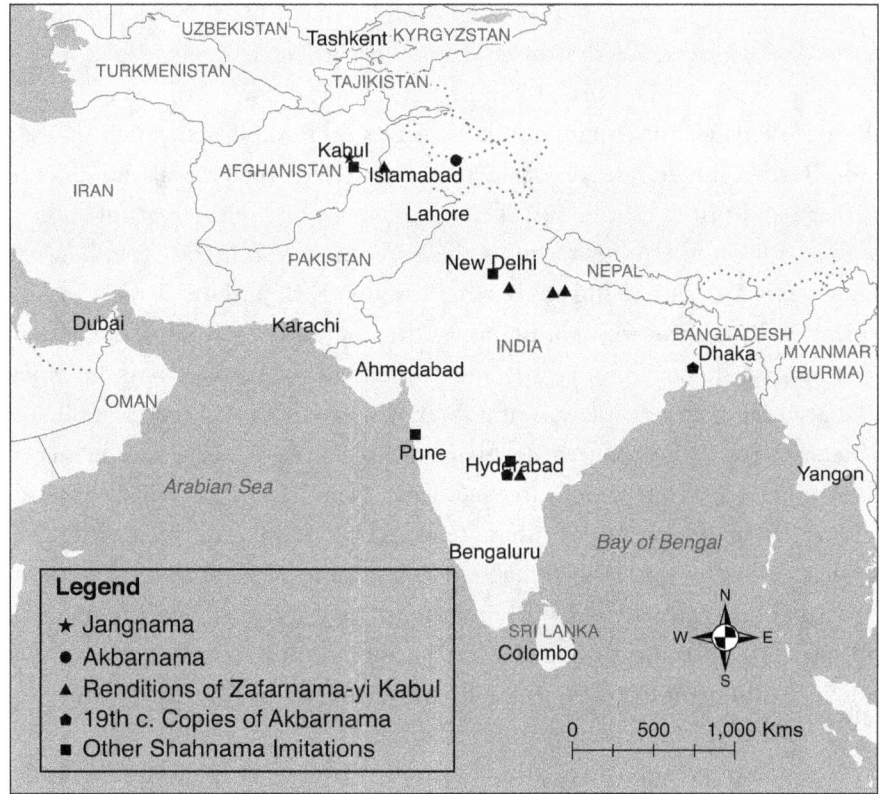

Figure 3.4 Market-place of Anglo-Afghan war-ballads and other Persian imitations of the *Shahanama* in nineteenth-century Afghanistan and South Asia.

Conclusion

The relationship between the war-ballads of the first Anglo-Afghan War and their prevalence throughout Afghanistan and South Asia is crucial for understanding the place of Persian literary culture in Afghanistan in the larger nineteenth-century Persianate world. The three texts featured here are bound together not only by their depictions of the Anglo-Afghan War, but also by the poetics they employ. Most importantly, works like *War Ballad*, *The Book of Akbar* and *The Victory Book of Kabul* helped create, and were supported by, a lively market-place for such texts. As the visual map in the preceding section indicates, these three works were part of a larger class of texts produced around the same time and in the same general vicinity.

The war-ballads of the first Anglo-Afghan War (and others like them) need not demonstrate the superiority of a particular literary trend at the expense of all others, as the discourse of 'literary return' in Persian literary history demands, or connote overt neo-classical sensibilities, which they do not. Rather, the production of the texts themselves, their circulation in oral, written and printed forms and their engagement by multiple sets of authors and patrons suffice to demonstrate the liveliness of this literary trend. While these texts may not be linked together through their authors' associations in a clearly defined collective or literary gathering (*anjuman*), along the lines of the Iranian 'literary return' movement, their story illustrates ways in which the prevalence and circulation of texts may help enrich the understanding of 'literary return' (or simply engagement with the 'masters') beyond a definition that appears solely applicable to what occurred in Iran or on stylistic grounds alone. The mere existence of these texts, to say nothing of the multilingual and cross-border space they inhabited, undermines any notion that the non-Iranian Persianate world of the nineteenth century remained uninterested in engaging with the ancient masters in any meaningful way – or, for that matter, indifferent to cultivating a discourse of literature centred on an imagined 'return' to certain figures dubbed 'masters'.

Nineteenth-century Afghanistan may not have witnessed a 'return' to the style of the ancients on the same terms as Iran. Nonetheless, how poets followed the classical tradition by imitating Firdawsi's canonic text demonstrates that at least one master's work remained a crucial enterprise with which to be engaged. Not unlike elsewhere in the eighteenth- and nineteenth-century Persianate world, the model of the masters in Afghanistan was utilised to help one find one's way in a politically chaotic and literary uncertain time – whether seeking to explain a contemporary event, such as war with an outside power, or trying to reconnect with a literary past deemed forgotten. If the meaning of 'literary return' is expanded beyond an Iranian-centric notion to include trends in textual production, debates concerning the imitation of the masters and circulating oral culture, then one can begin to view it as a set of normative practices operating across the Persianate world – that is, of course, if one wishes to maintain any adherence to the idea and importance of the category 'literary return' at all.

Notes

1. Diaries, journals and works of history produced around the time of the first Anglo-Afghan War and after are too numerous to mention. In addition to the works featured in this chapter, several notable texts recounting the war were composed in Persian by Afghans or other non-Europeans, such as: Shikarpuri, *Nava-yi maʿarik*; Shah Shujaʿ, *Vaqiʿat-i Shah Shujaʿ*. For an account of *Nava-yi maʿarik* and the circumstances of its composition, see Nawid, 'Historiography in the Sadduzai Era'. For a good bibliography of Persian and English sources related to the first Anglo-Afghan War see Dalrymple, *The Return of a King*. For insight into the British colonial apparatus and its understanding of Afghanistan at this time, see Hopkins, *The Making of Modern Afghanistan*. For the emergence of the Afghan State under Dust Muhammad Khan see Noelle, *State and Tribe*. For the impact of the British occupation on the Afghan economy and state formation, see Hanifi, *Connecting Histories in Afghanistan*.
2. On the dialogical process in Afghan history writing see Green, 'Introduction: A History of Afghan Historiography'. For an account of how the first Anglo-Afghan War was differentially depicted and memorialised by Afghan historians in the early twentieth century see Bakhtary, 'Fayz Mohammad Kāteb and Gholām Mohammad Ghobar's Divergent Allegories'.
3. Another war-ballad on the first Anglo-Afghan War from this period came to light in 1866–7 in Kabul from the shop of a perfumist. The work is anonymously written, though presumed to be the work of Mir Fayz al-Din bin Mir Imam al-Din Ahmad 'Darvish'. The work, based on an eye-witness account, includes information on the battles in and around Kabul and the various actors involved. See Ghubar, 'Jangnama nuskha khati'.
4. Green, 'Introduction: A History of Afghan Historiography', p. 50.
5. Noelle, *State and Tribe*, p. 38.
6. *Akbarnama* appeared in the pages of *Aryana* in 1948–9 and *Jangnama* in 1955–6.
7. The *Book of Akbar* appears to have circulated within the Afghan government prior to its publication, with one manuscript likely copied under the auspices of Habibullah's (r. 1901–19) court and another copied by the 'Office of News Reform in Kabul' in the mid-1930s. Along with a third manuscript copy from Peshawar, these copies were used to collate the print edition. See Kashmiri, *Akbarnama*, pp. 1–3. Only one manuscript of Ghulami's *War Ballad* is known to exist, cared for by the progeny of the famed national hero Mir Masjidi Khan,

likely circulating orally, primarily though not exclusively in the Kuhistan region. This manuscript formed the basis of the printed edition.
8. For the pivotal role played by Ahmad Ali Kuhzad in history writing and the reconceptualisation of Afghan history in the twentieth century see Green, 'From Persianate Pasts to Aryan Antiquity'. Green, 'The Afghan Discovery of Buddha'.
9. Nawid, 'Writing National History', p. 192.
10. For this process at work see Green, 'From Persianate Pasts to Aryan Antiquity'.
11. Hanifi, 'Colonial Production of Hegemony', p. 315.
12. The Kabul Literary Society was inaugurated by King Muhammad Nadir Shah (r. 1929–31) in 1931 and remained under the supervision of the king's secretariat and housed in the royal palace in Kabul. Hanifi, 'Colonial Production of Hegemony', p. 314. For the Kabul Literary Society's history and background see Ahmadi, 'Kabul Literary Society'. For a closer look at some of the Kabul Literary Society's activities see Fani, 'Becoming Literature', pp. 78–94.
13. Nawid, 'Writing National History', p. 189.
14. Farhadi, 'Anjoman-e Tarik-e Afganestan', p. 90. The Afghan Historical Society became affiliated with the Ministry of Culture in 1966. In 1978, it merged with the Academy of Sciences.
15. Habibi, 'Aryana'.
16. Nawid, 'Writing National History', p. 210. More recently, *War Ballad* and the *The Book of Akbar* have been situated within the context of the development of resistance poetry (*shi'r-i muqāvamat*) in modern Afghanistan. See e.g. Kazimi, 'Faryad-ha-yi mawzun'. For the interplay between archaeology and history writing in twentieth-century Afghanistan see Green, 'The Afghan Discovery of Buddha'. Green, 'From Persianate Pasts to Aryan Antiquity'.
17. Rashad, 'Darbara-yi zafarnama', p. 139.
18. Noelle-Karimi, 'Afghan Polities and the Indo-Persian Literary Realm', p. 77.
19. Green, 'Introduction: A History of Afghan Historiography', p. 9.
20. For information on the transnational characteristics of Afghan literary production, see Green, 'Introduction: Afghan Literature between Diaspora and Nation'.
21. Works of scholarship detailing the impact of the *Book of Kings* in these ways are too numerous to count. As an initial entrée into the references made here, see Askari, *The Medieval Reception of the Shahnama*. Melville, 'Rashīd al-Dīn and the Shāhnāmeh'. Lewis, 'The Shahnameh of Ferdowsi as World Literature'.

Melville '"Ali Yazdi and the *Shahname*'. Melville and van den Berg, *Shahnama Studies II*.
22. Rubanovich, 'Tracking the *Shahnama* in Medieval Persian Folk Prose', p. 33.
23. See Cornwall, 'Alexander and the Persian Cosmopolis, 1000–1500'.
24. Safa, *Hamasa sarayi dar Iran*, pp. 343–90.
25. Ibid., p. 354.
26. For the importance of the Alexander epic tradition to Persianate world more broadly, see Cornwall, 'Alexander and the Persian Cosmopolis, 1000–1500'.
27. Safa, *Hamasa sarayi dar Iran*, pp. 364–6.
28. Ibid., pp. 366–70. For a brief history of Qishm Island, including an account of events concerning Portuguese interference, see Potts, 'Qeshm Island'.
29. Amanat, '*Shahnameh-ye Naderi*', p. 296.
30. For information on the life and work of Saba see Aryanpur, *Az Saba ta Nima*, pp. 20–4.
31. For an overview of the role of Persian and Persian learning in Ottoman lands see Inan, 'Imperial Ambitions, Mystical Aspirations'.
32. Schmidt, 'The Reception of Firdausi's *Shahnama* among the Ottomans', p. 132.
33. Ibid., p. 133
34. Safa, *Hamasa sarayi dar Iran'*, p. 372.
35. Uluç, 'The *Shahanama* of Firdausi in the Lands of Rum', pp. 173–4.
36. For a brief overview of some of the uses of the *Shahnama* in South Asia during Mughal times see Sharma, 'Reading the Acts and Lives of Performers in Mughal Persian Texts', pp. 292–4.
37. Sharma, *Mughal Arcadia*, p. 138. For a brief overview of these two poets of Shahjahan's court and their poetic output see ibid., pp. 108–11.
38. Khan, 'Marvellous Histories', p. 533.
39. Ibid., pp. 534–6.
40. Ibid., p. 535.
41. Safa, *Hamasa sarayi dar Iran*, p. 374.
42. Noelle, *State and Tribe*.
43. The details of this paragraph come from Kuhzad, introduction to Ghulami, *Jangnama*.
44. Na'il, *Sukhan-sarayani*, p. 318.
45. Shamel, 'Afghanistan and the Persian Epic *Shahnamah*', p. 211.
46. Habib, 'Jumbish-i jangnama', p. 52.
47. Ghulami, *Jangnama*, p. 7. The reference to *Shab-i qadr* (in Persian) or *Laylat*

al-qadr (in Arabic) refers to the night when the Quran descended from the heavens and is commemorated each year towards the closing days of Ramadan.

48. Dupree, 'The First Anglo-Afghan War and the British Retreat of 1842', p. 524.
49. The extent to which Ghulami's tale circulated cannot be known definitively; however, in a predominantly non-literate society reliant on the oral transmission of tales and folklore it was likely vast. The *CIA World Factbook* placed the literacy rate in Afghanistan as of 2015 at 38.2 per cent.
50. For a similar example later in the nineteenth century and from where this concept is drawn see Edwards, 'Mad Mullahs and Englishmen'.
51. For information on *Jihad-i Akbar* see Green, 'Introduction: Afghan Literature between Diaspora and Nation', pp. 23–4. On Akbar Khan in the poetry of the Taliban see Hamid, 'Our Life, O Afghanistan' in Strick van Linschoten and Felix Kuehn, *Poetry of the Taliban*, pp. 121–2.
52. Habib, 'Jumbish-i jangnama-sarayi', p. 54.
53. Alexander Burnes, nicknamed 'Bukhara Burnes', was a British explorer and diplomat who was involved in the British occupation of Afghanistan and served as a political agent in Kabul following the removal of Dust Muhammad Khan from the throne. He was killed by a mob during the first Anglo-Afghan War in 1841 for reasons that likely included both his political activities and womanising among the locals.
54. Chihriqani-Barchaluyi and Shafaq, 'Bazgasht-i adabi dar shi'r-i Farsi-i Afghanistan', p. 58.
55. Habib, 'Jumbish-i jangnama-sarayi', p. 53.
56. Green, 'Introduction: A History of Afghan Historiography', p. 20.
57. Afaqi, 'Firdawsi-i Kashmir', p. 395. For a short biography of Kashmiri's life also see the entry on him in 'Adab-i Farsi dar Afghanistan', vol. 3, pp. 351–2.
58. Habib, 'Jumbish-i jangnama-sarayi', p. 55.
59. For a list of his other works see Afaqi, 'Firdawsi-i Kashmir', p. 396.
60. Ibid., p. 395.
61. See Habib, 'Jumbish-i jangnama-sarayi'.
62. Kashmiri, *Akbarnama*, p. 236.
63. See e.g. Tikku, *Persian Poetry in Kashmir*, pp. 204–7. Na'il, *Sukhan-sarayani*, pp. 271–4.
64. Na'il, *Sukhan-sarayani*, p. 313.
65. See Sharma, *Mughal Arcadia*, especially Ch. 4.
66. Meneghini, 'Kalim Kashani'.
67. Kashmiri, *Akbarnama*, pp. 14–15.

68. dam az ustādān-i ʿālī dihand/bi-khud nām-i ṣaḥib-kamālī nihand.
69. Kashmiri, *Akbarnama*, p. 15.
70. Ibid., p. 16.
71. Ibid., p. 17.
72. Ibid., p. 16.
73. Bland, 'Account of the Atesh Kedah', pp. 374–5. His translation.
74. Tikku, *Persian Poetry in Kashmir*, pp. 159–65.
75. Afaqi, 'Firdawsi-i Kashmir', p. 397.
76. Tikku, *Persian Poetry in Kashmir*, p. 165.
77. Ibid.
78. Ibid., pp. 188–9.
79. Kashmiri, *Akbarnama*, p. 235.
80. See e.g. Chiriqani-Barchaluyi and Shafaq, 'Bazgasht-i adabi', pp. 58–9.
81. See Kuhzad's introduction to Kashmiri, *Akbarnama*.
82. For the location of various manuscripts see Afaqi, 'Firdawsi-i Kashmir', p. 400. Storey, *Persian Literature*, section II, fasciculus II, p. 401. For the Bombay copy, see Sarfaraz, *A Descriptive Catalogue*, pp. 190–1. For the Calcutta copy, see Ivanow, *Concise Descriptive Catalogue*, p. 405.
83. Chiriqani-Barchaluyi and Shafaq, 'Bazgasht-i adabi', p. 59.
84. Storey, *Persian Literature*, section II fasciculus II, p. 402.
85. Sprenger, *A Catalogue*, p. 534 (no. 448).
86. *Fihrist-i kutub-i ʿArabi, Farsi va Urdu*, p. 248 (no. 203).
87. Storey, *Persian Literature*, section II, fasciculus II, p. 402.
88. Rieu, *Catalogue of the Persian Manuscripts*, vol. 3, p. 1038b (Or. 1961). This 'edition' comprises only extracts of the work, included within a manuscript featuring extracts of several other works compiled in 1850. It is now housed in the British Library.
89. Afaqi, 'Firdawsi-i Kashmir', p. 399.
90. Chiriqani-Barchaluyi and Shafaq, 'Bazgasht-i adabi' p. 59.
91. Compare Zhubal, *Tarikh-i adabiyat-i Afghanistan*, p. 264. Chiriqani-Barchaluyi and Shafaq, 'Bazgasht-i adabi', p. 59. Ghubar, 'Jangnama nuskha khati', pp. 2–3.
92. Rashad, 'Darbara-yi zafarnama-yi akbari', p. 144.
93. For two slightly different versions of this dedication see Zhubal, *Tarikh-i adabiyat-i Afghanistan*, pp. 274–5. Qasim Ali, *Zafarnama-yi Kabul*.
94. Rashad, 'Darbara-yi zafarnama-yi akbari', p. 139.
95. Ibid., pp. 157–8.

96. Munshi 'Abd al-Karim, *Muharaba-yi Kabul va Qandahar*, p. 55. This selection (and others cited in this section from Munshi 'Abd al-Karim's work) can also be found in Sara, 'Du ravayit az yik hamasa'.
97. For a more recent example of poetry which reflects how the emergence of new structures of power and social order were seen to have upturned societal norms and values in Afghanistan see Edwards, 'Words in the Balance'.
98. Munshi 'Abd al-Karim, *Muharaba-yi Kabul va Qandahar*, p. 65. Sara, 'Du ravayit az yik hamasa', p. 48.
99. Munshi 'Abd al-Karim, *Muharaba-yi Kabul va Qandahar*, p. 77. Sara, 'Du ravayit az yik hamasa', p. 49.
100. See Bakhtary, 'Fayz Mohammad Kāteb and Gholām Mohammad Ghobar's Divergent Allegories'.
101. See Ivanow, *Concise Descriptive Catalogue*, p. 12 no. 22. The text was also lithographed in Urdu by Matba'-i Masihi in 1852, under the title *Muharaba-yi Kabul dar Urdu*.
102. Questions remain about the timeline of the *Zafaranama-yi Kabul*'s composition, its distribution and the role played by the British, including the precise timeline of British sponsorship and whether the British sponsored the original composition in 1844 or the printed Agra version in 1855.
103. Munshi 'Abd al-Karim, *Muharaba-yi Kabul va Qandahar*, p. 2. Some sources offer evidence that Qasim Ali may not actually have participated in the war, and thus 'Abd al-Karim's claim must be considered inconclusive. See Rashad, 'Darbara-yi zafarnama-yi akbari', p. 141.
104. Munshi 'Abd al-Karim, *Muharaba-yi Kabul va Qandahar*, pp. 2–3.
105. See the epilogue to Qasim Ali, *Zafarnama-yi Kabul*.
106. Ibid., p. 25.
107. For information on the 'geography of the book' as a multi-faceted framework for understanding the production, distribution and circulation of texts see Ogborn and Withers, *Geographies of the Book*.
108. Heston, 'Pashto Oral and Popular Literature', p. 142.
109. Atkinson, *The Shah Nameh of the Persian Poet Firdausi*, p. xxiv.
110. Sheffield, 'Frankish Wine in Persian Bottles', p. 25.
111. Ibid., p. 4.
112. See 'Zafarnama (For General G. Lake)' in Ivanow, *Concise Descriptive Catalogue*, pp. 403–4.
113. Raj Kunwar, *Lahurnama*.

4

Debating Poetry on the Edge of the Persianate World: Arcot c.1850

One of the more curious aspects of *A'zam's Rosegarden* (*Tazkira-yi gulzar-i A'zam*), a biographical anthology (*tadhkira*) recounting the lives and works of Persian poets of mid-nineteenth-century Carnatic, is that the entry on the local poet Mawlavi Muhammad Mahdi 'Vasif' (d. 1873) spans more than twenty pages. The author of this work, who may or may not have been Muhammad Ghaws Khan Bahadur 'A'zam', the last Nawab of Arcot, clearly had a great deal to say about Vasif, who was still alive at the time of writing.[1] This is especially true when the length of this entry is compared to that of all the others, which at most amount to no more than a page or two.

The initial portion of the entry follows the long-established template of biographical anthologies by noting Vasif's birth, education and employment: he was born in 1802–3, studied Persian poetry with his father and taught at an East India Company (EIC) school for seven years. The entry remains positive in nature. The author notes that Vasif entered the Nawab's exclusive Persian poetic society in 1846 at the urging of one of its presiding heads and that among the attendees his 'face shone with reverence'.[2] On account of his many scholarly works, the author continues, Vasif reached a position of honour. There was, however, one work that the author of *A'zam's Rosegarden* viewed with the utmost disdain: Vasif's own biographical anthology of poets entitled *Mine of Jewels* (*Ma'dan al-jawahir*). 'It is not a secret', the author of *A'zam's Rosegarden* writes, 'that Vasif in his own *tadhkira* had criticised the words of poets in complete mockery and impudence. I have presented many of these [errors] in their appropriate place and written answers to them.'[3] So does the assault upon Vasif and his work begin.

The author proceeds methodically to list the errors found in Vasif's *tadhkira* on a variety of topics. He accuses Vasif of misunderstanding certain points of prosody (*ʿaruż*). He mentions that Vasif erroneously stated the death date of a certain poet, when it was well-known that the poet was alive and well after that date. He notes that Vasif mis-states the number of Arabic works of Mir Azad Bilgrami (d. 1786) as two, when in fact Bilgrami wrote seven. He even notes that Vasif was wrong to state a certain poet's largesse from a particular ruler as being 3,000 rupees, when in fact the actual sum was 2,000 rupees. Overall, the author of *Aʿzam's Rosegarden* goes to great lengths to nitpick over some very minute details of Vasif's work, challenging him wherever it can be determined that he mis-stated a fact, no matter how small.

On the surface, the quibbling is clearly an effort to present Vasif's general scholarship as careless, inattentive to details and generally unworthy. A much larger purpose, however, seems to motivate these critiques: the author was trying to undermine Vasif's trenchant criticism of the great South Asian poet ʿAbd al-Qadir 'Bidil' (d. 1721), whose work would later be considered the apogee of the so-called 'Indian Style' in Persian literary history. After presenting Vasif's opinion on Bidil, the author articulates his own argument and that of a few other prominent writers in support of the maligned poet.

This entry on Vasif is not the first we hear of him or his *Mine of Jewels*. In fact, the introduction to *Aʿzam's Rosegarden* states that it was Vasif's work that inspired this *tadhkira* in the first place:

> I inspected the *Mine of Jewels* by Vasif and I concluded clearly that the aforementioned work in many places did not penetrate the depths of poetic intricacies. His pen importuned upon the words of the able masters with unwarranted objections. Thus, the ocean of [my] temperament once again raged and the sea's pearl of [my] contemplation boiled; the pure answers of which I encased in this *tadhkira*.[4]

For all the hostile fireworks inaugurating *Aʿzam's Rosegarden*, the text was not, in fact, the first biographical anthology attributed to Nawab Muhammad Ghaws Khan, nor the only one of its time dedicated to the Persian poets of his court and its environs. Nor can it even be claimed that this work provides the most insightful account into the scope and nature of Persian literary activity at the Nawab's court. That text, which will be explored in detail further below, is *Binish's Notices* (*Tazkira-yi isharat-i Binish*). Rather, the value of *A'zam's Rosegarden* is found in the manner by which it frames the issue of the 'fresh' (*tāza*) style of poetry – the pre-eminent debate facing the greater Persianate literary world of the time – with local politics and personal rivalries among poets of mid-nineteenth-century Carnatic. This debate cuts to the heart of how the Persian poetic culture of Carnatic can be situated within the larger Persianate world at the time, in South Asia and beyond.

The introduction to *A'zam's Rosegarden* may begin with the justification that it was written as a rejoinder to another locally produced biographical anthology of poets, Vasif's *Mine of Jewels*. But by its conclusion, fittingly in its entry on Vasif himself, the work widens its lens beyond the local rivalries and specific errors of Vasif's text to a larger topic facing the legacy of Persian poetic evolution, one that was being discussed elsewhere in the Persianate world. The occurrence of such literary debates enriches our understanding of mid-nineteenth-century Carnatic's literary climate – at once exceedingly local yet still connected to the greater Persianate world. How such a situation unfolded is the story of this chapter.

The literary debates and rivalries of the Arcot court do not only highlight the vibrancy of Persian poetic culture occurring outside of Iran, a legacy dismissed and marginalised by larger renderings of Persian literary history maintaining the primacy of 'literary return' in Iran and the narrative of Persian's 'decline' in South Asia. Also, the example of Arcot demonstrates how poets in nineteenth-century South Asia grappled with the Persian canon, understood their poetry vis-à-vis the great 'masters' and sought to determine what constituted acceptable poetry accordingly. In other words, around the same time as the 'literary return' was in full flower in Iran, poets in South Asia also sought to re-evaluate their poetry in light of contemporary poetic trends, and that of the past, in a relatable fashion. Moreover, this example provides us with a case of what it was like to debate Persian poetry during a time when the Persianate world was fracturing, and in a place where the cosmopolitan value and use of Persian was dwindling.

The chapter begins with a brief history of the Nawabs of Arcot, an examination of the life and times of the last Nawab and the literary activities of his court. The focus then turns to the local network of Persian poets at Arcot and the rivalry among them. The chapter concludes with a discussion of poetic rivalry and how this competition relates to debates concerning the larger Persianate world.

Pivot of Persian: The Life and Times of Nawab Muhammad Ghaws Khan 'A'zam'

> Persian in Madras was like a body without a soul,
> Like the Messiah the sublime A'zam brought it to life.[5]

When Muhammed Ghaws Khan ascended the throne in 1825 under the care of a regent, the Nawabs of Arcot were no more than titular heads of state under the suzerainty of the British East India Company. The relative political and economic autonomy once achieved by Mughal-appointed governors and later independent rulers of the territory during the period from 1698 to 1801 was now over.[6] In 1801, the British leveraged accusations of political malfeasance and financial mismanagement to force the Nawabs to sign a treaty declaring the British right to select the next ruler and exercise suzerainty over the state in exchange for a stipend.[7] Nonetheless, as the political and financial fortunes of the state began to wane, the Walajahi court rose to new heights of princely splendour and lavishness, with a greater attention to 'the sacred and ceremonial functions of kingship and … rituals which exalted the status of the ruler and his kin'.[8] The Arcot state was well positioned in this regard prior to the treaty in 1801. It had become an attractive destination for poets, Sufis, scholars, administrators, artisans and military men as early as the reign of Saʿadatallah Khan, who was appointed governor (ṣūba-dār) of Carnatic in 1710. In the early eighteenth century and after, due to the disruption of patronage networks at other Muslim courts, Carnatic witnessed an influx of individuals looking to serve the state in a variety of capacities, leading to the appellation 'Shahjahanabad [i.e. Delhi] the small'.[9]

Policies during the forty-six-year reign of Muhammad Ali Walajah (r. 1749–95) helped continue the trend. Muhammad Ali's court attracted government servants, soldiers, jurists, literary men and Sufis in search of employment and patronage, all while he further developed administrative structures, absorbed subordinate vassals and imposed streamlined forms of revenue collection upon the populace.[10] Many of those venturing to Carnatic, like the Walajahi rulers themselves, were from among the north Indian urban gentry.[11] In this respect, the Arcot state under the Walajahis helped harbour and grow an Urdu-speaking Muslim elite. The Nawabs also employed groups of non-Muslims to fit their needs as an ambitious state in the southern part of the Subcontinent. Among them were the Niyogis, whose variegated linguistic skills allowed them to act as 'social and economic intermediaries between the local world of the village and the cosmopolitan world of the court'.[12] The Nawabs equally sought to incorporate and co-opt non-Islamic religious symbols, such as the patronage of Hindu places of worship, thereby practising a statecraft that transcended communal and religious boundaries.[13]

Crucial to the Arcot state's development as a centre of patronage for literary and scholarly activity was Muhammad Ali's decision to move his court from Arcot to a lavish residence at Chepauk next to Fort St George, Madras in 1766. The move to Madras marks a symbolic turn in the development of the Arcot state and is indicative of the further enmeshing of the activities of the court with that of the EIC. The employees and attendees of the court now found themselves in closer proximity to EIC officers, offices and institutions potentially in need of their services. This proximity allowed such individuals to better service both the Nawab's court and the EIC, which many would do later in the century and after. Local Muslim poets and scholars found easy employment teaching Persian, Arabic and Hindustani at the Company Madrasa or served the EIC in other capacities, such as private language tutors, interpreters or assistants.[14] The move to Madras also led the Arcot state to become more embroiled in financial dealings with the EIC, its officers and private individuals. This practice of borrowing large sums of money from outside sources proved detrimental to the long-term sovereignty of Arcot, eventually serving as one of the justifications for the 1801 treaty.

It was into such a courtly atmosphere that Muhammad Ghaws Khan found himself when he came to the throne in 1825. As was he just over one year old at the time, he was placed under the regency of his uncle, 'Azim Jah. More than half of Muhammad Ghaws Khan's life (he died aged thirty-one) was spent under a regent's control and devoted to educational activities that included, among other subjects, the study of Persian literature. His early engagement with Persian poetry in particular proved crucial in defining the cultural parameters of his court, his later literary activities and his overall poetic outlook. It informed and inspired his later rule as a Nawab invested

Figure 4.1 Portrait of the last Nawab of Arcot, Muhammad Ghaws Khan Bahadur 'Aʿzam' (d. 1855). Courtesy Royal House of Arcot.

in the promotion of Persian literary culture and as a participant in that culture as 'Aʿzam' ('the grandest', his pen name). During his reign as Nawab, Muhammad Ghaws Khan served as the promoter, protector and arbiter of Persian literary activity.

The young Nawab's early education followed established curricular norms and practices found throughout the Persianate world at that time. The curriculum was based on the study of Arabic, the Quran, the Islamic sciences, Persian literary texts and the art of Persian composition. On the surface, his education was not altogether exceptional compared to that of previous princes or the contemporary poets later active in his court, but this formative education would have a lasting impact.[15]

The Nawab's early association with the poet and scholar Sayyid Abu Tayyib Khan 'Vala' (d. 1848), for example, would affect the direction of literary developments and debates years later at his court. The young Nawab met Vala around the age of twelve and appointed him his poetry teacher in 1835.¹⁶ Under Vala's tutelage, he read a variety of Persian texts and was guided through the intricacies of poetic composition and stylistics. Vala became influential in poetic activities and debates during the Nawab's reign not only because he was the Nawab's teacher but through his instruction of other poets.

The Nawab's early education was also influenced by his introduction to the poetry of Nasir Ali Sirhindi (d. 1696), one of the great South Asian poets of the late Mughal period. The Nawab's admiration for the poetry and style of Sirhindi left a deep impression. He sought to imitate Sirhindi's style and recognised him as his model (*muqtadā*) in his later writing.¹⁷ Sirhindi's poetry too would be a central part of the literary affairs that consumed the Nawab's court and would continue to shape his own poetry.

Even though the Nawab of Arcot had become no more than a titular position by Muhammad Ghaws Khan's lifetime, the EIC nonetheless sought to influence his educational development. The Court at Madras, through its government agent at Chepauk, encouraged the Nawab to take his study of English and the 'branch[es] of Science' more seriously. The agent even attempted to coax the Nawab and his handlers into allowing him to spend the final years of his education at Calcutta, where the 'qualifications which were calculated to throw a lustre over the throne of his ancestors would be most readily acquired'.¹⁸ This suggestion, along with others, met with resistance. Eventually, the British authorities in Madras were forced to abandon their overtures. In their estimation, the Nawab's resistance was indicative of an individual indifferent to the future duties of his rule and of the overindulgent relatives charged with his care.

This view of the young Muhammad Ghaws Khan as a disinterested and lackadaisical prince at the centre of a disorganised court was only the initial formulation of the British impression of the Nawab. This impression persisted and developed further beyond his childhood with only slight modification. Later on, he was increasingly seen as a profligate ruler mired in debt and inattentive to his financial affairs. The Court of Directors in London was most critical of the Nawab, formulating their criticism of his financial affairs as a consequence both of his own actions and of his advisors' – the same factors referenced in its earlier criticism of his education. In response to a series of political letters in 1849 detailing recent financial developments, the Court of

Directors expressed its 'regret that extravagance and bad advisers have already involved this young Prince in heavy pecuniary embarrassments'.[19] There was indeed evidence of the Nawab's financial mismanagement and woes. He often found himself in arrears and seeking out assistance from the EIC or private citizens to lift him out of debt. In one memorable case, a group of Kashmiri merchants blocked the gate of the Nawab's court to prevent him from making the pilgrimage to Mecca until he paid them money he owed.[20] In the realm of learning and education, however, the British assessment could not be further from the truth. Whereas the British saw a disinterested prince making little progress in his studies, the Nawab was engaged in a more rigorous study of Persian poetry and literature. Under the pen name 'Aʿzam', the Nawab began composing Persian and Urdu poetry with increasing ease during his youth.

In the face of British suzerainty and increased management over military and political matters, the Nawab and his court sought to protect whatever was still in their control. In specific terms, this concerned the upbringing and education of the Nawab as an heir to the throne; more generally, it involved the cultural direction and composition of court activities. The Nawab was able to maintain control over cultural affairs at his court most prominently through his engagement with and promotion of literary activities. He collected books in Arabic and Persian on a wide array of topics and his royal library 'contained almost all of the eminent works in all the three languages [Arabic, Persian, Urdu] on the various branches of learning'.[21] He established several printing presses for publishing classical works in Arabic and Persian.[22] He oversaw construction of a state library in 1850 to house books and manuscripts collected from across South Asia and abroad.[23]

The realm of Persian literary-cultural activities firmly anchored the Nawab's court. He provided patronage and bestowed titles on poets. He founded a literary society as an officially sanctioned assembly that closely guarded its membership, and sought to establish standards of Persian poetry and delineate its proper composition. The Nawab took such deep pride in its establishment that he sent thirty-one copies of *Binish's Notices* (*Tazkira-yi isharat-i Binish*), a work devoted to recording the literary society's activities and the lives of participant members, to the Madras Court for distribution. It was the sole work sent by the Nawab to local British authorities.[24]

Nawab Muhammad Ghaws Khan was not only a patron of Persian literary activities, but also an active participant devoted to shaping their development. He composed his own verse in Persian and wrote two Persian *tadhkira*s (or had them commissioned in his name).[25] The dictionary *Sea of 'Ajam* (*Bahr-i 'Ajam*), by the poet and scholar Mawlavi Muhammad Husayn Qadiri 'Raqim' (d. 1888), exemplifies the attitude of recognising the Nawab as an esteemed Persian poet and critic. Raqim dedicates his work to the Nawab, not by celebrating his just rule, powers and beneficence, but by praising his poetic voice, critical discernment, command of language and comprehension of difficult topics.[26] More than being commended as the Nawab of Arcot, he is admired as the poet 'A'zam'.

The insistence of Muhammad Ghaws Khan and the Arcot court on promoting and maintaining an allegiance to Persian literary activity is certainly antithetical to the narrative of Persian's 'decline' in post-Mughal South Asia. There is no doubt that the Persian language found itself in a transitory role in eighteenth- and nineteenth-century South Asia, in particular on account of the rise of Urdu, English and other regional languages, as outlined in Chapter 2. Such developments were rapidly unfolding long before Muhammed Ghaws Khan came to the throne. Nonetheless, Persian remained relevant for the Nawabs of Arcot well into the middle of the nineteenth century, as it did for other locales. In the case of the Nawabs of Arcot, the continued adherence to Persian literary norms was both a matter of practicality and the assertion of cultural independence. The emergence and consolidation of the nascent state necessitated the development of bureaucratic models dependent on Persianate norms for which out-of-work cadres of littérateurs, courtiers and administrators from the North filled a ready need. Likewise, the proximity of the court to a seat of British power, which still relied on Persian-based bureaucratic norms to conduct business, granted the language a continued position of primacy as a medium of regal and official cultural power. For the Arcot court, which had little opportunity for political independence under British suzerainty, the promotion of Persian literary activity served as the most appropriate and recognisable linguistic and social medium for maintaining its cultural bona fides, both in terms of past practices and in accordance with the ongoing attitudes of the British. In the cultural and political nexus defining the relationship between the Arcot court and the EIC at Madras, these were roles Urdu was not yet equipped to fulfil.

Mapping Networks

The details and nuances of such a vibrant Persian literary culture at Arcot, how it functioned, who participated in it, and its place within the post-Mughal landscape, are best seen by looking at the Nawab's literary society. The poetic society of Nawab Muhammad Ghaws Khan, established in 1846 and lasting for roughly ten years until the Nawab's death, was an officially sanctioned affair that met once a week at the royal residence. Here, professional poets, scholars and court administrators congregated to recite their own verses, critique the poetry of their peers and engage in discussion. Even though several poets in attendance were known to compose both Persian and Urdu verse, including the Nawab himself, the society restricted its work to the composition and discussion of Persian poetry alone.

Most of the extant information relating to the Nawab's poetic society comes from Sayyid Murtaza 'Binish' (d. 1849) and his *Binish's Notices* (completed 1848–9).[27] The purpose of this work was to document the poetic society as well as the lives of other contemporary poets in the area of Carnatic. Binish died in 1849 and consequently was only able to witness the first years of the Nawab's poetic society; his biographical anthology nonetheless provides a wealth of information. It includes information on the poetic, familial and employment backgrounds of the society's members as well as other poets in Carnatic. By situating the society in the larger literary context of Carnatic, *Binish's Notices* catalogues the various inter-relationships among poets, administrators and elites composing Persian poetry during this time. Figure 4.2 presents a general overview of the network of poets as depicted by Binish. All the poets featured here were recorded in entries in *Binish's Notices*, but only a selection of them were members of the Nawab's poetic society. These latter individuals are marked by light grey circles. As can be seen from this network map, the poetic society and its members were part of a larger literary and social network extending beyond the confines of the Nawab's court. Lines between individual poets in this map designate either familial or instructional connections. Additional maps, found below, will discuss these relationships directly. Here, what is offered is a general overview of the interconnected world of poets in nineteenth-century Carnatic on the broadest of levels.

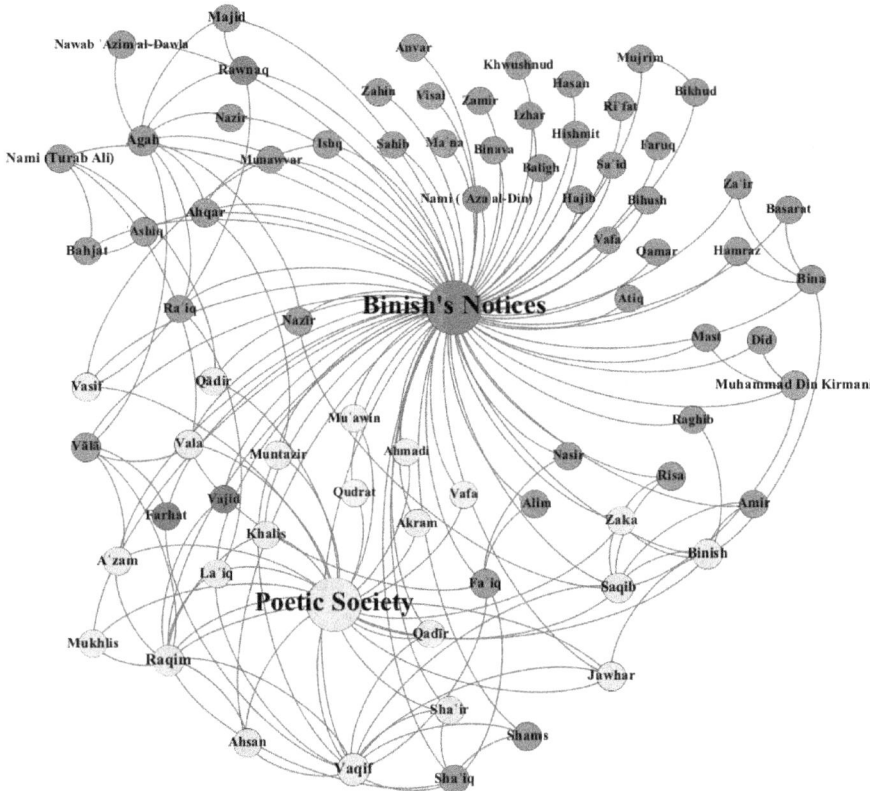

Figure 4.2 General overview of the literary networks of Carnatic as reconstructed from the biographical anthology of Persian Poets, *Binish's Notices* (1848–9).

The location of the poetic society at the Nawab's court made it an exclusive affair. The attendees were rigorously vetted, only being accepted by the Nawab or one of the assembly's leading figures. As a result, it mostly consisted of well-known poets, scholars and administrators employed at the court. These would be the key figures in the debates shaping the scope and direction of Persian literary activity during the Nawab's reign.

At the head of the poetic society was Raqim, a revered master of Persian poetry in Carnatic. He served as the instructor in poetry for many individuals during the time and received the title 'Mellifluous' (*shīrīn sukhan*) from the Nawab. When the Nawab's teacher Vala died in 1848, Raqim became the Nawab's instructor in poetry.[28] He also served as the headmaster of the

Nawab's madrasa, appointed to that position in 1851–2.²⁹ At the poetic society, however, his role was largely ceremonial. The actual managing of the society's meetings was left to two judges (*ḥakamayn mushāʿira*), the poets Miran Muhay al-Din 'Vaqif' (d. 1854) and Muhammad Qudratallah Khan Gupamavi 'Qudrat' (d. 1864).

Every poet present at the society had the ability to challenge the words of their peers by deeming them unacceptable and 'without proof from the words of the masters of language'. These challenges could result in possible embarrassment, erode the poet's confidence in presenting verses again or cause the accused to stop attending the society's gatherings in the future.³⁰ According to Binish, the two judges' mediation would end by sending the 'deficient one' on his way with 'his ignominy consigned by [their] resplendent thinking and sound reason'.³¹ In actuality, the record of Vaqif and Qudrat actually dismissing anyone from the society is less definitive.³²

Among the society's members were attendants of the Nawab's court and several individuals whose fathers had attained positions of distinction at the Arcot court previously.³³ Nearly all those present were born and raised around Arcot, and many had studied poetry with teachers like Vaqif or Raqim. The most notable exception to this local profile was the Baghdad-born poet Mirza 'Abd al-Baqi al-Sharif al-Rizvi 'Vafa' (d. 1856), whose travel and employment opportunities took him to Madras. Like many others he participated in the society at the Nawab's invitation. Due to his previous travel in Iran, the Nawab also requested that Vafa 'participate in the society and serve as arbiter of Persian discussions'.³⁴ Also present was Vasif, whose publication of the controversial biographical anthology, mentioned at the outset of this chapter, would initiate personal rivalries and poetic clashes at the Nawab's court.

The Nawab's poetic society did not encompass all Persian literary activity in mid-nineteenth-century Carnatic. Rather, it was part of a more extensive literary landscape. *Binish's Notices*, the window into the members, affairs and structure of the poetic society, makes this abundantly clear. The text contains a wealth of information, beyond the Nawab's court-sponsored activities, enabling one to identify a constellation of individuals for whom Persian poetry remained a preferred means of poetic expression. The *tadhkira* highlights the lives and careers of professional poets, scholars, elites, secretaries, administrators, judges, revenue collectors and teachers whose similarities in education and professional experience, not to mention the inter-relationships among them, reveal a social network of individuals for whom Persian poetry remained relevant in post-Mughal times. These individuals, no matter their particular career choice, moved in many of the same social, literary and scholarly circles.[35] Binish's biographical anthology provides a view of these associations and trends from the ground up, expressed through the poetic activities of various elites. Armed with this information, one can map an extensive world of Persian poetic culture in Carnatic.

Of the roughly seventy poets recorded in *Binish's Notices*, around two-thirds did not attend the poetic society, but nonetheless entered the purview of the author as men who continued to compose Persian poetry, particularly around Madras in the mid-nineteenth century. Indeed, to earn a spot in the work, one's presence in Madras or its environs seems to have been a prerequisite. Except for a few cases of poets situated in Hyderabad, whose presence Binish discovered through his brother Mir Mahdi al-Husayni 'Saqib' (d. after 1886/7), the poets included in Binish's work are restricted to the Nawab's domain and its immediate environs. Madras and its vicinity were home to the Nawab's court and the seat of British power, a vibrant metropolis providing an array of employment and poetic opportunities. Such opportunities attracted men from near and far and drew them into local bureaucratic and literary networks. Not unlike their predecessors (and in some cases their direct ancestors), who served as administrators and in other professional capacities for the Mughals, these men held a variety of professions but continued to compose Persian poetry.

Of the poets active in Carnatic at this time, some were affiliated to the court of the Nawab while others were employed by the East India Company. The poet Maulavi Taj al-Din 'Bahjat' (d. after 1854/5), for example, grew up in Madras and held various judicial positions under the British. He also composed a tract on the science of prosody (*'ilm-i 'arūż*), used by local students.[36] The poet 'Khwushnud' (d. after 1848–9) served as chief justice of the superior court in Madras, yet still found time to engage himself 'day and night' in *dhikr* (remembrance of God) and the composition of poetry that tended to be mystical (*'irfānī*) in nature.[37] The profiles of such individuals are by no means atypical of the world of Persian literary culture in South Asia, as the production of poetry extended well beyond the professional class of poets able to survive by their literary endeavours alone.

Men also came to Madras from afar, looking for opportunities and 'people of government' (*ahl-i ḥukūmat*) for whom they could put their skills to use.[38] The poet Mawlavi 'Abd al-Vudud ''Ashiq' (d. 1852), for example, hailed from near Allahabad and came from a family of administrators. He headed to Madras in accordance with the request of 'Europeans' (i.e. the British). He achieved positions in district tax collection in Natharnigar, before attaining the post of head tax-collector in Changalpit.[39] The poet 'Hasan' (d. 1842–3) came to Madras from Benares in search of employment, gaining an appointment as an instructor of Arabic and Persian to English officers at the Company school in Madras.[40] By coming to Madras, men like 'Ashiq and Hasan were entering a local network not just of administration and employment, but also one of poetry.

If it was the possibility of employment that drew them to the Nawab's domains in the first place, then it was their commitment to the composition of Persian poetry that brought them together and earned them a place in Binish's biographical anthology of poets. The conjunction of ample job opportunities and the presence of a literary culture allowed such a community to thrive. Participants could mix with like-minded men of letters, engage in debate and even instruct others in poetry. The local network of poets welcomed newcomers from beyond the region, as did the poetic society.[41] Such chances for individuals outside of the Nawab's domains were made possible because of the existence of a developed circle of local elites committed to the use and practice of Persian poetry.

The nature of this local network is available due to Binish's absolute insistence on providing the details of poets' educational and poetic backgrounds. His entries weave through each individual's poetic life, identifying with whom they studied instructional books in Persian, had their verses corrected, trained with in poetry, and generally came into contact with during the time of their development as poets. His information describes the connections among the individuals listed, enabling an enmeshed network not just of poets, but of brothers, sons, uncles, administrators and other elites to emerge. It is not uncommon for a biographical anthology to note such information, but Binish's listing of each poet's Persian educational and poetic background in such a deliberate and consistent manner results in more than a simple recording of basic biographical details. It gives his work its structural backbone and internal organisation; it allows it to become a ledger of collective memory. His *tadhkira* appears, equally, to be an effort to record those individuals who composed Persian poetry in mid-nineteenth-century Carnatic and an effort to emphasise an individual's 'Persian credentials' and poetic lineage. *Binish's Notices*, by its sheer focus on the array of individuals composing Persian poetry and their traceable poetic roots, stands as testament to the strength and position of Persian poetic culture in Carnatic during that time. It is not surprising that the Nawab sent copies of this work to his British counterparts, revealing as it was of the strength and maintenance of Persian poetic culture in his domain, a project that he valued above all else.

The intricate connections between the Persian poets of mid-nineteenth-century Carnatic through their training in poetry and family relationships are highlighted in Figure 4.3. Members of the Nawab's poetic society are once again indicated by light grey circles. The lines connecting various individuals denote either an educational or instructional relationship in poetry (dark lines) or a family relationship (light lines).

This map allows one to see with greater clarity just how enmeshed a network existed among these poets. One can see how the exclusive poetic society of the Nawab was situated and entangled among a much larger literary landscape and network of elites, connected through family bonds and poetic lineages. Situated within this larger literary landscape, the poetic society of Muhammad Ghaws Khan takes on a slightly different colour.

Writing Rivalry

Even within this geographically contained network around Carnatic, poets were actively engaged in poetic debates prevalent elsewhere in the Persianate world, including some beginning to appear in Qajar-era biographical anthologies. Much like poets elsewhere in South Asia and Iran at this time, the Carnatic poets debated the merits, value and characteristics of the 'fresh-speak' style, known for its inventive word choices, complicated literary acrobatics and overall juxtaposition with a 'simple' style of poetry. Evidence from biographical anthologies also dramatises the ways in which Carnatic poetic debates were framed by local politics – a volatile mix of aesthetic tastes,

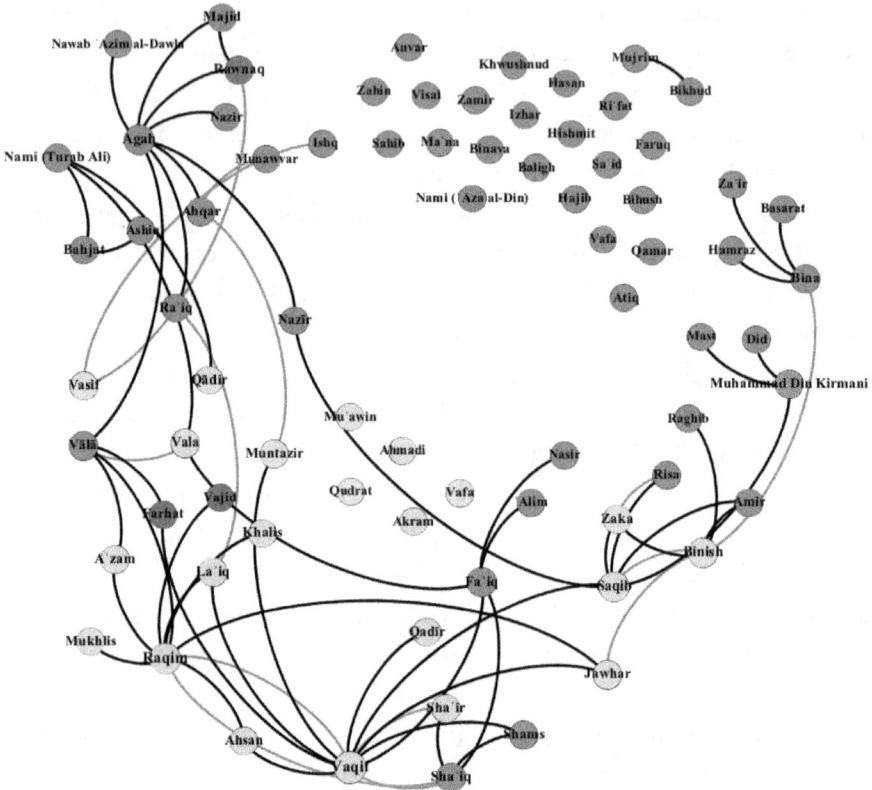

Figure 4.3 Network map of instructional and family connections among poets in nineteenth-century Carnatic.

personal rivalries and professional ties. Indeed, the debate over the 'fresh' style during the Nawab's time progressed along both poetic and personal lines.

In mid-nineteenth-century Carnatic, not necessarily unlike in other places, entry into disputations on poetics occurred through the writing of biographical anthologies. Unique to the Carnatic experience, however, is that the mid-nineteenth century witnessed an outpouring of biographical anthologies in a short time-span, with authors engaging in direct conversation with the previously written works of their contemporaries. In other words, authors positioned their own anthology as a response to the work of their peers, making *tadhkira* composition the preferred method of entering their opinions into the ledger of current debates and responding to contem-

Table 4.1 Major biographical anthologies and responses during the reign of Muhammad Ghaws Khan A'zam (d. 1855).

Title	Author	
Guldasta-yi Karnatik	Ra'iq	1832–3
Tazkira-yi Nata'ij al-afkar	Qudrat	1842
Tazkira-yi subh-i vatan	A'zam	1842–3
Ma'dan al-jawahir	Vasif	1844
Javab-i i'tirazat-i Vasif	Raqim	1845
Tazkira-yi isharat-i Binish	Binish	1848–9
Tazkira-yi gulzar-i A'zam	A'zam	1852–3
Hadiqat al-maram	Vasif	1853–4
Sham'-i mahfil-i sukhan	Sayyid 'Abd al-Latif	c.1862
Husn-i khitab va radd-i javab	Vasif	1870

poraries. From a quantitative perspective, Arcot witnessed one of the highest volumes of *tadkhira* production anywhere in the Persianate world during this time.

The Nawab himself entered the world of *tadhkira* production and poetic debate in 1842–3, around a year after he reached the age of maturity and attained the throne. *Dawn of Homeland* (*Tazkira-yi subh-i vatan*) appeared under his name and features a discussion of local Carnatic poets. Its publication signals the beginning of a remarkably productive period of *tadhkira* writing by a series of authors who collectively sought to shape the memory of Persian poets and poetry at the court and beyond.

The author of *Dawn of Homeland* expressly stated that he wished to position his work at least as an addendum to the recently composed *Bouquet of Carnatic* (*Guldasta-yi Karnatik*) completed in 1828–33 by the poet 'Ra'iq' (d. c.1832–4). The author of *Dawn of Homeland* justifies his work as a response to what he found lacking in the accounts of the poets presented in Ra'iq's anthology, a common justification in producing *tadhkira*s of Persian poets. He resolved to offer commemorations of some additional notable poets of his time. The result was modest.[42]

A year later, in 1844, the poet Vasif completed his controversial work entitled *Mine of Jewels*, which more fully set in motion the debates at Arcot over poetics and larger questions of Persianate literary history. This work is no longer extant and even the nature of its original distribution is in question.

What is known of *Mine of Jewels* comes from the reactions it elicited among Vasif's opponents and detailed in other works. Vasif's opponents accused him of unduly criticising Mawlana Baqir Agah (d. 1805), the pre-eminent poetic instructor of Arcot during the time, and Nasir Ali Sirhindi, whose poetry the Nawab sought to imitate in his own work. According to Binish, Vasif in *Mine of Jewels* 'made shameless insults referring to Nasir Ali Sirhindi and other masters and treated most of [their] poetry without decorum'.[43] The specifics of Vasif's 'insults' are not indicated.

To grasp the grounds of Vasif's criticisms, one must consider Vasif's own poetic pedigree and personal relationships compared to his contemporaries'. Unlike many of his contemporaries or even predecessors, Vasif cannot be connected to any of the major poetic networks prevalent at Arcot. Instead he was a man apart: neither his poetic lineage, family background nor employment directly crossed paths with the Nawab and his inner circle. Figure 4.4 depicts the networks of poetic instruction at Arcot and highlights the isolation of Vasif. In this map, individual nodes vary according to size, with the larger nodes indicating those poets who were more central to the network as a whole. For example, the centrality of Vaqif, who served as one of the judges of the Nawab's poetic society and was a pre-eminent instructor in poetry of the time, occupies the largest node. Equally prominent for his centrality in the overall network at Arcot is the prominent figure of Agah, who Vasif supposedly unduly criticised in his work. The main poets caught up in the drama of the court, namely Agah, the Nawab (A'zam), Raqim and Vasif, are highlighted with a darker colour for easier identification. Vasif's position in the network, unlike the other three individuals', was marginal and can been by his location in one of the outer rims of the network.

Vasif's poetic instruction in Persian came primarily at the hands of his father 'Rawnaq', who according to Binish favoured a 'simple' (*sāda*) type of poetry.[44] The preference for such a style of poetry and its effect on Vasif's poetic outlook, while not to be over-emphasised, can be seen in the way Vasif instructed his son, ''Ishq'. 'Ishq's poetry, like that of his grandfather Rawnaq, is described as being that of a simple style, hinting that Vasif's family had a predilection for that style of poetry in the training of their offspring.[45] Vasif's early exposure and commitment to such a simple style helps to explain his opposition to the poetry of Sirhindi and other like-minded poets being imi-

ARCOT c. 1850 | 181

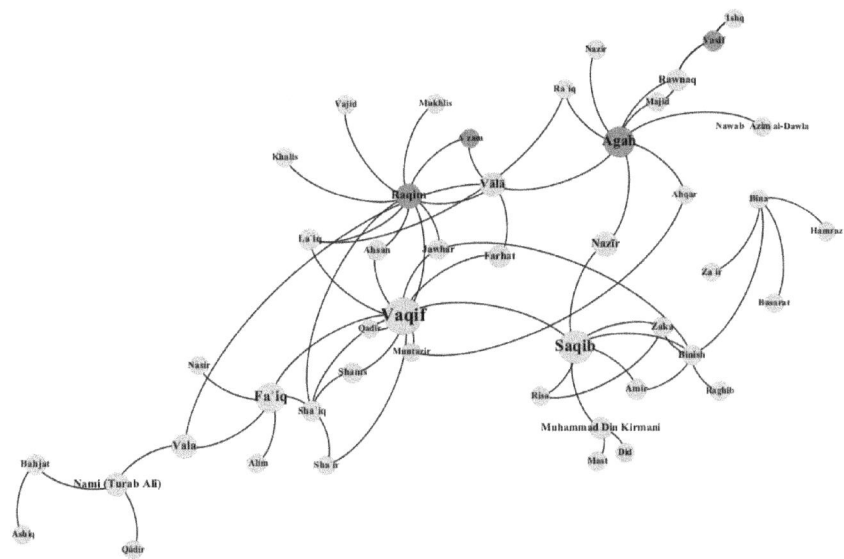

Figure 4.4 Network map of poetic instruction in nineteenth-century Carnatic and the isolation of the poet Vasif.

tated during the time.[46] While most poets active in Carnatic were instructed and influenced by each other, and were primarily focused on the more complicated 'fresh style', Vasif and his family were in a realm apart.

Binish further emphasises Vasif's differences from his contemporaries by noting that he was 'more in the company with the eloquent ones of *'Ajam'* and 'acquainted with many of their conversations'.[47] The full meaning of Binish's comment is not made clear, but the implication that Vasif had a poetic outlook distinct from his colleagues by being more engaged with the poets and conversations of *''Ajam'* is suggestive. Though geographic fault lines had not yet fully cast a shadow over different styles of Persian poetry, equating the 'fresh' style with Indian-born poets and a 'return' poetry with poets from Iran, Binish's comment hints that such lines were beginning to form.

The most likely association Binish was making between Vasif and *'Ajam*, however, was one that meant to align the poet with native speakers of Persian, not the geographic locale of Iran or Iranian-born poets per se. One element of the debate about poetics in the South Asian context centred on questions about one's poetic ability based on native language, that is, whether a poet was a native speaker of Persian or not.[48] Questions about one's ability to 'speak for Persian poetry', or perhaps more accurately 'speak Persian poetry', based on one's native tongue are raised later by the author of *A'zam's Rosegarden*. Nonetheless, the possibility should not be discarded that the borders of what constituted *'Ajam* for poets in South Asia was beginning to morph from a geographic space encompassing an expansive Persianate world to one restricted to Iran. That this conceptualisation remained at a distance from the Iran-centric notion of *'Ajam* emerging around the same time in Zand and Qajar biographical anthologies, as noted in Chapter 1, makes it all the more intriguing.[49] It is indicative of a general awareness by multiple literary communities that the structure and foundations of the Persianate world – at least as understood through poetry – were being reconfigured.

Vasif's aloofness from the networks and styles of other poets prevalent at Carnatic, his education and instruction of his own son in a 'simple' style of poetry and his greater familiarity with the poets and debates of *'Ajam* suggest a likely result: Vasif was increasingly viewed as an opponent of the 'fresh' style and its poetics. When the dust of the personal animus that hovered over the debates between Vasif and his opponents is finally cleared away, the difference in poetic opinions driving the debate becomes evident. But first the dust over Vasif's 'insults' would have to settle.

The response to Vasif's criticism of Agah, Sirhindi and others as outlined in *Mine of Jewels* was swift. A year later, Raqim (one of the Nawab's closest associates) penned his answer in a tract entitled *An Answer to Vasif's Objections (Javab-i i'tirazat-i Vasif)*. Raqim's outright disdain for Vasif and his recent work were made clear from the outset. His criticism firmly focused on what he perceived to be Vasif's breach of decorum (*adab*), chiding him for his 'scoffing, cursing, and reproach of the eminent learned men and grand orators'.[50] Raqim goes on to note that he beseeched Vasif to remove such 'baseless objections' from his work but the latter refused. Raqim summed up his feelings in the following poem:

> When Vasif wrote the *tadhkira*
> in which he made his reproach clearly
> Upon the words of the chosen poet
> Sayyid Nasir Ali Vali [Sirhindi]

Also to disgrace the esteemed Agah
> he used impoliteness [stemming from] impurity of the heart

Raqim found in this year in history
> the sigh of awareness from the Zulfiqar of Ali.[51]

This account differs significantly from the way Vasif later remembered the exchange. A full quarter-century after Raqim offered his indictment, Vasif addressed the matter in a work that appeared in 1870 entitled *The Beauty of Discourse and Rebuttal* (*Husn-i khitab va radd-i javab*). This work sought to address thirty-seven allegations that Raqim had made against Vasif.[52] His recollection could not be further from what Raqim had penned twenty-five years earlier. According to Vasif's version of events, not only did he willingly submit his earlier work to Raqim for inspection, but he also was amenable to having the 'unsound and reprehensible' portions related to Sirhindi (about 'three to four pages') removed.[53] When Raqim 'opposed the settlement', having noted that 'you [Vasif] are older than me and your skills in the Persian language are apparent', Vasif considered the matter closed.[54] Only it wasn't: Raqim penned his pamphlet shortly thereafter, and a quarter-century later Vasif was still trying to set the record straight. The difference between the accounts of Vasif and Raqim is striking and reveals how their rivalry was based upon personal enmity as much as differing notions of poetry. On the personal level, each poet attempted to prove that his own conduct was proper while his rival's was not, Raqim claiming that Vasif remained at fault for being unwilling to remove the disparaging remarks after he had asked him to do so, and Vasif accusing Raqim of being in the wrong for apparently acknowledging that he, Vasif, should leave the work as is, but then reneging on his word.

It is worth noting that the opinions offered by Vasif in *Mine of Jewels* may not have been made solely according to poetic tastes. His criticism, or 'shameless insults' as Binish called them, may have had a personal element as well, particularly his comments concerning Agah. Vasif himself was not a direct student of Agah, but his father Rawnaq was, making the criticism of the pre-eminent poetic instructor of Carnatic somewhat puzzling (Figure 4.4). This is especially true since Agah and Rawnaq worked together to correct the poetic verses of the one-time presumptive heir to the throne, Taj al-Umara' Ali Husayn Khan 'Majid'. The relationship between Rawnaq and Agah, however, may have been somewhat complicated by the politics of royal succession. Upon the death of Nawab 'Umdat al-Umara' in 1801, his son Majid was passed over for the throne (on the recommendation of the British) in favour of Muhammad Ghaws Khan's grandfather Nawab 'Azim al-Dawla. This occurred when Taj al-Umara' refused to play by the new set of rules established by the British. With Nawab 'Azim al-Dawla on the throne, instead of Majid, Rawnaq's star at the court may have fallen. Unlike Agah, Rawnaq did not train the new Nawab in poetry; rather, his fortune may have been solely tied to the rejected Majid, who, in any case, would die later in 1801. When Majid died, both his personal effects and the state library, which had been his and his father's possession, passed into the hands of the new Nawab.[55] Rawnaq withdrew to Hyderabad, and Agah continued to wield influence with the royal family through those poets trained by him. If Vasif wanted to interpret such events as a rivalry that resulted in the waning of his father's influence at the court, then he would not need to imagine much. Vasif certainly held Majid in great esteem.[56]

Such are the complications of the professional and political dynamics among literati at a courtly centre. But Binish gives no indication in his anthology that the rivalry between Raqim and Vasif was much of an issue during the time of the poetic society's gathering. In fact, if one is to believe Binish, then the entire rivalry between the two poets never really reached fever pitch at all, at least during the time of his writing. If, by downplaying the affair, Binish believed he could ease the rivalry between the two men or possibly erase it altogether, he would be sorely disappointed. With the publication of *A'zam's Rosegarden* in the Nawab's name in 1852–3, Vasif's circumstances would change. No longer were his reputation, scholarship and opinions about poetry being questioned by a fellow poet, albeit by the Nawab's instructor and companion, but in a work bearing the Nawab's name. The publication of *A'zam's Rosegarden*, not the tract by Raqim from several years earlier, would lead Vasif to challenge Raqim's claims against him. Moreover, *A'zam's Rosegarden* best encapsulates the debates vexing Carnatic poets about their place in the Persianate world and literary history.

Speaking for Persian

The personal clashes, poetic rivalries and debates over poetics at the court of Nawab Muhammad Ghaws Khan reached their apogee with the publication of *A'zam's Rosegarden* in 1852–3. This work, more than any preceding or following it, laid bare the substance of conflicts among poets at the Arcot court. Here one gains the fullest understanding of what exactly Vasif wrote in his *Mine of Jewels* that so upset his rivals (beyond the various 'insults') and warranted a head-on response. Here too one begins to understand how the poets at Carnatic fit into larger debates around poetry in a crumbling Persianate world.

The idea that *A'zam's Rosegarden* was composed as a rejoinder to Vasif's *Mine of Jewels* is evident from the outset, reinforcing again how authors used the genre to set the record straight on poetic matters, and how *tadhkira* production at the Nawab's court remained a competitive venture. The introduction, however, offers only a general justification for the *tadhkira* and is no more than an opening salvo against Vasif. The bulk of the impressions and criticisms are found in the entry on Vasif himself, some four hundred pages later (due to the alphabetical organisation of the work). The entry spans some twenty pages and includes the author's critique and challenges to his biographical anthology composed several years earlier. Overall, it attempts to question the work's scholarship, culminating with its objection to Vasif's portrayal of the South Asian poet Bidil, whose work would later be considered the apogee of the complex 'fresh' style in Persian literary history.

Significantly, it is Vasif's discussion of Bidil, rather than his criticism of Agah and Sirhindi (two personages close to the Nawab's heart and that of his coterie), that the author wishes to address most forcefully. This approach underscores that Vasif's work was not viewed merely as a breach of proper conduct on the basis of his personal 'insults', but also as one that opposed a certain type of poetry, presumably exemplified by Bidil. The status of the 'fresh-speak' style in general, if not Bidil's poetry in particular, occupied several South Asian authors and poets, as will be seen below.[57] The opening of Vasif's opinion of Bidil, as cited in *A'zam's Rosegarden*, runs as follows:

Concerning Mirza Bidil he [Vasif] wrote that 'the Mirza, mercy upon him, in his God-given insight toward the creation of meanings, started to produce some foundations for fresh conversations. He gained an abode in the eyes of Indians, like a pupil. However, in the eyes of the eloquent ones of *'Ajam*, his invented terms appeared [as] inverting the rules of poetry and excessive, which seemed like a pain-causing mote in the eye's socket. Consequently, they started finding fault in his work. Mawlavi Azad Bilgrami, who was a distinguished learned man of equitable temperament ... says that the noble Quran, even though it is the wondrous words of God the almighty, descended suitable to the idioms of Arab men of correct speech so to be closer [i.e. easier] to comprehension. Thus, in the Persian language, when even a [poet of] unquestionable perfection like Bidil invents words, how could the people of ordinary speech accept him? For instance, in his elegy for his own son, he writes:

Whoever was gracefully planting two steps
    had a staff in their palm from my finger.'[58]
har-ki du qadam khirām mī-kāsht
    az angushtam 'asā bi-kaf dāsht.

Vasif's insistence, in the above passage, that supporters and opponents of Bidil's poetry were divided along fault lines, with Indians in the former camp and the 'eloquent ones of *'Ajam*' in the latter, is of primary importance here. It is this division that defines Vasif's opinion and should be seen as strongly indicative of the manner in which the boundaries of *'Ajam* were being reconfigured and understood. Again, the 'eloquent ones of *'Ajam*' in this context are not necessarily synonymous with 'eloquent ones of Iran' or 'Iranians' – a distinction bestowed upon them by later historians – but more likely correspond to 'eloquent ones whose native tongue was Persian', leaving necessarily ambiguous the question of birthplace. Nonetheless, this does not detract from the fact that differences in poetic taste were being ascribed to different groups, whether one was a native or a non-native speaker of Persian. Indeed, what constituted the boundaries of *'Ajam*, or the world of Persian speakers, was shrinking.

The fact that it was a South Asian poet and scholar in the nineteenth century making this claim, not an Iranian one of the nineteenth or twentieth century writing within an Iranian nationalist discourse, makes this distinction all the more interesting. Vasif, it may be said, was a part of what the literary scholar Shamsur Rahman Faruqi sees as a tendency of nineteenth-century South Asian poets to more definitively and uniformly disparage the Persian poetry of South Asians at the expense of the 'purity' of poetry composed by native Persian speakers.[59]

Vasif was not alone in viewing Bidil's poetry as a lightning rod, or even unique in choosing the particular expression 'to gracefully plant' (*khirām kāshtan*) to criticise the poetry of Bidil and to judge his poetics. This expression became a favourite target of many South Asian commentators in the eighteenth and early nineteenth centuries. The author of *A'zam's Rosegarden* references these commentators to provide support for his own opinion of Bidil's poetry. The inclusion of these earlier opinions underscores their accessibility in mid-nineteenth-century Carnatic, made possible by advanced techniques in printing and copying (some of which were adopted by the Nawab himself) and by increased book-centred learning and knowledge in late Mughal times.[60] The presence of these contemporary opinions in *A'zam's Rosegarden* is a testament to the vibrancy of the nineteenth-century South Asian book market and to the manner in which biographical anthologies augmented the transmission and circulation of ideas and texts during this era.[61]

A'zam's Rosegarden continues with a pastiche of the opinions of Agah (d. 1805), Mir Azad Bilgrami (d. 1786), Khan-i Arzu (d. 1756) and Mirza Muhammad Hasan 'Qatil' (d. 1817) regarding the poetry of Bidil and, more generally, the use of idioms in Persian poetry. Opinions range from an outright dismissal of Bidil's usage to the rejection of Bidil's critics. The latter three commentators addressed the use of the expression 'to gracefully plant' directly in their respective works: Mir Azad in *The Royal Treasury* (*Khizana-yi 'amira*); Arzu in *The Assembly of Delicacies* (*Majma' al-nafa'is*); and Mirza Qatil in *The Tree of Desires* (*Shajarat al-amani*).

The opinion of Agah, however, is offered first and is based on an 'abbreviated epistle' focused on the structure of language in prose and poetry. Agah comments in his letter that all languages are susceptible to new idioms, even if the great orators of Arabic and Persian would prefer that such usages did not enter poetry or prose.[62] Agah's argument is a defence of Bidil and affirms his right to use new idioms. The author of *A'zam's Rosegarden* then presents the opinions of Azad, Arzu and Qatil in succession and notes that all three have said that the words of Bidil 'went against the usage of the Persians' (*khilāf-i muḥāvara-yi Fārsīyān*). In this statement we have an initial indication that the general dismissal of Bidil's poetry was one founded on linguistic, not geographical, affiliation. The author then notes that Mir Azad believed that Bidil 'had invented some strange things in the Persian language that people of everyday speech do not accept', a slight variation on the same statement by Mir Azad that Vasif included in his *Mine of Jewels*.[63]

Summarising the opinion of Arzu, the author of *A'zam's Rosegarden* relates that Arzu too recognised Bidil as having instigated bold usages in Persian, which people across South Asia accept.[64] This passage makes no precise reference to 'Persians' (*Fārsīyān*), but its very omission makes apparent the demarcation between their unstated opinion, on the one hand, and the people of South Asia who accept Bidil's poetry and its invented terms on the other. Although Arzu criticises Bidil for using idioms that run counter to accepted speech, his overall judgement of the poet in *The Assembly of Delicacies* is overwhelmingly positive. He refers to the poet as his teacher and defends him generally against criticism.[65]

The author of the *A'zam's Rosegarden* concludes with the opinion of Qatil, who, more plainly than the previous two commentators, remarks on how critiques of Bidil's poetry are founded on extra-literary criteria, such as Bidil's Indian identity. Qatil is perhaps an ideal candidate for detecting such complexities and subtle shifts in the identity politics of literary discourse. Born a Bhandri Khatri and named Diwani Singh, he became an accomplished writer and a convert to Shi'i Islam.[66] Qatil wrote the following regarding Bidil:

> Such do they relate of Mirza Bidil, mercy upon him, that in the elegy of his own son he created the idiom 'to gracefully plant' and the reason is on account of the Mirza's Indian-ness (*Hindī būdan-i Mīrzā*). If he had been from the soil of Isfahan or another locale in Iran (*az khāk-i Iṣfahān yā dīgar bilād-i Īrān*), then no one would reproach him.[67]

Qatil's opinion, hinging on Bidil's 'Indian-ness' as the source of his plight among critics, aligns best with that of the author of *A'zam's Rosegarden*. The author of *A'zam's Rosegarden* goes on to offer a justification for the use of 'to gracefully plant' as an acceptable phrase given the poetics of Bidil's poetry. But it is Bidil's homeland of South Asia, rather than that of Iran, that preoccupies the author. It is the clearest indication yet among the opinions offered that geographic fault-lines perhaps do have a role to play in this debate for some of its participants. No matter that both the *South Asia*-born Vasif and Azad Bilgrami viewed Bidil's poetics as problematic. It is the undue chastisement that the great South Asian poet has endured for not being born in Iran, and presumably for not being a native speaker of Persian, that draws the author's ire. Building on Qatil's example, the author of *A'zam's Rosegarden* offers the following summation:

> The source of the attack of the Iranians (*Īrāniyān*) relating to the curse and scorn of the exalted Mirza [Bidil] is, one, the Indian origin (*Hindī nizhād būdan*) of this esteemed master and, two, the Sunni religion of this man of excellence. But if this celebrated one had been from Iran then they would have elevated him to the ninth clime and would have brought his spell-shattering (*bāṭil al-siḥr*) poems to the status of inimitability (*i'jāz*). From the time of Abu al-Hasan Rudaki Samarqandi Turani, who is the point of reference (*marjaʿ*) of all poets of Iran and Turan, until today not one of Iran's poets appears whose speech is immune to various types of offenses both by way of idiom as well as by way of prosody, rhyme, and so on. What justice that they leave all [their poets] alone but only make trouble with the Mirza?[68]

The author's scathing attack on Iranian critics who 'made trouble' with the poetry of Mirza Bidil on the basis of his 'Indian-ness' and 'Indian race' (not to mention his Sunni background) seems to imply that these critics of Bidil hailed from Iran. Indeed, scattered throughout the various citations on Bidil in *A'zam's Rosegarden* are references to 'Iranians', 'eloquent ones of *'Ajam*', 'the Persians' and 'the soil of Isfahan'. Persian literary history has often focused on how poets located in nineteenth-century Iran railed against the 'fresh' style of poetry, of which Bidil's poetry is considered the apogee, in initiating an exclusively Iranian literary movement seeking to 'return' Persian poetry to the styles of the classical masters. A natural conclusion to draw is that the author of *A'zam's Rosegarden* and his contemporaries were aware of the existence and critiques of this Iran-based 'return' movement.

The citations in *A'zam's Rosegarden* provide no indication that this was the case. Nor do biographical anthologies composed in South Asia around the same time recognise any type of literary movement burgeoning in Iran that sought to 'return' Persian poetry to the styles of the classical masters. Consider, for example, *Consequences of Thoughts* (*Nata'ij al-afkar*), composed at the Nawab's court ten years earlier in 1842 by Qudrat, an appointed judge of the Nawab's poetic society. This work covers Persian poets during and prior to the author's own time (in South Asia and elsewhere) and is well-sourced.[69] Among the works Qudrat consulted was Azar's *Firetemple* (*Atishkada*), one of the earliest criticisms of the complicated style of poetry that came to be associated in literary historiography with the so-called 'Indian Style'. Yet, Qudrat shows no awareness of such critiques dominating literary circles in Iran. His entries on several poets later considered among the founders of the 'return' movement fail to portray these poets as having initiated a major movement antithetical to the 'fresh' style of poetry exemplified by Bidil.[70] Earlier biographical anthologies, like *Ibrahim's Pages* (*Tazkira-yi suhuf-i Ibrahim*), composed in 1790–1, likewise provide no evidence that an Iranian programme of literary reform was received in South Asia. Even though such works contain several entries on poets later considered crucial to the 'return' movement in Iran, there is little mention of such poets' stylistic affinities or distastes. In fact, the emphasis of these entries is not on a new poetic movement, but on the poets' relationship to the mayor of Isfahan Mirza 'Abd al-Wahhab, as outlined in Chapter 2.[71] Available evidence leads to the conclusion that a movement in Isfahan antithetical to poetry such as Bidil's had not yet reached South Asia. *Ibrahim's Pages* remarks on a controversy surrounding Bidil's use of idioms, but offers no indication that this controversy was known to poets of the Isfahani Circle discussed in Chapter 2.

The lack of recognition in South Asian *tadhkira*s of a supposedly contemporaneous 'literary return' movement based in Iran, which sought to distance itself from a particular literary style, should not be surprising. The idea that the 'return' movement in Iran was a response to a poetic style is primarily the construction of late nineteenth- and twentieth-century literary historians looking to justify and rationalise an argument claiming that Iranian poets rescued Persian poetry from its decline in other locales, particularly in South Asia. As Chapter 2 argued, a closer examination of the poetry and attitudes of the early founders of the 'return' movement in Isfahan makes clear that they were significantly more interested in seeking out patronage and reconstituting the role of the poet in society.

The critiques over Bidil's 'Indian-ness' appear to have been contained within South Asia itself. The 'Iranians' of *A'zam's Rosegarden* were most likely Indo-Iranians (whose native tongue was Persian) based in South Asia. In other words, criticisms of Bidil's poetry at this time were not connected to the writings of any specific community of poets based in Iran. Later literary histories, of course, would try to make this association by portraying Bidil's poetry as the apogee of the 'fresh' style, soon to be denigrated as the 'Indian Style'.[72]

The debate over Bidil's poetry may appear at odds with *A'zam's Rosegarden* immersion in the local literary politics and rivalries of mid-nineteenth-century Carnatic. In its introduction, *A'zam's Rosegarden* was positioned as a rejoinder to *Mine of Jewels*, in which the author Vasif 'made shameless insults' concerning Agah and Sirhindi. By the end of the work, it widens its lens beyond the local rivalries and the specific errors of Vasif's text to consider the broader issues of Persian poetic development and the place of Bidil's poetry in it. It does not show any receptivity to ideas emanating from an embryonic literary movement in Iran concerned with different poetic styles.

Nonetheless, while the debate in Arcot was not in conversation with those emerging in Iran, they do exhibit similarities. Indeed, Isfahan-based poets of the eighteenth and nineteenth centuries clearly sought to hark back to models of more 'simple' verse. They did so, however, not because of a stylistic preference for 'simple' verse over more 'complicated' verse. Rather they followed such a programme because the simplicity of previous classical masters, in particular in the ode (*qaṣīda*), provided the most fundamental model for re-establishing the role of the poet as an actor bestowing praise and receiving patronage in the aftermath of the downfall of the Safavids and destruction of Isfahan. As receiving patronage was the primary aim of these Isfahan-based poets, the imitation of the ode of the 'masters' was a more appropriate modelling device than the more complicated lyric (*ghazal*) of the 'fresh' style. It was not until later in the nineteenth century and the firm re-establishment of poetic patronage at the Qajar court in Tehran that debates over poetic style were awarded a position of primacy in an emergent 'return' movement. It was at this time that authors based in Iran began to ascribe literary style to geographical location, namely, a 'simple' style for Iran and 'complicated' style for everywhere else.

The important intersection between style and geography, however, was already rearing its head in lyric poetry and debates in eighteenth-century South Asia, albeit in less than uniform ways. Jane Mikkelson, through her close reading of lyrics by Sa'ib (d. 1677–8), Bidil and Hazin (d. 1766), highlights how metaphors of geography and place informed attitudes of literary belonging, exile and aesthetic sensibilities, which included, in the case of Hazin, a desire to map the binary of 'Iran' and 'India' (and 'Iranians' and 'Indians') onto notions of what constituted acceptable poetic verse.[73] But this attitude of Hazin represented an extreme example of defining poetic rivalry according to a real-world geographical binary separating 'Iran' and 'India'; the other two poets were more ambiguous about associating geography and style in such a concrete way. However, even in the case of Hazin, it is at times difficult to decipher how he may have weighed the importance of geographical belonging when articulating attitudes towards style. In writing of debates over proper Persian poetics in the eighteenth century, the intellectual historian Arthur Dudney correctly points out that discussions about poetic style featuring elements of geographic rivalry 'were framed primarily in terms of temporality, that is, old styles versus new styles. Geographical differences are a distant secondary concern in the critical literature.'[74] For example, while the well-documented debate between Arzu (d. 1756) and the aforementioned Hazin may be easy to slot as one pitting an Indian representing an 'Indian Style' against an 'Iranian' in opposition to it, this was by no means the prime mover of their rivalry. The major difference between the two interlocutors and how they understood contrasting poetic styles does not concern geographical (or ethnic) rivalry, but rather differing opinions over strict adherence to the discourse of the ancients: Hazin believed in such adherence, while Arzu saw this opinion as one of unwarranted conservatism.[75]

But while a difference over poetics may have out-trumped ethnic and geographic rivalry in eighteenth-century North India, the situation seems to have been reversed a century or so later in South India. A debate that began over the acceptability of Bidil's idioms ended by associating differences of literary opinion with ethnic and geographical difference. By carefully assembling select passages of Bilgrami, Arzu and Qatil, and reframing them with his own, the author of *A'zam's Rosegarden* appears to have flipped the terms of the debate. Unlike a century earlier, the author of *A'zam's Rosegarden* concludes that differences in opinions about poetics are indeed grounded in questions of ethnicity and birthplace. Such an opinion serves as an important indicator of how the connectivity and fissures of a multi-regional Persianate literary sphere were being conceived at the time of its breaking in a place where Persian would not be maintained as a national language.

While it may be convenient to relate this Carnatic controversy over Bidil and the role of his 'Indian-ness' to the nascent 'return' movement in Iran, this does not prove to be the case. The debate over Bidil's poetry in Carnatic was not one that pitted Iranian-born poets against those born in South Asia, but it was nonetheless a dispute increasingly shaped by fault-lines marking distinctions between South Asians, Indo-Iranians and the territory of Iran. Notably, the author of *A'zam's Rosegarden* reserved his ire not for the South Asian opponents of Bidil, but for those 'Iranian' critics and poets who seemed more preoccupied with Bidil's place of birth and native tongue than his poetry. While it was the critique of the Indian-born Vasif that precipitated the need to defend Bidil, it was the Indo-Iranian critics whom the author chastised most. In other words, the debate over Bidil's poetry in nineteenth-century Carnatic was a South Asian one, yet the culprits critiquing the great South Asian poet's work were increasingly being seen as 'Iranians'. The inability, however, to specifically relate these deliberations to any Iranian or Indo-Iranian interlocutors, or concomitant debates favouring ethno-geographic differences over stylistic ones, makes determining why discussions over Bidil's poetry progressed as they did extremely difficult. It is perhaps the most curious element of Persian literary culture at Carnatic.

The debate over Bidil's poetry, and who was critiquing it, is a long way from where *A'zam's Rosegarden* began, namely, as immersed in the local literary politics and rivalries of mid-nineteenth-century Carnatic. That *A'zam's Rosegarden* engaged with the poetry of Bidil and the larger question of poetic development and consolidated relatively recent opinions on the matter says a great deal about Persian literary culture at the Arcot court. It speaks to how the Arcot court fits into our larger understanding of Persian literary historiography at a time when the Persianate world was in its final throes.

A'zam's Rosegarden demonstrates that the debate over Bidil's poetry, which would later appear in the broader context of the history of the so-called 'Indian Style', was relevant in mid-nineteenth-century Arcot. The poets of Arcot may have framed the discussion according to local politics and personal rivalries, but they nonetheless were engaged in a contemporary and wider-reaching dialogue taking place at several locations within the Persianate world at a time of its fracturing and ultimate disappearance.[76] Even though the Persian literary world was on shaky grounds in mid-nineteenth-century South Asia, the literary atmosphere of Arcot proved to be resilient in its ability to remain engaged with these ongoing debates taking place elsewhere. This multi-regional debate on assessing a particular style of contemporary verse in light of canonic authority was, of course, not uniform in the manner it developed, nor in the outcomes it produced. Rather, it manifestly itself differently on account of the local circumstances and cultural preoccupations faced by diverse groups of poets. In Iran, for example, Zand- and Qajar-era authors began to indict a whole corpus of poetry over its poetics. The debates in Arcot, on the other hand, were more grounded in discussing the merit and appropriateness of Bidil's choice of words and poetry, without necessarily seeking to indict a whole poetic style.[77] In other words, debates among poets in Arcot (and elsewhere in South Asia) certainly resemble those in Iran even if the resultant impact was different. In this way, the example of Arcot points to how, during the time when the foundations of the Persianate world were becoming dislodged, poets in different locales were similarly conceptualising their place within in it according to a shared literary canon and debates about poetic authority.

Conclusion

When Nawab Muhammad Ghaws Khan died without heir in 1855, the EIC took the opportunity to formally annex his dynasty's territorial possessions and end the reign of the Nawabs once and for all. The Nawab's uncle and one-time regent, 'Azim Jah, attempted to attain the position of Nawab for himself, but was instead relegated to the role of Prince of Arcot, and given that title. This royal household remained in existence when India became independent in 1947 and continues until today.

The death of Muhammad Ghaws Khan not only marked the end of

Walajahi rule in Carnatic, but also ended an era promoting Persian literary activities encompassing his reign and that of his predecessors. The absence of a local court dedicated to the support of Persian literary activities, the consequent lack of available employment opportunities for individuals versed in Persian administrative technologies and the insistence of the British on shaping the area's educational activities according to their own criteria all led to Persian literary culture in Carnatic losing much of its importance and lustre. The Nawab's Madrasa, which he founded in 1851 to instruct students in both religious and secular sciences, was converted into an English highschool in 1859. Many instructors appointed to teach Arabic, Persian and Islamic theology were dismissed.[78] The East India Company's own madrasa at Fort St George College, which once employed local poets to serve as instructors in Persian and Arabic, was also converted into a high-school.[79]

Fate was no more kind to individuals whose livelihood depended on Persian retaining its cultural and official status at the court, whether they were poets and scholars receiving patronage or administrators. Those seeking to continue to capitalise on their skills in and knowledge of Persian for employment turned to Hyderabad. The poet Raqim, for example, following the death of the Nawab and his dismissal from the Nawab's school, eventually migrated to Hyderabad and obtained employment there.[80]

Works in Persian continued to be produced by poets and scholars in Carnatic after the Nawab's reign, but with less frequency.[81] If biographical anthologies may be taken as reflective of contemporary literary climates, then the last biographical anthology dedicated to the poets of Carnatic during this time does little to belie the notion that the vibrancy of Persian literary culture declined precipitously. Sayyid ʿAbd al-Latif's *The Candle of Poetry's Gathering* (*Shamʿ-i mahfil-i sukhan*), composed c.1862, appears only as a shell of the many *tadhkira*s discussed above that featured detailed accounts of the individuals, activities and debates occurring around Persian in Carnatic. Few of the major poets who had helped shape the direction of Persian literary culture only a decade or so earlier are mentioned. When they are, all that is offered is the scantest of biographical details. This could certainly mean no more than that the author had a personal proclivity for brevity, or only a paucity of information and texts accessible to him. But its depiction of Persian literary activity less than a decade after the Nawab's death represents a stark contrast to the time of his poetic society, their debates, and the overall literary climate outside of the court. Those days were in the past.

Closing the chapter on the Nawab's literary activities was left to Vasif. After the Nawab's death, he attempted to restore his honour by levelling claims against the authenticity of Nawab's own writings. He addressed the issue of the authenticity of the two biographical anthologies appearing under the Nawab's name in a work entitled *The Garden of Intention* (*Hadiqat al-maram*), which dealt with the learned men of Madras and Hyderabad. The work was not printed until 1862–3, several years after the Nawab's death.[82] In this work Vasif offers strong words about Vala, the Nawab's first instructor in poetry. He writes:

> He [Vala] was among the people of knowledge but he made people dumb-witted and envious. He used to teach Nawab Ghaws Khan, after his studies, cunningly [hidden] from people. He used to address the Nawab as 'Khan Sahib' and thus, because of this, he used to claim for himself that he [was] the greatest of poets and the most eloquent of orators.[83]

Vasif goes on to accuse Vala of trickery for appropriating Ra'iq's *Bouquet of Carnatic* from Ra'iq's heirs, which formed the basis of the Nawab's *Dawn of Homeland*, discussed above. Vasif also accused Vala of being the true author of *A'zam's Rosegarden*, which appeared under the Nawab's name. Since Vala died in 1848, and the work did not appear until several years later, it is more likely that it was the Nawab's other teacher in poetry and rival of Vasif, Raqim, who was the true author. Vala, who began educating the Nawab when the future ruler was twelve years old, appears to be the more likely candidate for the authorship of *Dawn of Homeland*. The Nawab's authorship of either *tadhkira* bearing his name remains uncertain. Perhaps more important than this controversy itself is that Vasif sustained this personal and poetic rivalry well into his later years, beyond the lives of the Nawab, Vala and the very existence of the Arcot state.

Vasif's persistence is a testament to the state of Persian literary culture as it existed in mid-nineteenth-century Carnatic, which resulted from a fortunate conjunction of factors. In particular, this vibrant poetic environment was the result of the Nawab's personal interest in Persian, his promotion of literary activities and the plethora of employment opportunities available for individuals skilled in Persian, both at the Nawab's court and with the EIC in Madras. If the case of Carnatic reveals anything about the shifting position of Persian in post-Mughal South Asia in general, it is how a ruler's personal investment in Persian's cultural value could intersect with local employment opportunities to create beneficial conditions for a thriving literary culture. Listening to the voices accumulated in the various 'homeless' texts of Arcot, one experiences the vitality of literary activity, debate and rivalry that is the legacy of the last Nawab and the poets of his court when the Persianate world was crumbling. In the case of Arcot, the tale of Persian literary culture in nineteenth-century South Asia was not one of outright decline, but a story of re-articulations and renewals, driven by the local politics, personalities and networks of an educated elite. Their tussles over the poetry of Bidil, and the manner in which it was framed both by local rivalries and regional opinions, demonstrate their relevance to historiographical debates in Persianate literature. Their discussion over what constituted acceptable poetry according to the classical canon, and who 'speaks for Persian', directly relates to those later debates occupying literary history writing in the nineteenth and twentieth centuries, for far too long narrowly defined on a national, rather than a multi-regional, basis. But more than anything else, it provides an example of what it was like for one literary community experiencing poetic life when a shared Persianate sphere was breaking apart.

Notes

1. While the English and Persian sources of the time refer to this successor state as 'the Carnatic State' and those who ruled over it as the 'Nawabs of Carnatic', the region of Carnatic is significantly larger than that which the Nawabs actually controlled. Therefore, when referring to later Nawabs, such as Muhammad Ghaws Khan Bahadur, I have opted for the 'Nawab of Arcot', as it more accurately reflects the scope of the Nawabs' domains. 'Carnatic' will be used when discussing trends in the larger region around the court and state.
2. 'A'zam', *Tazkira-yi gulzar-i A'zam*, p. 398. The work was composed in 1852–3.
3. Ibid.
4. *Tazkira-yi gulzar-i A'zam*, p. 6.
5. By the poet Ahmadi, cited in Kokan, *Arabic and Persian*, p. 417. All Persian and Arabic quotations appearing in Kokan are translated by me, unless otherwise stated.

6. For a general background on the emergence of the Arcot state in the late seventeenth century see Ramaswami, *Political History*. In understanding how the state's emergence is partially defined by successes in gaining greater control over the flow of external commerce and local ports of entry, see Alam and Subrahmanyam, 'Trade and Politics'.
7. Ramaswami, *Political History*, p. 375.
8. Bayly, *Saints, Goddesses, and Kings*, p. 223.
9. Ibid., pp. 153–4.
10. Phillips, 'A Successor to the Moguls', p. 366.
11. Bayly, *Saints, Goddesses, and Kings*, p. 155.
12. Wagoner, 'Precolonial Intellectuals', p. 796.
13. Bayly, *Saints, Goddesses, and Kings*, p. 168.
14. Vatuk, 'Islamic Learning', pp. 49–50. The Company Madrasa was replaced by Fort St George College, which opened in 1812.
15. For the education of princes at the Mughal court see Faruqui, *The Princes of the Mughal Empire, 1504–1719*, pp. 77–82. For more general trends in Perso-Islamic education in South Asia see Robinson 'Perso-Islamic Culture in India from the Seventeenth to Early Twentieth Century'.
16. Kokan, *Arabic and Persian*, p. 368.
17. Ibid., p. 351. The poet Binish observed that the foundation of the Nawab's poetry (*pāya-yi sukhan*) was based on that of Sirhindi's. Binish, *Tazkira-yi isharat-i Binish*, p. 44.
18. Madras Letter to Court, Foreign Department, 14 February 1837, no. 3.
19. Madras Letter from Court, Foreign Department, 6 February 1849, no. 2.
20. Ibid.
21. Kokan, *Arabic and Persian*, p. 359.
22. Ibid., p. 352.
23. Ibid., pp. 359–60.
24. Madras Letter from Court, Foreign Department, 18 October 1854, no. 3. Unfortunately, the Political Letter from the Madras Court to the Court of Directors (3 June 1854, no. 1) recording the receipt of the copies of *Binish's Notices* and their associated comments could not be located. All that is known from the transaction is a response of the Court of Directors to the Madras Court stating: 'We presume that this work, of which thirty-one copies have been presented to your Government by the Nuwaub, has been compiled under the directions of His Highness. We approve your having thanked His Highness for those copies and having distributed them in accordance with his wishes.'

25. The two *tadhkira*s were *Tazkira-yi subh-i vatan* (completed 1842–3) and *Tazkira-i gulzar-i Aʿzam* (completed 1852–3).
26. Raqim, *Bahr-i ʿAjam*, p. 2.
27. The poetic society is variously referred to in contemporary sources as 'Aʿzam's society' (*mahfil-i Aʿzam*), 'Aʿzam's poetic gathering' (*mushāʿira-yi Aʿzam*), or simply 'poetic gathering' (*mushāʿira*) or society (*mahfil*).
28. Binish, *Tazkira-yi isharat-i Binish*, p. 85.
29. Kokan, *Arabic and Persian*, p. 411.
30. Binish, *Tazkira-yi isharat-i Binish*, p. 39.
31. Ibid.
32. See e.g. ibid., p. 108.
33. See e.g. ibid., pp. 51, 91, 108.
34. Ibid., p. 123.
35. Vatuk, 'Islamic Learning', p. 51.
36. Binish, *Tazkira-yi isharat-i Binish*, p. 51.
37. Ibid., p. 70.
38. Ibid., pp. 67–8.
39. Ibid., p. 95.
40. Ibid., pp. 67–8.
41. Ibid., p. 72.
42. Raʾiq's work included the biographies of seventy poets from late eighteenth- and early early nineteenth-century Carnatic. The author of *Dawn of Homeland* enlarged the entries to include twenty others and expanded upon some of the poetic selections. Ivanow, *Concise Descriptive Catalogue*, pp. 7–10.
43. Binish, *Tazkira-yi isharat-i Binish*, p. 124.
44. Ibid., p. 82.
45. Ibid., p. 98.
46. This was not the first time Sirhindi's poetry had featured in debates about acceptable poetic style in South Asia. The poet Hazin Lahiji, a frequent critic of the 'fresh-speak' style, referred to Sirhindi's poetry as 'incomprehensible' a century or so earlier. See Mikkelson, 'Of Crows and Parrots', p. 525.
47. Ibid., p. 124.
48. See Faruqi, 'Unpriviledged Power'.
49. For information on the shifting and increasingly shrinking geographic meaning of *ʿAjam*, see Sharma, 'Redrawing the Boundaries of ʿAjam'. Sharma is particularly interested in the changing meaning of *ʿAjam* as it pertains to the literary discourse of Iranian-born and Western historians.

50. Raqim, *Javab-i i'tirazat-i Vasif*, cited in Kokan, *Arabic and Persian*, p. 413.
51. 'Zulfiqar' refers to the famous sword of Ali, the fourth Caliph of Islam and son-in-law of the Prophet Muhammad. Raqim, *Javab-i i'tirazat-i Vasif*, cited in Kokan, *Arabic and Persian*, pp. 413–14.
52. *Husn-i khitab va radd-i javab*, cited in Kokan, *Arabic and Persian*, p. 406.
53. Ibid.
54. Ibid.
55. Kokan, *Arabic and Persian in Carnatic*, p. 234.
56. Ibid., p. 407.
57. For some general information on the poetry of Bidil and his impact see Becka, 'Bedil and Bedilism'. Shafi'i-Kadkani, *Sha'ir-i ayina-ha*.
58. A'zam, *Tazkira-yi gulzar-i A'zam*, p. 402. Vasif's recounting of Mir Azad Bilgrami's opinion does not exactly correspond to the impression of Bidil's poetry in Azad's original statement. Vasif's rendition is actually more positive towards the great poet, whereas Mir Azad's original statement strikes a more incredulous tone regarding Bidil's 'invention contrary to language'. Azad, *Khizana-yi 'amira*, p. 153.
59. See Faruqi, 'Unprivileged Power'.
60. Green, 'The Uses of Books in a Late Mughal Takiyya'.
61. On the role and impact of Persian lithography during this time see Shah, 'Sustaining Authority in Persian Lithographed Books'.
62. A'zam, *Tazkira-yi gulzar-i A'zam*, pp. 405–6.
63. dar zabān-i Fārsī chīz-hā-yi gharīb ikhtirā' nimūda ki ahl-i muḥāvara qabūl na-dārand. A'zam, *Tazkira-yi gulzar-i A'zam*, p. 406.
64. Ibid.
65. Kia, 'Contours of Persianate Community', p. 280.
66. Alam and Subrahmanyam, 'Eighteenth-Century Historiography', pp. 423–5.
67. A'zam, *Tazkira-yi gulzar-i A'zam*, p. 407. For the original quotation, see Qatil, *Shajarat al-amani*, pp. 13–14.
68. A'zam, *Tazkira-yi gulzar-i A'zam*, p. 407.
69. For a brief background on *Tazkira-yi nata'ij al-afkar* see Naqavi, *Tazkira-navisi*, pp. 553–5.
70. See e.g. Qudrat, *Tazkira-yi nata'ij al-afkar*, p. 664.
71. Khalil, *Suhuf-i Ibrahim*, pp. 74 and 92.
72. For the important role of Bidil in Persian literary historiography see Schwartz, 'The Local Lives of a Transregional Poet'.
73. See Mikkelson, 'Of Parrots and Crows'.

74. Dudney, 'Sabk-e Hendi and the Crisis of Authority', p. 4.
75. Ibid., pp. 4–5.
76. For example, in places like Samarkand and Bukhara, similar debates were occurring around the vitality and viability of the dominant 'fresh style' of poetry and whether it was the most appropriate poetic style to express pressing contemporary concerns facing society. Poets began to strive to produce poetry that could address local concerns, such as educational reform, and other did so by relying on 'simpler' models drawn from the classical canon. See Schwartz, 'The Local Lives of a Transregional Poet', pp. 99–101. 'Ayni, *Nimuna-yi dabiyat-i Farsi.*
77. I would like to thank Hajnalka Kovacs for her clarification of this point.
78. Kokan, *Arabic and Persian in Carnatic*, p. 517.
79. Ibid., p. 518.
80. Ibid., p. 411.
81. See e.g. Hadi, *Dictionary of Indo-Persian Literature*, pp. 736–56.
82. The work was published at Madras, but Vasif most likely wrote it in Hyderabad. He migrated there in 1853–4 to take a position at the *Dar al-ʿulum*, much like his adversary Raqim.
83. *Hadiqat al-maram*, cited in Kokan, *Arabic and Persian in Carnatic*, p. 355.

Conclusion

The emergence of Persian literature as the national literature of Iran, like that of national literatures elsewhere, has been marked 'by the assertion of the national literary language as superior to its cosmopolitan antecedents, better suited to contemporary circumstances, or more accessible to a larger public'.[1] Large quantities of information – ill-fitting within an account of Persian literary history and retro-fitted for the purposes of the Iranian nation – remain obstructed, obscured and elided. The idea of 'literary return' has been the most effective tool in achieving such ends.

The idea of 'literary return' – that some poets in eighteenth- and nineteenth-century Iran revived Persian poetry by returning to the styles of the classical masters, while poets outside of Iran did not – has left much historiographical debris in its wake: the conflation of the writing of Persian literary history with that of Iran's own; the assertion of a greater proprietary right by Iran over the classical 'masters'; and the erasure from history of many facets of Persian literary culture occurring outside of Iran's borders. Most crucially, the idea of 'literary return' has served as an interjection in Persian literary history seeking to revitalise literature in Iran on a national basis while effectively dismissing aspects of Persian literary history occurring elsewhere. Recognising the historiographical problem of 'literary return' in writing about Persian literature and addressing what can be done to rectify it has been the major aim of this book.

The preceding chapters have sought to challenge this conceptualisation of 'literary return' by re-depicting Persian literary culture in the eighteenth and nineteenth centuries through an emphasis on different literary communities in operation across a fracturing Persianate world. The poetic assemblies of the Safavid–Qajar interregnum in Isfahan, the *Book of Kings*-inspired war ballads of the first Anglo-Afghan War and the literary activity of a court in South India all represent episodes of historically contingent literary communities engaged with the classical canon of the masters in order to better understand and depict their place within the shifting landscape of the eighteenth- and nineteenth-century Persianate world. Rather than being a time defined by the grandiose revival of poetry in Iran and its stagnation elsewhere in Central and South Asia, the literary climate of the eighteenth- and nineteenth-century Persianate world remains ripe for the comparison and exploration of shared and divergent literary practices and orientations on a multi-regional basis. Comparing the experiences of coeval literary communities, whether in the eighteenth and nineteenth centuries or during other eras, helps establish a comparative field by which to commensurably explore the (a)symmetrical elements and characteristics of an ever-changing literary and cultural Persianate sphere.

The construction of 'literary return' as a conceptual category, as noted in the introduction, has impacted the writing of Persian literary history in several discrete ways. First, the genesis narrative of 'literary return', covered over with an Iranian nationalist sheen, has overshadowed important aspects relating to the literary history of Iran and obscured how the 'return' movement actually came into being. Second, the exclusive emphasis on literary trends in eighteenth- and nineteenth-century Iran has ignored critical elements of Persian literary culture outside Iran during that time. Finally, the desire to define literary history of the eighteenth and nineteenth centuries solely according to the stylistic proclivities of individual poets, and merely relate these poets to the canonic master they sought to imitate, makes for a restrictive depiction of Persian literary phenomena heading into the modern period.

Chapter 1 critically examined the historiography of 'literary return' through an analysis of Zand- and Qajar-era authors and the scholarship of their successors in twentieth-century Iran and elsewhere. It argued for how the accepted notion of 'literary return' has diminished many of the social and political conditions that actually helped nurture the movement's growth and allowed it to take shape. This chapter also included information related to eighteenth- and nineteenth-century Persian literary culture pertaining to South Asia and Afghanistan. In the case of South Asia, scholarship has understood Persian within a narrative of 'decline', overrun by the emergence of English and Urdu. While the rise of English and Urdu no doubt displaced the social and literary predominance of Persian, such a narrative cannot account for the many revisions and afterlives of Persian literary culture in post-Mughal South Asia – the literary activity of the court of the last Nawab of Arcot being but one example. With regard to Afghanistan, a brief reexamination of literary history in the eighteenth and nineteenth centuries highlighted the multiplicity of poetic practice, whether promoted by the state or otherwise. Poetic practice during this time was not solely devoted to imitating the poetry of ʿAbd al-Qadir Bidil, for which Afghanistan is overwhelmingly known; Afghan poets engaged with the poetry of the classical masters as well. The chapter also raised questions about the relationship between literary historiography in Afghanistan and Iran, in particular the manner in which Afghan literary historians have grappled with the notion of 'literary return' in the writing of their country's literary past from the early twentieth century up until the present. Persianate literary history, whether in relation to the eighteenth and nineteenth centuries or writ large, must better strive to integrate the national and regional historiographies of South Asia and Afghanistan, often as told by their own scholars.

Chapter 2 reconstructed the circumstances, associations and environments that were relevant to the Isfahani Circle of poets who would later be enshrined as the founders of the 'literary return' movement in Iran. It was argued that the 'literary return' movement emerged for reasons beyond a mere distaste for a particular style, known at the time as 'fresh-speak' (*tāza-gūʾī*), and to later authors as the 'Indian Style' (*sabk-i Hindī*). The attitudes and perceptions of the Isfahani Circle, many of which were highlighted through an examination of their poetry, related to an unease with the role of the poet in society, the chaotic political environment in post-Safavid times and the loss of patronage. On account of these experiences, this group of poets inaugurated a desire to recreate a community of socially connected and like-minded poets striving to find a place for themselves in Iran's post-Safavid landscape. This does not imply that the Isfahani Circle of poets cared little for poetics; rather, that such attitudes towards poetic style were of secondary importance, at least initially. Following the guidance and style of the masters, especially in constructing and exchanging poems of praise, was relied upon as the most adept vehicle for strengthening intra-community bonds in the absence of a patron. Contrary to the appearance of the 'literary return' movement at the court of Fath Ali Shah several decades later, when an established patron was well in place, these Isfahan-based poets were less wedded to a particular style of poetry simply because it mirrored that of the classical masters. The ways in which the poets at Fath Ali Shah's court engaged with the styles of the masters, what this implies for their approach to the literary canon, how it may have shaped their self-recognition as a literary community and the manner in which this instantiation of literary return may differ from the experiences of the early founders of the 'return' movement is a story for another time. The directed focus on the Isfahani Circle of poets was, first and foremost, meant to unravel the myth-making surrounding the 'literary return' movement's process of becoming and remove the nationalist sheen that would later define conceptions of 'literary return' as a category of historiography for everything that succeeded it.

Chapters 3 and 4 looked outside of Iran to consider literary trends in Afghanistan and South Asia concomitant with the emergence of 'literary return' in Iran. Both cases demonstrate how poets, scholars and littérateurs outside Iran remained engaged with the poetry of the masters in the nineteenth century in their own ways. These chapters were offered as case studies of literary communities equally adept at channelling the classical canon in the nineteenth century, similar to their counterparts in Iran.

Chapter 3 turned its attention to a series of war-ballads (*jangnāma*s) composed in response to the first Anglo-Afghan War and in imitation of Firdawsi's *Book of Kings* (*Shahnama*). It contended that the production of these texts created a market-place of the masters, stretching across Afghanistan and South Asia and spanning oral, written and print culture. The existence in the nineteenth century of such a market-place – one predicated upon the desire of poets to use the model of the masters to narrate a contemporary event – raises intriguing questions about 'literary return' as a historiographical category. While different from the emergence of the 'literary return' movement in Iran, the war-ballads of the first Anglo-Afghan War make the case for a definition of 'literary return' as a potentially more expansive phenomenon able to account for a wider range of phenomena. Such a definition can help explicate and connect trends outside nineteenth-century Iran that remained indebted to the style, circulation and role of the masters as well as an engagement with the classical canon.

The literary activity at the court of the last Nawab of Arcot, the subject of Chapter 4, demonstrated how the debates and rivalries at a small South Indian court addressed issues of poetics and divisions over accepted styles. These debates culminated in a questioning of the use of idioms in the poetry of ʿAbd al-Qadir Bidil and that of poetry in general. With the poetry of Bidil serving as a lightning-rod, these discussions served as a bridge to others, such as the acceptability of 'simple' versus 'complicated' styles and the division between native or non-native speakers of Persian. Such discussions, while operating in isolation from the 'literary return' movement in Iran, can nonetheless be linked to debates about what constituted 'literary return' among nineteenth- and twentieth-century authors in Iran. Like those later Iranian authors, poets at Arcot grappled with how certain types of poetry related to the classical canon and what constituted acceptable verse. In other words, at least one literary community in nineteenth-century South Asia precipitated the delimiting conceptual parameters of 'literary return' that would feature in later Persian literary history writing. The literary experiences and debates at Arcot are equally revealing for what they say about how a literary community experienced the undoing of the Persianate world in a place where the Persian language would not retain national prominence.

The literary communities surrounding the production of the Anglo-Afghan War ballads and at the court of the last Nawab of Arcot, like the Isfahani Circle of poets in Iran, all point to how various groups engaged with the poetry and prestige of the masters when the Persianate world was breaking apart. This should not be taken to mean that the manner in which the 'literary return' movement developed self-consciously in Iran and gained support at the court of the Qajar monarch Fath Ali Shah has an exact equivalent elsewhere in the Persianate world. Nor could it. The construction of 'literary return' as an exclusively national category of literary prestige for Iran makes it prima facie impossible to find a replica elsewhere. But this does not mean that communities and literary phenomena outside of Iran were disengaged from certain aspects that would go on to define 'literary return', namely the grappling with the poetry of the masters to articulate one's place in a shifting Persianate world and one's relationship to the classical Persian canon. To explore such a possibility, through an examination of how different actors debated and grappled with the place of the masters during uncertain times, whether in a chaotic Isfahan, in response to occupation and war with a colonial power, or in a court emerging after the break-up of the Mughal Empire, helps us to re-imagine a more integrated Persian literary history in the eighteenth and nineteenth centuries.

Note

1. Beecroft, *An Ecology of World Literature*, p. 200.

Bibliography

Archives

Aligarh Muslim University. Aligarh, India.
National Archives of India. New Delhi, India.
National British Library. London, UK.
Salar Jung Museum. Hyderabad, India.

Sources in Persian

Afaqi, Sabir, 'Firdawsi-i Kashmir', *Vahid* 7.4 (1970–1), pp. 394–407.
Akhavan-Sales, Mehdi, 'Nima mardi bud mardistan', *Andisha va Hunar* no. 7 (April 1960).
Akhtar, Ahmad Bayg, *Tazkira-yi Akhtar*, 'Abd al-Rasul Khayyampur (ed.) (Tabriz: Shirkat-i Chap-i Kitab-i Azarbayjan, 1964).
Anushah, Hasan et al. *Danishnama-yi adab-i Farsi*, 6 vols (Tehran: Sazman-i Chap va Intisharat-i Vizarat-i Farhang va Irshad-i Islam, 2001–5).
Aryanpur, Yahya, *Az Saba ta Nima: tarikh-i 150 sal-i adab-i Farsi*, 2 vols (Tehran: Intisharat-i Zavvar, 2000), 7th edn.
Asghari, Mahmud Ali, 'Jaigah-i dawra-yi bazgasht dar sabk-shinasi', *Rushd-i Amuzish-i Zaban va Adab-i Farsi* no. 96 (Winter 2010–11), pp. 4–9.
''Ashiq' Isfahani, Muhammad, *Divan-i 'Ashiq Isfahani*, M. Darvish (ed.) (Tehran: Sazman-i Intisharat-i Javidan, 1964).
'Ayni, Sadriddin, *Nimuna-yi adabiyat-i Farsi*, 3 vols (Samarkand, 1925).
'Azad', Ghulam Ali al-Husayni al-Wasiti al-Bilgrami, *Khizana-yi 'amira* (Cawnpore: Newal Kishor, 1871). HathiTrust Digital Library. <https://babel.hathitrust.org/cgi/pt?id=njp.32101076206505> (last accessed 10 December 2018).
'Azar' Baygdili, Lutf Ali, *Divan-i Azar*, Hasan Sadat-Nasiri and Ghulam Husayn Baygdil (eds), (Tehran: Javidan, 1987).

'Azar' Baygdili, Lutf Ali, *Atishkada-yi Azar*, Jaʿfar Shahidi (ed.) (Tehran: Muʿassasa-yi Nashr-i Kitab, 1958).

'Azar' Baygdili, Lutf Ali, *Atishkada* (Bombay: n.p., 1881–2).

'Aʿzam', Muhammad Ghaws Khan Bahadur, *Tazkira-yi gulzar-i Aʿzam*, yuniverseti no. 20 Farsi tadhkira, Aligarh Muslim University Oriental Manuscript Collection, Aligarh, India, 1854.

Bahar, Muhammad Taqi, *Bahar va adab-i Farsi: majmuʿa-yi yiksad maqala az Malik al-shuʿara Bahar*, 2 vols, Muhammad Gulban (ed.) (Tehran: Shirkat-i Sihami Kitab-ha-yi Habibi, 1992).

Baygdili, Ghulam Husayn, 'Nigarish bar bazgasht-i adabi', *Kayhan-i Farhangi* 41 (July–Aug. 1987), pp. 33–5.

'Binish', Sayyid Murtaza, *Tazkira-yi isharat-i Binish*, Sharif Husayn Qasimi (ed.) (Delhi: Indo-Persian Society, 1973).

Chihriqani-Barchaluyi, Riza and Ismaʿil Shafaq, 'Bazgasht-i adabi dar shiʿr-i Farsi-i Afghanistan', *Funun-i Adabi* 4.2 (2012–13), pp. 52–68.

Daʾirat al-maʿarif Aryana, vol. 3 (Kabul: Anjuman-i Aryana Daʾirat al-maʿarif Afghanistan, 1956).

Dihgan-Nizhad, Murtaza and Luqman Dihqan-Nayri and Ahmad ʿAqili, 'Barrassi-i tarikhi va arzyabi-i juryan-i adabi-i Isfahan dar qarn-i davazdahum (az suqut-i Safaviyya ta zuhur-i Qajar)', *Pizhuhish-ha-yi Tarikhi* 6 (Summer 2010), pp. 25–44.

Dunbuli, ʿAbd al-Razzaq, *Tajribat al-ahrar wa tasliyat al-abrar*, Hasan Qazi Tabatabaʾi (ed.), (Tabriz: Danishgah-i Tabriz, 1970–1).

Dunbuli, ʿAbd al-Razzaq, *Nigaristan-i dara*, A. Khayyampur (ed.) (Tabriz: Mahall-i Furush; Kitabfurushi-i Tehran, 1963).

Falsafi, Nasr Allah, 'Tarikh-i qahva va qahva-khana dar Iran' in *Chand maqala-yi Tarikhi va adabi* (Tehran: Intisharat-i Danishgah-i Tehran, 1963–4), pp. 271–83.

Farshidvard, Khusraw, *Darbara-yi adabiyat va naqd-i adabi*, 2 vols (Tehran: Amir Kabir, 1984–5).

Fihrist-i kutub-i ʿArabi, Farsi va Urdu makhzuna-yi Kutub Khana-yi Asafiyya Sarkar-i ʿAli (Hyderabad: Kutub Khana-yi Asafiyya Sarkar-i ʿAli, 1928–36.)

Garrusi, Fazil Khan, *Tazkira-yi anjuman-i Khaqan* (Tehran: Intisharat-i Rawzana, 1997–8).

Ghaznavi, Muhammad Akbar Sana, *Tarikh-i adabiyat-i Dari* (Kabul: Mayvand, 2007).

Ghubar, Mir Ghulam Muhammad, *Afghanistan dar masir-i tarikh*, 2 vols in one (Kabul: Mayvand, 2001).

Ghubar, Mir Ghulam Muhammad, 'Jangnama nuskha khati manzum dar nasf-i duvvum-i qarn-i sizdah hijri', *Aryana* 6.11 (1948–9), pp. 1–5.

'Ghulami' Kuhistani, Muhammad Ghulam, *Jangnama* (Kabul: Matbaʻa-yi Dawlati, 1957).

Gulchin-i Maʻani, Ahmad, *Tarikh-i tazkira-ha-yi Farsi*, 2 vols (Tehran: Intisharat-i Kitabkhana-yi ana'i, 1984–5).

Gulchin-i Maʻani, Ahmad, *Maktab-i vuquʻ dar shiʻr Farsi* (Tehran: Bunyad-i Farhang-i Iran, 1970).

Habib, Asadullah, 'Jumbish-i jangnama-sarayi dar shiʻr-i Dari sada-yi nuzdah Afghanistan', *Khurasan* 2.1 (1981–2), pp. 49–64.

'Hatif' Isfahani, Sayyid Ahmad, *Divan-i Hatif Isfahani*, Mahmud Shahrukhi and Muhammad ʻAlidust (eds) (Tehran: Intisharat-i Mishkat; Daftar-i Tahqiq va Nahsr-i Baharan, 1992).

Hidayat, Riza Quli Khan, *Majmaʻ al-fusaha'*, 6 vols, Mazahir Musaffa (ed.) (Tehran: Muʻassasa-yi Matbuʻat Amir Kabir, 1957–61).

Husayni, Hasan, *Bidil, Sipihri, va sabk-i Hindi* (Tehran: Surush, 1988–9).

Imdad, Hasan, *Anjuman-ha-yi adabi-i Shiraz: az avakhir-i qarn-i dahum ta imruz* (Shiraz: Navid-i Shiraz, 2008–9).

Karimi-Hakkak, Ahmad, 'Pusht-i rang-ha-yi khazan: ta'ammulati darbara-yi zaban-i shiʻr-i Farsi dar Hind', *Iran Nameh* 8.2 (Spring 1990), pp. 225–45.

Kashmiri, Hamid Allah, *Akbarnama* (Kabul: Anjuman-i Tarikh, 1951–2).

Kazimi, Muhammad Kazim, 'Faryad-ha-yi mawzun: shiʻr-i muqavamat dar Afghanistan', *Sura Andisha* 24 (2006), pp. 76–81.

Khalil, Ali Ibrahim Khan, *Suhuf-i Ibrahim: tazkira-yi shuʻara-yi Farsi (sada-yi duvaz-dahum)*, ʻAbid Raza Bidar (ed.) (Patna: Khuda Bakhsh Oriental Public Library, 1978).

Khatami, Ahmad, *Pizhuhishi dar nasr va nazm-i dawra-yi bazgasht-i adabi* (Tehran: Arman, 1995).

al-Latf, ʻAbd al-Latif al-Husayni, *Shamʻ-i mahfil-i sukhan* (Madras: Matbaʻ Mazhar al-ʻAja'ib, 1862).

Mahdavi, Muslih al-Din, *Tazkirat al-qubur, ya, Danishmandan va buzurgan-i Isfahan* (Isfahan: Kitabfurushi-i Saqafi-i Isfahan, 1969–70).

Mawla'i, Muhammad Sarvar, 'Bazgasht-i adabi dar Afghanistan', *Sukhan* 19.1 (June 1969), pp. 60–7.

Munshi ʻAbd al-Karim, *Muharaba-yi Kabul va Qandahar* (Lucknow: Matbaʻ-i Mustafa'i-i Muhammad Khan Mustafa, 1850–1).

'Mushtaq' Isfahani, Sayyid Ali, *Divan-i ghazaliyat va qasaʾid va rubaʿiyat-i Mushtaq*, Husayn Makki (ed.) (Tehran: Intisharat-i ʿIlmi, 1984).

Naʾil, Husayn, *Sukhan-sarayani az sada-yi sizdahum* (Kabul: Akadimi-i ʿUlum-i Afghanistan, Markaz-i Zaban-ha va Adabiyat, Instituti-i Zaban va Adab-i Dari, 2003–4).

Naʾil, Husayn, *Sayri dar adabiyat-i sada-yi sizdahum* (Kabul: Matbaʿa-yi Dawlati, 1981–2).

Nazimi, Latif, 'Darbara-yi bazgasht-i adabi Afghanistan', *Pashtun Zhagh* 36.1 (1976–7).

Nuʿmani, Shibli, *Shiʿr-i ʿAjam*, trans. Muhammad Taqi Fakr Daʿi Gilani, 5 vols (Tehran, n.p., 1935–57).

Pahlavan-Zada, Muluk, 'Qahva-khana-ha-yi ʿasr-i Safavi, farhang va adabiyat' in *Girdhamayi-i maktab-i Isfahan: majmuʿa-yi maqalat-i adabiyat*, vol. 1 (Tehran: Farhangistan-i Hunar-i Jumhuri-i Iran, 2008–9), pp. 29–56.

'Qasim Ali', *Zafarnama-yi Kabul*, British Library Manuscript Collection, Or. 1961, British National Library, 1844–5.

'Qatil', Muhammad Hasan, *Shajarat al-amani* (Cawnpore, 1865–6). HathiTrust Digital Library. <https://babel.hathitrust.org/cgi/pt?id=njp.32101076320728> (last accessed 10 December 2018).

Qavim, ʿAbd al-Qayyum, *Mururi bar adabiyat-i muʿasir-i Dari az 1259 ta 1380* (Kabul: Intisharat-i Saʿid, n.d.).

'Qudrat', Muhammad Qudratallah Khan Gupamavi, *Tazkira-yi nataʾij al-afkar* (Bombay: Sultani-yi Bombay, 1957).

Raj Kunwar, *Lahurnama*, Salar Jung Museum Manuscript Collection, 824 nm/a.

'Raqim', Muhammad Husayn, *Bahr-i ʿAjam*, College of Fort William Collection, no. 527, National Archives of India, New Delhi, India.

Rashad, Puhand ʿAbd al-Shakur, 'Darbara-yi zafarnama-yi akbari va nazim-i an', *Aryana* 44.2 (1986–7), pp. 137–69.

'Sabahi' Bidguli Kashani, Sulayman, *Divan-i Sabahi-i Bidguli*, Ahmad Karami (ed.) (Tehran: Talar-i Kitab, 1987).

'Sabahi' Bidguli Kashani, Sulayman, *Divan-i Sabahi Bidguli*, H. Partaw Bayzaʾi and ʿAbbas Kaymanish 'Mushfiq Kashani' (eds) (Tehran: Kitabfurushi Zavvar, 1959).

Sadat-Nasiri, Hasan, 'Bazgasht-i adabi', *Yaghma* 17.19 (1964), pp. 424–30.

Safa, Zabihullah, *Hamasa sarayi dar Iran: az qadimtarin ʿahd-i tarikhi ta qarn-i chahardahum-i hijri* (Tehran: Amir Kabir, 1954).

Sara, 'Du ravayit az yik hamasa: barrasi-i muqayisa Akbarnama-yi Munshi

Qasim Jan va Akbarnama-yi Hamid Kashmiri', *Aryana* 39.3 (1981), pp. 40–64.

Shahbaz, Iraj, 'Guftugu ba ustad-i Vasif Bakhtari, sha'ir va pizhuhishgar-i Afghan: Bidil-gira'i dar Afghanistan', *Shi'r* 29 (Winter 2001), pp. 16–21.

Shafaq, Riza-Zada, *Tarikh-i adabiyat-i Iran* (Tehran: Vizarat-i Farhang, 1963).

Shafi'i-Kadkani, Muhammad Riza, *Sha'ir-i ayina-ha: barrasi-i sabk-i Hindi va shi'r-i Bidil* (Tehran: Mu'assasa-yi Intisharat-i Agah, 1987).

Shah Shuja', *Vaqi'at-i Shah Shuja'* (Kabul: Mayvand; Peshawar Saba Kitabkhana, 2003).

Shamisa, Sirus, *Sabk-shinasi-i shi'r* (Tehran: Mitra, 2015–16).

Shams-Langarudi, Muhammad, *Maktab-i bazgasht: barrasi-i shi'r-i dawra-ha-yi Afshariyya, Zandiyya, Qajariyya* (Tehran: Nashr-i Markaz-i Isfand, 1996).

Shikarpuri, Mirza 'Ata Muhammad, *Nava-yi ma'arik* (Peshawar: Markaz-i Nasharat-i Mayvand, 2000).

Shirzadfar, Mihr al-Zaman, *Isfahan dar dawran-i Afshar va Zand* (Isfahan: Sazman-i Farhangi Tafrihi-i Shahrdari-i Isfahan, 2009).

Shushtari, Mir 'Abd al-Latif Khan, *Tuhfat al-'alam va dhayl al-tuhfah*, Samad Muvahhid (ed.), (Tehran: Kitabkhana-yi Tahuri, 1984).

'Tabib' Isfahani, 'Abd al-Baqi, *Divan-i Tabib Isfahani*, Mujtaba Burzabadi Farahani (ed.), (Tehran: Intisharat-i Sana'i, 199–?).

Tamimdari, Ahmad, 'Adabiyat-i 'asr-i Safavi, inhitat ya taraqqi' in *Girdhamayi-i maktab-i Isfahan: majmu'a-yi maqalat-i adabiyat*, vol. 1 (Tehran: Farhangistan-i Hunar-i Jumhuri-i Iran, 2008–9), pp. 77–91.

Tughyani, Ishaq, 'Isfahan va tahavvul-i shi'r-i Parsi dar 'asr-i Safaviyya' in *Girdhamayi-i maktab-i Isfahan: majmu'a-yi maqalat-i adabiyat*, vol. 2 (Tehran: Farhangistan-i Hunar-i Jumhuri-i Iran, 2008–9), pp. 37–50.

Zarrinkub, 'Abd al-Husayn, *Naqd-i adabi: justju dar usul va ravish-ha va mabahis-i naqqadi ba barrasi dar tarikh-i naqd va naqqadan* (Tehran: Amir Kabir, 1990).

Zhubal, Muhammad Haydar, *Tarikh-i adabiyat-i Afghanistan* (Kabul: Mayvand, 2008).

Zipoli, Riccardo, *Chira sabk-i Hindi dar dunya-yi gharb sabk-i baruk khunda mi-shavad?* (Tehran: Anjuman-i Farhangi-i Italiya, 1984).

Sources in English

Abe, Naofumi, 'The Politics of Poetics in Early Qajar Iran: Writing Royal-Commissioned *Tazkera*s at Fath-'Ali Shāh's Court', *Journal of Persianate Studies* 10 (2017), pp. 129–57.

Abisaab, Rula Jurdi, *Converting Persia: Religion and Power in the Safavid Empire* (London; New York: I. B. Tauris, 2004).

'Afghanistan', *The World FactBook Online*, US Central Intelligence Agency. <https://www.cia.gov/library/publications/the-world-factbook/geos/af.html> (last accessed 20 December 2018).

Ahmad, Aziz, *Studies in Islamic Culture in the Indian Environment* (New Delhi: Oxford University Press, 1964).

Ahmadi, Wali, 'Kabul Literary Society', *Encyclopedia Iranica Online*, 2012. <http://www.iranicaonline.org/articles/kabul-literary-society> (last accessed 20 December 2018).

Ahmadi, Wali, *Modern Persian Literature in Afghanistan: Anomalous Visions of History and Form* (London; New York: Routledge, 2008).

Ahmadi, Wali, 'The Institution of Persian Literature and the Genealogy of Bahar's "Stylistics"', *British Journal of Middle Eastern Studies* 31.2 (Nov. 2004), pp. 141–52.

Alam, Muzaffar, 'The Culture and Politics of Persian in Precolonial Hindustan', in Sheldon Pollock (ed.), *Literary Cultures in History: Reconstructions from South Asia* (Berkeley: University of California Press, 2003), pp. 131–98.

Alam, Muzaffar, 'The Pursuit of Persian: Language in Mughal Politics', *Modern Asian Studies* 32.2 (1998), pp. 317–49.

Alam, Muzaffar, *The Crisis of Empire in Mughal North India: Awadh and the Punjab, 1707–1847* (Delhi; New York: Oxford University Press, 1986).

Alam, Muzaffar and Sanjay Subrahmanyam, 'Trade and Politics of the Arcot *Nizamat* (1700–1732)', in Muzaffar Alam and Sanjay Subrahmanyam (eds), *Writing the Mughal World: Studies on Culture and Politics* (New York: Columbia University Press, 2012), pp. 339–95.

Alam, Muzaffar and Sanjay Subrahmanyam, 'Eighteenth-Century Historiography and the World of the Mughal *Munshi*', in Muzaffar Alam and Sanjay Subrahmanyam (eds), *Writing the Mughal World: Studies on Culture and Politics* (New York: Columbia University Press, 2012), pp. 396–428.

Alam, Muzaffar and Sanjay Subrahmanyan, *Indo-Persian Travels in the Age of Discoveries, 1400–1800* (Cambridge: Cambridge University Press, 2007).

Alam, Muzaffar and Sanjay Subrahmanyan, 'The Making of the Munshi', *Comparative Studies of South Asia, Africa, and the Middle East* 24.2 (2004), pp. 61–72.

Algar, Hamid, 'Akundzada', *Encyclopedia Iranica Online*, 2011. <http://www.iranicaonline.org/articles/akundzada-playwright> (last accessed 7 December 2018).

Amanat, Abbas, '*Shahnameh-ye Naderi* and the Revival of Epic Poetry in Post-Safavid

Iran', in Ali-Asghar Seyed-Ghorab (ed.), *The Layered Heart: Essays on Persian Poetry, A Celebration in Honor of Dick Davis* (Washington, DC: Mage, 2019), pp. 295–318.

Amanat, Abbas, 'Introduction: Iranian Identity Boundaries: A Historical Overview', in Abbas Amanat and Farvin Vejdani (eds), *Iran Facing Others: Identity Boundaries in a Historical Perspective* (New York: Palgrave Macmillan, 2012), pp. 1–33.

Amanat, Abbas, 'Legend, Legitimacy and Making a National Narrative in the Historiography of Qajar Iran (1785–1925)', in Charles Melville (ed.), *A History of Persian Literature*, vol. X, Persian Historiography (London; New York, I. B. Tauris, 2012), pp. 292–366.

Amin, Camron Michael, '*Mujassama-ī būd mujassama-ī nabūd*: The Image of the Safavids in 20th Century Iranian Popular Historiography', in Judith Pfeiffer and Sholeh A. Quinn (eds) in collaboration with Ernest Tucker, *History and Historiography of Post-Mongol Central Asia and the Middle East: Studies in Honor of John E. Woods* (Wiesbaden: Harrassowitz, 2006), pp. 343–59.

Ansari, Ali M., *The Politics of Iranian Nationalism in Modern Iran* (Cambridge: Cambridge University Press, 2012).

Ashraf, Assef, 'Introduction: Pathways to the Persianate', in Abbas Amanat and Assef Ashraf (eds), *The Persianate World: Rethinking a Shared Sphere* (Leiden; Boston: Brill, 2018), pp. 1–14.

Askari, Nasrin, *The Medieval Reception of the Shahnama as a Mirror for Princes* (Leiden; Boston: Brill, 2016).

Atkinson, James (trans.), *The Shah Nameh of the Persian Poet Firdausi* (edited and abridged), Rev. J. A. Atkinson (ed.) (London; New York: Frederick Warne & Co., 1886).

Axworthy, Michael (ed.), *Crisis, Collapse, Militarism & Civil War: The History & Historiography of 18th Century Iran* (Oxford: Oxford University Press, 2018).

Axworthy, Michael, *Empire of the Mind: A History of Iran* (London: Hurst, 2007).

Bakhtary, Elham, 'Fayz Mohammad Kāteb and Gholām Mohammad Ghobar's Divergent Allegories of an Afghan Rebellion', *Journal of Persianate Studies* 11 (2018), pp. 203–33.

Bayly, C. A., *The Birth of the Modern World, 1780–1914: Global Connections and Comparisons* (Malden, MA: Blackwell, 2004).

Bayly, C. A., *Empire and Information: Intelligence Gathering and Social Communication in India, 1780–1870* (Cambridge; New York: Cambridge University Press, 1996).

Bayly, C. A., *Indian Society and the Making of the British Empire* (Cambridge; New York: Cambridge University Press, 1987).

Bayly, Susan, *Saints, Goddesses, and Kings: Muslims and Christians in South India Society, 1700–1900* (Cambridge; New York: Cambridge University Press, 1989).

Becka, Jiri, 'Bidel and Bidelism', in Jan Rypka, *History of Iranian Literature*, Karl Jahn (ed.), (Dordrecht, Holland: D. Reidel, 1968), pp. 515–20.

Becka, Jiri, 'Tajik Literature from the 16th Century to the Present', in Jan Rypka, *History of Iranian Literature*, ed. Karl Jahn (Dordrecht: D. Reidel, 1968), pp. 486–7.

Beecroft, Alexander, *An Ecology of World Literature: From Antiquity to the Present Day* (London; New York: Verso, 2015).

Beers, Theodore S., 'The Biography of Vahshi Bāfqi (d. 991/1583) and the *Tazkera* Tradition', *Journal of Persianate Studies* 8.2 (2015), pp. 195–222.

Bland, N., 'Account of the Atesh Kedah, a Biographical Work on the Persian Poets, by Hajji Lutf Ali Beg of Ispakan', *Journal of the Royal Asiatic Society of Great Britain and Ireland* 7.2 (1843), pp. 345–92.

Bredi, Daniela, 'Remarks on *Ara'ish-e Mahfil* by Mir Sher 'Ali Afsos', *The Annual of Urdu Studies* vol. 14 (1999), pp. 33–53.

Browne, Edward Granville, *Literary History of Persia*, 4 vols (Cambridge: Cambridge University Press, 1928–30).

Chatterjee, Kumkum, *The Cultures of History in Early Modern India: Persianization and Mughal Culture in Bengal* (New Delhi: Oxford University Press, 2009).

Cohn, Bernard, *Colonialism and Its Forms of Knowledge* (Princeton: Princeton University Press, 1996).

Cornwall, Owen, 'Alexander and the Persian Cosmopolis, 1000–1500', unpublished PhD dissertation, Columbia University, 2016.

Dabashi, Hamid, *The World of Persian Literary Humanism* (Cambridge, MA: Harvard University Press, 2012).

Dale, Stephen F., *The Muslim Empires of the Ottomans, Safavids, and Mughals* (Cambridge: Cambridge University Press, 2010).

Dalrymple, William, *The Return of a King: The Battle for Afghanistan, 1839–1842* (New York: Alfred A. Knopf, 2013).

Das, Sisar Kumar, *Sahibs and Munshis: An Account of the College at Fort William* (Calcutta: Orion, 1978).

Datla, Kavita, 'A Worldly Vernacular: Urdu at Osmania University', *Modern Asian Studies* 43.5 (2009), pp. 1,117–48.

Dhavan, Purnima, 'Marking Boundaries and Building Bridges: Persian Scholarly

Networks in Mughal Punjab', in Nile Green (ed.), *The Persianate World: The Frontiers of a Eurasian Lingua Franca* (Oakland: University of California Press, 2019), pp. 159–73.

Dhavan, Purnima and Heidi Pauwels, 'Controversies Surrounding the Reception of Valī "Dakhanī" (1665?–1707?) in Early Tażkirahs of Urdu Poets', *JRAS Series 3*, 25.4 (2015), pp. 625–46.

Digby, Simon. 'Travels in Ladakh, 1820–1821: The Account of Moorcroft's Persian *Munshi*, Hajji Sayyid 'Ali, of His Travels', *Asian Affairs* 29.3 (1998), pp. 299–311.

Digby, Simon, 'An Eighteenth Century Narrative of a Journey from Bengal to England: Munshi Ismaʻil's *New* History', in Christopher Shackle (ed.), *Urdu and Muslim South Asia: Studies in Honour of Ralph Russell* (London: School of Oriental and African Studies, 1989), pp. 49–65.

Dudney, Arthur, 'Testing the Limits of Comparatism: The Quarrel of the Ancients and Moderns in Persian and Urdu Literary Culture', talk given at the Institute for South Asian Studies, University of California, Berkeley, 5 April 2018.

Dudney, Arthur, 'Metaphorical Language as a Battleground for Tradition and Newness in Late Mughal Persian', *International Journal of Persian Literature* 2 (2017), pp. 138–60.

Dudney, Arthur, 'Sabk-e Hendi and the Crisis of Authority in Eighteenth-Century Indo-Persian Poetics', *Journal of Persianate Studies* 9.1 (2016), pp. 60–82.

Dupree, Louis, 'The First Anglo-Afghan War and the British Retreat of 1842: The Functions of History and Folklore', *East and West* 26.3/4 (Sept.–Dec. 1976), pp. 503–29.

Eaton, Richard M., 'The Persian Cosmopolis (900–1900) and the Sanskrit Cosmopolis (400–1400)' in Abbas Amanat and Assef Ashraf (eds), *The Persianate World: Rethinking a Shared Sphere* (Leiden; Boston: Brill, 2018), pp. 63–83.

Edwards, David B., 'Words in the Balance: The Poetics of Political Dissent in Afghanistan', in Dale F. Eickelman (ed.), *Russia's Muslim Frontiers: New Directions in Cross-cultural Analysis* (Bloomington and Indianapolis: Indiana University Press, 1993), pp. 114–29.

Edwards, David B., 'Mad Mullahs and Englishmen: Discourse in the Colonial Encounter', *Comparative Studies in Society and History* 31.4 (Oct. 1989), pp. 649–70.

Fani, Aria, 'Becoming Literature: The Formation of *Adabiyat* as an Academic Discipline in Iran and Afghanistan (1895–1945)', unpublished PhD dissertation, University of California, Berkeley, 2019.

Farhadi, R., 'Anjoman-e Tarik-e Afganestan', *Encyclopedia Iranica Online*, 2011. <http://www.iranicaonline.org/articles/anjoman-e-tarik-e-afganestan> (last accessed 31 January 2019).

Faruqi, Shamsur Rahman, 'A Stranger in the City: The Poetics of *Sabk-e Hindi*', *The Annual of Urdu Studies* 19 (2004), pp. 1–93.

Faruqi, Shamsur Rahman, 'A Long History of Urdu Literary Culture, Part 1: Naming and Placing a Literary Culture', in Sheldon Pollock (ed.), *Literary Cultures in History: Reconstructions from South Asia* (Berkeley: University of California Press, 2003), pp. 805–63.

Faruqi, Shamsur Rahman, 'Unprivileged Power: The Strange Case of Persian (and Urdu) in Nineteenth Century India', *The Annual of Urdu Studies* 13 (1998), pp. 3–30.

Faruqi, Shamsur Rahman, 'Constructing a Literary History, a Canon, and a Theory of Poetry: Ab-e Hayat (1880) by Muhammad Husain Azad (1830–1910)', *Social Scientist* 23.10/12 (Oct.–Dec. 1995), pp. 70–97.

Faruqui, Munis D., *The Princes of the Mughal Empire, 1504–1719* (Cambridge: Cambridge University Press, 2012).

Ferdowsi, Ali, 'The "Emblem of the Manifestation of the Iranian Spirit": Hafiz and the Rise of the National Cult of Persian Poetry', *Iranian Studies* 41.5 (Dec. 2008), pp. 667–91.

Fisher, Michael H., 'Conflicting Meanings of Persianate Culture: An Intimate Example from Colonial India and Britain', in Nile Green (ed.), *The Persianate World: The Frontiers of a Eurasian Lingua Franca* (Oakland: University of California Press, 2019), pp. 225–41.

Fisher, Michael H., 'Teaching Persian as an Imperial Language in India and in England during the late 18th and early 19th Centuries', in Brian Spooner and William L. Hanaway (eds), *Literacy in the Persianate World: Writing and the Social Order* (Philadelphia: University of Pennsylvania Museum of Archaeology and Anthropology, 2012), pp. 328–58.

Fisher, Michael H., *Counterflows to Colonialism: Indian Travellers and Settlers in Britain 1600–1857* (Delhi: Permanent Black, 2004).

Fisher, Michael H., 'The Office of Akhbar Nawis: The Transition from Mughal to British Forms', *Modern Asian Studies* 27.1 (1993), pp. 45–82.

Fisher, Michael H., *Indirect Rule in India: Residents and the Residency System, 1764–1858* (Delhi: Oxford University Press, 1991).

Firuzkuhi, K. Amiri, ''Asheq Esfahani', *Encyclopedia Iranica Online*, 1987. <http://www.iranicaonline.org/articles/aseq-esfahani-aqa-mohammad-kayyat-or-in-

one-account-mohammad-khan-a-persian-poet-of-the-12th–18th-century> (last accessed 17 December 2018).

Gallagher, Catherine and Stephen Greenblatt, *Practicing New Historicism* (Chicago; London: University of Chicago Press, 2000).

Gheissari, Ali, 'Iran's Dialectic of the Enlightenment: Constitutional Experience, Transregional Connections, and Conflicting Narratives of Modernity', in Ali M. Ansari (ed.), *Iran's Constitutional Revolution of 1906 and the Narratives of Enlightenment* (London: Gingko Library, 2016), pp. 15–47.

Green, Nile, 'Introduction: The Frontiers of the Persianate World (ca. 800–1900)', in Nile Green (ed.), *The Persianate World: The Frontiers of a Eurasian Lingua Franca* (Oakland: University of California Press, 2019), pp. 1–71.

Green, Nile, 'From Persianate Pasts to Aryan Antiquity: Transnationalism and Transformation in Afghan Intellectual History, c. 1880–1940', *Afghanistan* 1.1 (2018), pp. 26–67.

Green, Nile, 'The Afghan Discovery of Buddha: Civilizational History and the Nationalizing of Afghan Antiquity', *International Journal of Middle East Studies* 49.1 (2017), pp. 47–70.

Green, Nile, 'Introduction: A History of Afghan Historiography', in Nile Green (ed.), *Afghan History through Afghan Eyes* (Oxford: Oxford University Press, 2017), pp. 1–51.

Green, Nile. *The Love of Strangers: What Six Muslim Students Learned in Jane Austen's London* (Princeton: Princeton University Press, 2015).

Green, Nile, 'Introduction: Afghan Literature between Diaspora and Nation', in Nile Green and Nushin Arbabzadah (eds), *Afghanistan in Ink: Literature Between Diaspora and Nation* (New York: Columbia University Press, 2013), pp. 1–30.

Green, Nile, 'Urdu as an African Language: A Survey of Source Literature', *Islamic Africa* 3:2 (2012), pp. 173–99.

Green, Nile, *Bombay Islam: The Religious Economy of the West Indian Ocean, 1840–1915* (Cambridge: Cambridge University Press, 2011).

Green, Nile, 'The Uses of Books in a Late Mughal Takiyya: Persianate Knowledge Between Person and Paper', *Modern Asian Studies* 44 (2010), pp. 241–65.

Habibi, A., 'Aryana', *Encyclopedia Iranica Online*, 2011. <http://www.iranicaonline.org/articles/aryana-bulletin-of-the-historical-society-of-afghanistan> (last accessed 20 December 2018).

Hadi, Nabi, *Dictionary of Indo-Persian Literature* (New Delhi: Indira Gandhi National Centre for the Arts, Abhinav, 1995).

Hakala, Walter, *Negotiating Languages: Urdu, Hindi, and the Definition of Modern South Asia* (New York: Columbia University Press, 2016).

Hanaway, Jr, William L., 'Is There a Canon of Persian Poetry?', *Edebiyat* 4.1 (1993), pp 4–12.

Hanaway Jr, William L., 'Bazgasht-e Adabi', *Encyclopaedia Iranica Online*, 1989. <http://www.iranicaonline.org/articles/bazgast-e-adabi> (last accessed 7 December 2018).

Hanifi, M. Jamal, 'Colonial Production of Hegemony through the "Loya Jerga" in Afghanistan', *Iranian Studies* 37.2 (Jun. 2004), pp. 295–322.

Hanifi, Shah Mahmoud, *Connecting Histories in Afghanistan: Market Relations and State Formation on a Colonial Frontier* (Stanford, CA: Stanford University Press, 2011).

Hermansen, Marcia K. and Bruce B. Lawrence, 'Indo-Persian Tazkiras as Memorative Communications', in David Gilmartin and Bruce B. Lawrence (eds), *Beyond Turk and Hindu: Rethinking Religious Identities in Islamicate South Asia* (Gainesville, FL: University of Florida Press, 2000), pp. 149–75.

Heston, Wilma, 'Pashto Oral and Popular Literature', in Philip G. Kreyenbroek and Ulrich Marzolph (eds), *Oral Literature of Iranian Languages: Kurdish, Pashto, Balochi, Ossetic, Persian & Tajik*, Companion vol. II to *A History of Persian Literature* (London: I. B. Tauris, 2010), pp. 135–66.

Hodgson, Marshall G. S., *The Venture of Islam: Conscience and History in a World Civilization*, vol. 2 (Chicago: University of Chicago Press, 1974).

Hohendahl, Peter Uwe, *Building a National Literature: The Case of Germany, 1830–1870* (Ithaca: Cornell University Press, 1989).

Hopkins, B. D., *The Making of Modern Afghanistan* (New York: Palgrave Macmillan, 2012).

Inan, Murat Umut, 'Imperial Ambitions, Mystical Aspirations: Persian Learning in the Ottoman World' in Nile Green (ed.), *The Persianate World: The Frontiers of a Eurasian Lingua Franca* (Oakland: University of California Press, 2019), pp. 75–92.

Ivanow, Wladimir, *Concise Descriptive Catalogue of the Persian Manuscripts in the Collections of the Asiatic Society of Bengal, First Supplement* (Calcutta: Asiatic Society of Bengal, 1927).

Jabbari, Alexander, 'The Making of Modernity in Persianate Literary History', *Comparative Studies of South Asia, Africa, and the Middle East* 36.3 (Dec. 2016), pp. 418–34.

Karimi-Hakkak, Ahmad, 'Continuity and Creativity: Models of Change in Persian

Poetry, Classical and Modern', in Ali-Asghar Seyed-Ghorab (ed.), *The Layered Heart: Essays on Persian Poetry, a Celebration in Honor of Dick Davis* (Washington, DC: Mage, 2019), pp. 25–54.

Karimi-Hakkak, Ahmad, 'Language Reform Movement and its Language: The Case of Persian' in Björn H. Jernudd and Michael J. Shapiro (eds), *The Politics of Language Purism* (Berlin; Boston: De Gruyter Mouton, 2011), pp. 81–104.

Karimi-Hakkak, Ahmad, *Recasting Persian Poetry: Scenarios of Poetic Modernity in Iran* (Salt Lake City: University of Utah Press, 1995).

Kashani-Sabet, Firoozeh, *Frontier Fictions: Shaping the Iranian Nation, 1804–1946* (Princeton: Princeton University Press, 1999).

Keshavmurthy, Prashant, *Persian Authorship and Canonicity in Late Mughal Delhi: Building an Ark* (London: Routledge, 2016).

Khan, Pasha M., 'Marvellous Histories: Reading the *Shahnamah* in India', *Indian Economic and Social History Review* 49.4 (2012), pp. 527–56.

Khazeni, Arash, *Sky Blue Stone: The Turquoise Trade in World History* (Berkeley: University of California Press, 2014).

Kia, Mana, 'Indian Friends, Iranian Selves, Persianate Modern', *Comparative Studies of South Asia, Africa and the Middle East* 36.3 (2016), pp. 398–417.

Kia, Mana, 'Imaging Iran before Nationalism: Geocultural Meanings of Land in Azar's Ateshkadeh', in Kamran Scot Aghaie and Afshin Marashi (eds), *Rethinking Iranian Nationalism and Modernity* (Austin: University of Texas Press, 2014), pp. 89–112.

Kia, Mana, 'Contours of Persianate Community, 1722–1835', unpublished PhD dissertation, Harvard University, 2011.

Kia, Mehrdad, 'Persian Nationalism and the Campaign for Language Purification', *Middle Eastern Studies* 34.2 (April 1998), pp. 9–36.

Kinra, Rajeev, *Writing Self, Writing Empire: Chandar Bhan Brahman and the Cultural World of the Indo-Persian State Secretary* (Oakland: University of California Press, 2015).

Kinra, Rajeev, 'Make it Fresh: Time, Tradition, and Indo-Persian Literary Modernity', in Anne Murphy (ed.), *Time, History and the Religious Imaginary in South Asia* (London; New York: Routledge, 2011), pp. 12–39.

Kinra, Rajeev, 'Fresh Words for a Fresh World: Taza-Gui and the Poetics of Newness in Early Modern Indo-Persian Poetry', *Sikh Formations* 3.2 (2007), pp. 125–49.

Kokan, Muhammad Yosouf, *Arabic and Persian in Carnatic, 1710–1960* (Madras: Ameera, 1974).

Kolbas, E. Dean, *Critical Theory and the Literary Canon* (Boulder, CO: Westview Press, 2001).

Lal, Mohan, *Travels in the Panjab, Aghanistan, & Turkistan, to Balk, Bokhara, and Herat; a Visit to Great Britain and Germany* (London: W. H. Allen, 1846).

Lambton, Ann K. S., 'Persian Biographical Literature', in Bernard Lewis and P. M. Holt (eds), *Historians of the Middle East* (London: Oxford University Press, 1964), pp. 141–51.

Lanzillo, Amanda, 'The Politics of Persian Language Education in Colonial India', *Ajam Media Collective Online*, 31 January 2018. <https://ajammc.com/2018/01/31/late-indo-persian/> (last accessed 12 December 2018).

Lefevere, André, *Translation, Rewriting, and the Manipulation of Literary Fame* (London; New York: Routledge, 2017).

Lehmann, Fritz, 'Urdu Literature and Mughal Decline', *Mahfil* 6.2/3 (1970), pp. 125–31.

Lewis, Franklin, 'The Shahnameh of Ferdowsi as World Literature', *Iranian Studies* 48.3 (2015), pp. 313–36.

Levine, Robert S., *Dislocating Race and Nation: Episodes in Nineteenth-Century American Literary Nationalism* (Chapel Hill: University of North Carolina Press, 2008).

Losensky, Paul, 'Introduction: Symposium on the Eighteenth-Century Fracturing of the Persianate World', *Journal of Persianate Studies* 2.2 (2009), pp. 145–7.

Losensky, Paul, 'Poetic and Eros in Early Modern Persia: *The Lovers' Confection* and *The Glorious Epistle* by Muhtasham Kashani', *Iranian Studies* 42.5 (2009), pp. 745–64.

Losensky, Paul, 'Vahshi Bafqi', *Encyclopedia Iranica Online*, 2004. <http://www.iranicaonline.org/articles/vahshi-bafqi> (last accessed 14 December 2018).

Losensky, Paul, *Welcoming Fighani: Imitation and Poetic Individuality in the Safavid–Mughal Ghazal* (Costa Mesa, CA: Mazda, 1998).

Macaulay, Thomas Babington, 'Minute on Education', 2 February 1835. <http://www.columbia.edu/itc/mealac/pritchett/00generallinks/macaulay/txt_minute_education_1835.html> (last accessed 12 December 2018).

McChesney, Robert D., 'The Anthology of Poets: *Muzzakir al-Ashab* as a Source for the History of Seventeenth-Century Central Asia', in Michel M. Mazzaoui and Vera B. Moreen (eds), *Intellectual Studies on Islam: Essays Written in Honor of Martin B. Dickson* (Salt Lake City: University of Utah Press, 1990), pp. 57–84.

Madras Letter from Court, Foreign Department, 18 October 1854, no. 3, National Archives of India, New Delhi, India.

Madras Letter from Court, Foreign Department, 6 February 1849, no. 2, National Archives of India, New Delhi, India.

Madras Letter to Court, Foreign Department, 14 February 1837, no. 3, National Archives of India, New Delhi, India.

Marashi, Afshin, 'Parsi Textual Philanthropy: Print Commerce and the Revival of Zoroastrianism in Early 20th-Century Iran', in Alka Patel and Touraj Daryaee (eds), *India and Iran in the Longue Durée* (Irvine: University of California Jordan Center for Persian Studies, 2017), pp. 125–42.

Marashi, Afshin, 'Patron and Patriot: Dinshah J. Irani and the Revival of Indo-Iranian Culture', *Iranian Studies* 46.2 (2013), pp. 185–206.

Marashi, Afshin, *Nationalizing Iran: Culture, Power, and the State, 1870–1940* (Seattle: University of Washington Press, 2011).

Matini, J., 'Azar Bigdeli', *Encyclopedia Iranica Online*, 2011. <http://www.iranicaonline.org/articles/azar-bigdeli-hajj-lotf-ali-big> (last accessed 17 December 2018).

Matthee, Rudi, 'Coffee in Safavid Iran: Commerce and Consumption', *Journal of the Economic and Social History of the Orient* 37.1 (1994), pp. 1–32.

Mazzaoui, Michel M., 'Islamic Culture and Literature in Iran and Central Asia in the Early Modern Period', in Robert L. Canfield (ed.), *Turko-Persian in Historical Perspective* (Cambridge: Cambridge University Press, 1991), pp. 78–103.

Melville, Charles, 'Rashīd al-Dīn and the Shāhnāmeh', *Journal of the Royal Asiatic Society, Series 3*, 26:1–2 (2016), pp. 201–14.

Melville, Charles, '"Ali Yazdi and the *Shahname*', in Forogh Hashabeiky (ed.), *International Shahname Conference: The Second Millenium, Conference Volume*, Department of Linguistics and Philology, Uppsala University, Sweden, 15–16 October 2011 (Uppsala: Uppsala Universitet, 2014), pp. 117–33.

Melville, Charles and Gabrielle van den Berg (eds), *Shahnama Studies II: The Reception of Firdausi's Shahnama* (Leiden; Boston: Brill, 2012).

Meneghini, Daniela, 'Kalim Kashani', *Encyclopedia Iranica Online*, 2012. <http://www.iranicaonline.org/articles/kalim-kasani> (last accessed 21 December 2018).

Meskoob, Shahrokh, *Iranian National Identity and the Persian Language 900–1900, The Roles of the Court, Religion, and Sufism in Persian Prose Writing*, Michael C. Hillman (trans.), John R. Perry (ed.) (Washington, DC: Mage, 1992).

Metcalf, Barbara D., 'Urdu in India in the 21st Century: A Historian's Perspective', *Social Scientist* 31.5/6 (June 2003), pp. 29–37.

Mikkelson, Jane, 'Of Parrots and Crows: Bīdil and Ḥazīn in Their Own Words'

Comparative Studies of South Asia, Africa, and the Middle East 37.4 (2017), pp. 510–30.
Minault, Gail, 'Delhi College and Urdu', *Annual of Urdu Studies* 14 (1999), pp. 119–34.
Mohiuddin, Momin. *The Chancellery and Persian Epistolography under the Mughals* (Calcutta: Iran Society, 1971).
Moin, A. Azfar, *The Millennial Sovereign: Sacred Kingship and Sainthood in Islam* (New York: Columbia University Press, 2012).
Naim, C. M., 'Mughal and English Patronage of Urdu Poetry: A Comparison', in Barbara Stoler Miller (ed.), *The Powers of Art: Patronage in Indian Culture* (Delhi; New York: Oxford University Press, 1992), pp. 259–76.
Nawid, Senzil, 'Writing National History: Afghan Historiography in the Twentieth Century', in Nile Green (ed.), *Afghan History through Afghan Eyes* (London; Oxford: Oxford University Press, 2017), pp. 185–210.
Nawid, Senzil, 'Historiography in the Sadduzai Era: Language and Narration', in Brian Spooner and William Hanaway (eds), *Literacy in the Persianate World: Writing and the Social Order* (Philadelphia: University of Pennsylvania Museum of Archaeology and Anthropology, 2012), pp. 234–78.
Noelle, Christine, *State and Tribe in Nineteenth-Century Afghanistan: The Reign of Amir Dost Muhammad Khan (1826–1863)* (Richmond, Surrey: Curzon, 1997).
Noelle-Karimi, Christine, 'Afghan Polities and the Indo-Persian Literary Realm: The Durrani Rulers and their Portrayal in Eighteenth-Century Historiography', in Nile Green (ed.), *Afghan History through Afghan Eyes* (London; Oxford: Oxford University Press, 2017), pp. 53–77.
Oesterheld, Christina, 'Campaigning for a Community: Urdu Literature of Mobilisation and Identity', *The Indian Economic and Social History Review* 54.1 (2017), pp. 43–66.
Ogborn, Miles, and Charles W. J. Withers (eds), *Geographies of the Book* (Farnham; Burlingon, VT: Ashgate, 2010).
Orsini, Francesca, 'Between *Qasbas* and Cities: Language Shifts and Literary Continuities in North India in the Long Eighteenth Century', *Comparative Studies of South Asia, Africa and the Middle East* 39.1 (2019), pp. 68–81.
Osterhammel, Jürgen, *The Transformation of the World: A Global History of the Nineteenth Century*, trans. Patrick Camiller (Princeton: Princeton University Press, 2015).
Pauwels, Heidi, 'Literary Moments of Exchange in the 18th Century: The New Urdu Vogue Meets Krishna Bakhti', in Alka Patel and Karen Leonard

(eds), *Indo-Muslim Cultures in Transition* (Leiden; Boston: Brill, 2012), pp. 61–84.

Pellò, Stefano, 'Persian Poets on the Streets: The Lore of Indo-Persian Poetic Circles in Late Mughal India', in Francesca Orsini and Katherine Butler Schofield (eds), *Telling and Texts: Music, Literature, and Performance in North India* (Cambridge: Open Book Publishers, 2015), pp. 303–26.

Perkins, David, *Is Literary History Possible?* (Baltimore; London: The Johns Hopkins University Press, 1992).

Pernau, Margrit, 'The *Delhi Urdu* Akhbar Between Persian Akhbarat and English Newspapers', *The Annual of Urdu Studies* 18 (2003), pp. 105–31.

Perry, John R., 'Language Reform in Turkey and Iran', *International Journal of Middle East Studies* 17.3 (Aug. 1985), pp. 295–311.

Perry, John R., *Karim Khan Zand: A History of Iran, 1747–1779* (Chicago: University of Chicago Press, 1979).

Perry, John R., 'The Last Safavids, 1722–1773', *Iran* 9 (1971), pp. 59–69.

Phillips, Jim, 'A Successor to the Moguls: The Nawab of the Carnatic and the East India Company, 1763–1785', *The International History Review* 7.3 (Aug. 1985), pp. 364–89.

Potts, Daniel T., 'Qeshm Island', *Encyclopedia Iranica Online*, 2004. <http://www.iranicaonline.org/articles/qeshm-island> (last accessed 20 December 2018).

Pritchett, Frances, 'A Long History of Urdu Literary Culture, Part 2: Histories, Performances, and Masters', in Sheldon Pollock (ed.), *Literary Cultures in History: Reconstructions from South Asia* (Berkeley: University of California Press, 2003), pp. 864–911.

Qamber, Akhtar (trans.), *The Last Musha'irah of Delhi: A Translation into English of Farhatullah Baig's Modern Urdu Classic, Delhi ki akhri shama'* (New Delhi: Orient Longman, 1979).

Rahimieh, Nasrin, 'Four Iterations of Persian Literary Nationalism', in Meir Litvak (ed.), *Constructing Nationalism in Iran: From the Qajars to the Islamic Republic* (London; New York: Routledge, 2017), pp. 40–55.

Rahman, Munibar, 'Mirza Asad-Allah Khan Galeb', *Encyclopedia Iranica Online*, 2012. <http://www.iranicaonline.org/articles/galeb> (last accessed 24 December 2018).

Rahman, Tariq, 'Urdu as an Islamic Language', *Annual of Urdu Studies* 21 (2006), pp. 101–19.

Rahman, Tariq, 'Decline of Persian in British India', *South Asia: Journal of South Asian Studies* 22.1 (1999), pp. 47–62.

Rahmany, Mirwais, and Hamid Stanikzai (trans.), *Poetry of the Taliban*, Alex Strick van Linschoten and Felix Kuehn (eds) (New York: Columbia University Press, 2012).

Ramaswami, N. S., *Political History of Carnatic under the Nawwabs* (New Delhi: Abhinav, 1984).

Rieu, Charles, *Catalogue of the Persian Manuscripts of the British Museum* (London: British Museum, 1879).

Ringer, Monica, 'Reform Transplanted: Parsi Agents of Change amongst Zoroastrians in Nineteenth-Century Iran', *Iranian Studies* 42.4 (Sept. 2009), pp. 549–60.

Ríos-Font, Wadda C., 'Literary History and Canon Formation', in David T. Gies (ed.), *The Cambridge History of Spanish Literature* (Cambridge: Cambridge University Press, 2009), pp. 15–35.

Robinson, Chase F., *Islamic Historiography* (Cambridge: Cambridge University Press, 2003).

Robinson, Francis, 'Perso-Islamic Culture from the Seventeenth to the Early Twentieth Century', in Robert Canfield (ed.), *Turko-Persia in Historical Perspective* (Cambridge: Cambridge University Press, 1991), pp. 104–31.

Rubanovich, Julia, 'Tracking the *Shahnama* in Medieval Persian Folk Prose', in Charles Melville and Gabrielle van den Berg (eds), *Shahnama Studies II: The Reception of Firdausi's Shahnama* (Leiden; Boston: Brill, 2012), pp. 11–34.

Russell, Ralph (ed.), *The Oxford India Ghalib: Life, Letters, and Ghazals* (New Delhi; New York: Oxford University Press, 2003).

Russell, Ralph, *The Pursuit of Urdu Literature: A Select History* (London and New Jersey: Zed Books, 1992).

Rypka, Jan, *History of Iranian Literature*, Karl Jahn (ed.) (Dordrecht: D. Reidel, 1968).

Sarfaraz, 'Abd al-Qadir, *A Descriptive Catalogue of the Arabic, Persian and Urdu Manuscripts in the Library of the University of Bombay* (Bombay: University of Bombay, 1935).

Savory, Roger, *Iran under the Safavids* (Cambridge: Cambridge University Press, 1980).

Schimmel, Annemarie, *Islamic Literatures of India* (Wiesbaden: Otto Harrassowitz, 1973).

Schmidt, Jan, 'The Reception of Firdausi's *Shahnama* among the Ottomans', in Charles Melville and Gabrielle van den Berg (eds), *Shahnama Studies II: The Reception of Firdausi's Shahnama* (Leiden; Boston: Brill, 2012), pp. 121–39.

Schwartz, Kevin L., 'A Transregional Persianate Library: The Production and

Circulation of *Tadhkira*s of Poets in the 18th and 19th Centuries', *International Journal of Middle East Studies*, forthcoming.

Schwartz, Kevin L., 'The Curious Case of Carnatic: The Last Nawab of Arcot (d. 1855) and Persian Literary Culture', *Indian Economic and Social History Review* 53.4 (2016), pp. 533–60.

Schwartz, Kevin L., 'The Local Lives of a Transregional Poet: 'Abd al-Qader Bidel and the Writing of Persianate Literary History', *Journal of Persianate Societies* 9.1 (2016), pp. 83–106.

Schwartz, Kevin L., 'Bazgasht-i Adabi (Literary Return) and Persianate Literary Culture in Eighteenth and Nineteenth Century Iran, India, and Afghanistan', unpublished PhD dissertation, University of California, Berkeley, 2014.

Shah, Zahra, 'Sustaining Authority in Persian Lithographed Books: Publishers and Printing in North India, c. 1835–57', *South Asian Studies* 33.2 (2017), pp. 137–48.

Shamel, Shafiq, 'Afghanistan and the Persian Epic *Shahnama*: Historical Agency and the Epic Imagination in Afghan and Afghan–American Literature', in Nile Green and Nushin Arbabzadah (eds), *Afghanistan in Ink: Literature Between Diaspora and Nation* (New York: Columbia University Press, 2013), pp. 209–27.

Sharma, Sunil, 'Fā'iz Dihlavī's Female-Centered Poems and the Representation of Public Life in Late Mughal Society', in Kishwar Rizvi (ed.), *Affect, Emotion, and Subjectivity in Early Modern Muslim Empires: New Studies in Ottoman, Safavid, and Mughal Art and Culture* (Leiden: Brill, 2017), pp. 168–84.

Sharma, Sunil, *Mughal Arcadia: Persian Literature at an Indian Court* (Cambridge, MA: Harvard University Press, 2017).

Sharma, Sunil, 'Reading the Acts and Lives of Performers in Mughal Persian Texts', Francesca Orsini and Katherine Butler Schofield (eds), *Telling and Texts: Music, Literature, and Performance in North India* (Cambridge: Open Book Publishers, 2015), pp. 283–302.

Sharma, Sunil, 'Redrawing the Boundaries of 'Ajam in Early Modern Persian Literary History', in Abbas Amanant and Farvin Vejdani (eds), *Iran Facing Others: Identity Boundaries in a Historical Perspective* (New York: Palgrave Macmillan, 2012), pp. 51–64.

Sharma, Sunil, 'From 'Āesha to Nur Jahān: The Shaping of a Classical Persian Poetic Canon of Women', *Journal of Persianate Societies* 2.2 (2009), pp. 148–64.

Sharma, Sunil, 'The City of Beauties in Indo-Persian Poetic Landscape', *Comparative Studies of South Asia, Africa and the Middle East* 24.3 (2004), pp. 73–81.

Shafieioun, Saeid, 'Some Critical Remarks on the Migration of Iranian Poets to India in the Safavid Era', *Journal of Persianate Studies* 11 (2018), pp. 155–74.
Sheffield, Daniel J., 'Frankish Wine in Persian Bottles: Patronage, Sovereignty, and Gender in the *Georgenama* of Mulla Firuz', unpublished paper.
Smith, Matthew C., 'Betrayed by Earth and Sky: Poetry of Disaster and Restoration in Eighteenth-Century Iran', *Journal of Persianate Studies* 11 (2018), pp. 175–202.
Smith, Matthew C., 'Literary Connections: Bahar's *Sabkshenasi* and the *Bazgasht-e Adabi*', *Journal of Persianate Studies* 2.2 (2009), pp. 194–209.
Smith, Matthew C., 'Literary Courage: Language, Land and the Nation in the Works of Malik al-Shu'ara Bahar', unpublished PhD dissertation, Harvard University, 2006.
Spooner, Brian, 'Persian, Farsi, Dari, Tajiki: Language Names and Language Policies' in Harold F. Schiffman (ed.), *Language Policy and Language Conflict in Afghanistan and Its Neighbors: The Changing Politics of Language Choice* (Leiden: Brill, 2011), pp. 89–117.
Spooner, Brian and William L. Hanaway, 'Introduction: Persian as *Koine*: Written Persian in World-Historical Perspective', in Brian Spooner and William L. Hanaway (eds), *Literacy in the Persianate World: Writing and the Social Order* (Philadelphia: University of Pennsylvania Museum of Archaeology and Anthropology, 2012), pp. 1–68.
Sprenger, Aloys, *A Catalogue of the Arabic, Persian, and Hindu'sta'ny Manuscripts of the Libraries of the King of Oudh* (Calcutta: J. Thomas, 1854).
Stark, Ulrike, 'Politics, Public Issues and the Promotion of Urdu Literature: Avadh Akhbar, the First Urdu Daily in Northern India', *Annual of Urdu Studies* 18 (2003), pp. 66–95.
Storey, C. A. *Persian Literature: A Bio-Bibliographical Survey* (London: Luzac, 1927).
Syed, Muhammad Aslam, 'How Could Urdu be the Envy of Persian (rashk-i-Farsi)!: The Role of Persian in South Asian Literature in Culture', in Brian Spooner and William L. Hanaway (eds), *Literacy in the Persianate World: Writing and the Social Order* (Philadelphia: University of Pennsylvania Museum of Archaeology and Anthropology, 2012), pp. 279–310.
Tabor, Nathan L. M., 'Heartless Acts: Literary Competition and Multilingual Association at a Graveside Gathering in Eighteenth-Century Delhi', *Comparative Studies of South Asia, Africa and the Middle East* 39.1 (2019), pp. 82–95.
Tavakoli-Targhi, Mohamad, *Refashioning Iran: Orientalism, Occidentalism, and Historiography* (New York: Palgrave, 2001).
Tavakoli-Targhi, Mohamad, 'Contested Memories: Narrative Structures and

Allegorical Meanings of Iran's Pre-Islamic History', *Iranian Studies* 29.1–2 (Winter–Spring 1996), pp. 149–75.

Tikku, G. L., *Persian Poetry in Kashmir, 1339–1846* (Berkeley: University of California Press, 1971).

Trivedi, Madhu, *The Making of Awadh Culture* (Delhi: Primus, 2010).

Uluç, Lale, 'The *Shahanama* of Firdausi in the Lands of Rum', in Charles Melville and Gabrielle van den Berg (eds), *Shahnama Studies II: The Reception of Firdausi's Shahnama* (Leiden; Boston: Brill, 2012), pp. 161–80.

Vasilyeva, Ludmila, 'The Indian Mushairah: Traditions and Modernity', in Satyanarayana Hegde (ed.), *An Informal Festschrift in Honor of the Manifold Lifetime Achievements of Shamsur Rahman Faruqi* (2010–), pp. 1–18. <http://www.columbia.edu/itc/mealac/pritchett/00urduhindilinks/srffest/> (last accessed 12 December 2018).

Vatuk, Sylvia, 'Islamic Learning at the College of Fort St. George in Nineteenth-century Madras', in Thomas R. Trautmann (ed.), *The Madras School of Orientalism: Producing Knowledge in Colonial South India* (New Delhi: Oxford University Press, 2009), pp. 48–73.

Vaziri, Mostafa, *Iran as Imagined Nation: The Construction of National Identity* (New York: Paragon House, 1993).

Vejdani, Farzin, 'Indo-Iranian Linguistic, Literary, and Religious Entanglements between Nationalism and Cosmopolitanism, ca. 1900–1940', *Comparative Studies of South Asia, Africa, and the Middle East* 36.3 (Dec. 2016), pp. 435–54.

Vejdani, Farzin, *Making History in Iran: Education, Nationalism, and Print Culture* (Stanford: Stanford University Press, 2015).

Wagoner, Phillip B., 'Precolonial Intellectuals and the Production of Colonial Knowledge', *Comparative Studies in Society and History* 45.4 (Oct. 2003), pp. 783–814.

Werner, Christoph, 'Taming the Tribal Native: Court Culture and Politics in Eighteenth Century Shiraz', in Albrecht Fuess and Jan-Peter Hartung (eds), *Court Cultures in the Muslim World: Seventeenth to Nineteenth Centuries* (London; New York: Routledge, 2011), pp. 221–34.

Yarshater, Ehsan, 'The Indian or Safavid Style: Progress of Decline?' in Ehsan Yarshater (ed.), *Persian Literature, Columbia Lectures on Iranian Studies No. 3* (Albany, NY: Bibliotheca Persica, 1988), pp. 249–88.

Zastoupil, Lynn and Martin Moir (eds), *The Great Indian Education Debate: Documents Related to the Orientalist–Anglicist Controversy, 1781–1843* (Richmond: Curzon Press, 1999).

Zia-Ebrahimi, Reza, *The Emergence of Iranian Nationalism: Race and the Politics of Dislocation* (New York: Columbia University Press, 2016).

Zilli, Ishtiyaq, 'Development of *Insha* Literature till the End of Akbar's Reign', in Muzaffar Alam, Francoise 'Nalini' Delvoye and Marc Gaborieau (eds), *The Making of Indo-Persian Culture: Indian and French Studies* (New Delhi: Manohar, 2000), pp. 309–49.

Index

'Abd al-Majid Darvish, 90, 99, 105
'Abd al-Rahman Khan, 50–1, 55–6, 137
Ahmad Shah Durrani, 50, 52, 133, 134
'Aisha Durrani, 52
Akbar Khan *see* Muhammad Akbar Khan
Akbarnama (*Book of Akbar*), 124–8, 137–45, 150–2
Akhavan-Sales, Mehdi, 47
'Akhtar' Garrusi, Ahmad Bayg, 88
Akhundzada, Mirza Fath Ali, 11
ancients *see* classical Persian poets
Anvari, 38, 43, 53, 94, 96–7, 111–12
Arcot
  Arcot State, 166–71
  literary networks, 172–7, 180–2
  literary production, 178–95
Aryana, 125–7
Aryana Encyclopedia, 56
Aryanpur, Yahya, 14
''Ashiq' Isfahani, Aqa Muhammad, 91, 94, 100, 105–6
Atishkada (*Firetemple*), 41, 82, 88, 103, 190
Awadh State, 64
Azad Bilgrami, 143, 164, 186–8, 193
'A'zam', Muhammad Ghaws Khan Bahadur, 163–71, 179, 194–7, 206
'Azar' Baygdili, Lutf Ali, 41, 48, 81–5, 88–9, 90, 91–2, 93, 94, 95–8, 100, 104–5, 116, 142–3, 149
  biography, 102–3
  poetry, 95–8, 101–2 106–15
  see also Isfahani Circle of poets

Bahadur Shah II, 65
Bahar, Muhammad Taqi, 13–14, 19, 20
  periodisation of Persian literature, 35–40
bāzgasht-i adabī see literary return
'Bidil', 'Abd al-Qadir, 164, 185–94, 197, 204, 206

Afghanistan, 51–53, 55–6
  Timur Shah's court, 52–3
  see also 'Indian style' and *tāza-gū'ī* (fresh-speak)
'Binish', Sayyid Murtaza, 172, 180–4;
  see also Isharat-i Binish (*Binish's Notices*)
biographical anthologies *see tadhkira*
Book of Kings see *Shahnama*

Carnatic *see* Arcot
classical Persian poets, 12–14, 18–23
  Afghanistan, 53–8

Dunbuli, 'Abd al-Razzaq 'Maftun', 41–5, 48, 88–9, 90, 92, 93, 94, 99–100, 104–5
Dust Muhammad Khan, 134–6, 137, 144

East India Company (EIC), 131, 154, 163, 175–6
  munshis, 60–2
  Nawabs of Arcot, 166–71, 194–5, 197

Farshidvard, Khusraw, 14
Fath Ali Shah, 14, 42, 45, 46–7, 88, 91, 93, 115, 117, 131, 205, 206
Firdawsi, 20, 38, 43, 97, 111–12, 124, 125, 129, 140, 150, 156; *see also Shahnama*
Fort William College, 67–8

Garrusi, Muhammad Fazil Khan, 41–2, 43, 44, 45
Ghalib, 67, 69
Ghubar, Ghulam Muhammad, 58
Ghulam 'Mushafi' Hamdani, 67
'Ghulami' Kuhistani, Muhammad Ghulam, 124, 134–8, 150–2

Gulzar-i A'zam (*A'zam's Rosegarden*), 1–2, 163–5, 184–94

Hafiz, 13, 20, 38, 53, 55, 89, 93
Hajji Muhammad Ranani, 86, 104–6, 107, 112
Hamid Allah Kashmiri, 124, 137–44, 149, 150–2
'Hatif' Isfahani, Sayyid Ahmad, 84–5, 90, 91–2, 94, 100, 116, 140
  poetry, 95–8, 104–115
  see also Isfahani Circle of poets
Hazin Lahiji, 192
Hidayat, Riza Quli Khan, 41, 48
  and 'literary return', 43–6
Historical Society of Afghanistan, 125–6, 134, 135

'Indian style', 14–15, 18, 37, 107, 194, 204
  Afghanistan, 51–3
  depictions, 38–40
  relationship to 'literary return', 38, 40–3, 82–5, 165, 189–92
  scholarship, 39–40
  see also *tāza-gū'ī* (fresh-speak)
'Iraqi style of poetry, 36–7, 55, 89
Isfahan
  destruction (1722), 85–7
  'literary return', 87–90
Isfahani Circle of poets, 84–5, 115–18, 139, 140, 143, 190, 204–5
  literary bonds, 95–8, 104–5
  literary networks, 91–4, 100–1
  poetry, 90, 92, 94–8, 107–15
  see also 'Azar', 'Hatif', Mirza 'Abd al-Wahhab, 'Mushtaq', and 'Sabahi'
Isharat-i Binish (*Binish's Notices*), 165, 170, 172–7; see also Arcot and 'Binish'

jangnāma
  first Anglo-Afghan War, 57–8, 124–30, 133, 150–6, 205
  genre, 130–3
Jangnama (*War Ballad*) of 'Ghulami', 124–8, 134–7, 150–2
Jones, William, 9

Kalim Kashani, 14, 53, 132, 139
Karim Khan Zand, 81, 86, 88–9, 90, 99, 103, 105–6
Khan-i Arzu, 187–8, 192, 193

Khaqani, 94, 139, 141
Khurasani style of poetry, 36–7, 55
Kuhzad, Ali Ahmad, 125, 134, 135

Library of Congress, 1–3
linguistic nationalism in Iran see Persian language reform
literary nationalism, 6, 10, 12–16, 202–3
  and cosmopolitanism 17–18, 202–3
literary networks
  Arcot, 172–7, 180–2
  Isfahan, 91–4, 100–1
'literary return'
  Afghanistan, 20, 53–58, 129–30, 143–4, 151, 156, 204
  as literary nationalism 6, 10, 12–16, 202–3
  Bahar, 37–8
  general, 3–5, 202
  modern impressions, 47
  Qajar court, 23, 42–8, 56–7, 91, 93, 117, 191–2, 206
  relationship to 'Indian style', 38, 40–3, 82–5, 165, 189–92
  standard narrative, 12–15
  Zand and Qajar impressions, 41–6, 83, 117–18; see also Dunbuli and Hidayat
literary societies
  Arcot, 170, 172–7
  Isfahan, 88–90, 91, 97–107

Ma'dan al-jawahir (*Mine of Jewels*), 163–5, 180–7
Majma' al-fusaha' (*Assembly of the Eloquent*), 43–6; see also Hidayat
maktab-i vuqū' (realist school), 89
Mawlana Baqir Agah, 180, 182, 183–4, 187, 191
Mir 'Abd al-Latif Khan Shushtari, 94
Mir Masjidi Khan, 134–6
Mir Taqi Mir, 66–7
Mirza 'Abd al-Wahhab, 81, 83, 85, 92, 97, 107, 113, 116–17
  and Isfahani Circle of poets, 98–104
Mohan Lal, 61–2
Mughals, 3, 14, 132
  break-up, 59–60, 63–4, 68–9
  relationship to Persian, 59, 60, 63–5, 139
Muhammad Akbar Khan 136, 137, 142, 147–8, 152

Muhammad Ali Walajah, 166–7
Muhammad Husayn Azad, 67
Muʿizzi, 20, 107–10
munshi, 60–2, 68
'Mushtaq' Isfahani, Sayyid Ali, 94
   historiographical treatment 42–3, 45
   literary society, 88–90, 91, 97, 100–1, 104–5, 107
   see also Isfahani Circle of poets

Nadir Shah, 60, 86, 90, 99, 102, 131
Nashat Isfahani, 20, 92–3
Nasir Ali Sirhindi, 169, 180, 182, 191
nationalism
   Afghanistan, 125–7
   Iran 6–9
   see also literary nationalism, 'literary return', Persian language reform
'Naziri' Nishapuri, Muhammad Husayn, 42, 45, 89, 116
Nizami, 43, 97, 111–12, 131
Nuʿmani, Shibli, 15, 21

orientalism, 6–9, 71

Persian language reform, 10–12
Persian 'literary decline'
   in Iran, 12–14
   in South Asia, 59–72, 165, 171, 197, 203–4
Persian poetic canon
   classical Persian poets, 12–14, 18–23
   formation, 17–23, 48, 93–4
   tāza-gūʾī (fresh-speak), 39–40
Persian secretary *see* munshi
Persianate world
   background, 3–5
   cosmopolitanism, 16–19, 202
poetic assemblies *see* literary societies

Qasim Ali, 124, 127–8, 144–52
'Qatil', Mirza Muhammad Hasan, 187, 188–9, 193
'Qudrat', Muhammad Qudratallah Khan Gupamavi, 174, 190

'Rafiq' Isfahani, 92, 94, 100, 105–6, 115, 140
'Raqim', Mawlavi Muhammad Husayn Qadiri, 171, 173–4, 180, 181, 182–4, 195, 196
Rekhta, 63, 64–5

Rudaki, 92, 97, 109, 189
Rumi, 13, 53, 139, 141

Saʿadat Khan Nasir, 66–7
'Saba' Kashani, Fath Ali Khan, 20, 93, 131
'Sabahi' Bidguli, Sulayman, 84–5, 90, 92, 94, 104–5, 106, 116, 140
   poetry, 95–98, 107–15
   see also Isfahani Circle of poets
sabk (style), 18–19
sabk-i Hindī see 'Indian style'
Saʿdi, 13, 43, 53, 89, 97, 111–12, 139, 141
Safa, Zabihullah 130
Safavids, 85
   relationship to poetry, 12–15, 44, 89
Sahba, 91, 94, 100, 105–6
Saʾib, 15, 53, 192
Shafaq, Riza-Zadah, 13, 36
Shah ʿAlam II, 63, 65
Shah Shujaʿ, 51, 54 134, 136, 146, 147, 151
Shahamat Ali, 61
Shahnama, 27, 57–8, 109, 112, 124, 125, 129, 140, 205
   imitations, 93, 130–3, 134–8, 149–54
   Mughals, 132
   Ottomans, 131–2
   Safavids, 131–2
   see also jangnāma
shahr-āshūb (city-disturber), 66
'Shamil', Sayyid Muhammad Muhsin, 55–6
Shir Ali Khan, 54, 56
Shujaʿ al-Dawla, 64

'Tabib' Isfahani, Mirza ʿAbd al-Baqi, 92, 105
'Tabib' Isfahani, Mirza Muhammad Nasir, 92, 97, 105
tadhkira
   as source, 24, 91, 93–4, 117
   at Arcot, 178–84
   definition, 23
   Urdu, 66–7
Tarzi, Ghulam Muhammad, 55–6
Tarzi, Mahmud 50, 55
tāza-gūʾī (fresh-speak), 15, 39–40, 151, 165, 177–8, 181, 182, 185, 189, 204; *see also* 'Bidil' and 'Indian style'
Timur Shah Durrani
   Bidil assemblies, 51–3

Urdu language, 59–60, 62–72, 171
    musha'ira, 65, 68–9
'Urfi Shirazi, 14, 53

'Vala', Sayyid Abu Tayyib Khan, 168–9, 173, 196
'Vali' Dakhani, 64
'Vaqif', Miran Muhay al-Din, 174, 180, 181
'Vasif', Mawlavi Muhammad Mahdi, 163–5, 174, 179–84, 196–7

'Vasil', Muhammad Nabi Kabuli, 55–6

war-ballads *see jangnāma*

Zafarnama-yi Kabul (*Victory Book of Kabul*), 124, 127–8, 144–52
'Zamiri' Isfahani, Kamil al-Din Husayn, 42, 45, 89, 116
Zarrinkub, 'Abd al-Husayn, 14

EU representative:
Easy Access System Europe
Mustamäe tee 50, 10621 Tallinn, Estonia
Gpsr.requests@easproject.com